We are pleased to present to you this special, collectors' edition of this book documenting a fascinating story from the 19th Century heritage of our home city, Elizabethtown, Kentucky.

Hardin County Historical Society
P.O. Box 381
Elizabethtown, KY 42702

Ron Elliott, author

_____ of 300
Printed 2013

AMERICAN EL DORADO

AMERICAN EL DORADO

THE GREAT DIAMOND HOAX of 1872

BY **RON ELLIOTT**

Acclaim Press

MORLEY, MISSOURI

Acclaim Press
— Your Next Great Book —
P.O. Box 238
Morley, MO 63767
(573) 472-9800
www.acclaimpress.com

Book Design: Tiffany Glastetter; M. Frene Melton
Cover Design: Kimberly Paul

Library of Congress Cataloging-in-Publication Data

Elliott, Ron, 1943-
   American El Dorado: The Great Diamond Hoax of 1872 / by Ron Elliott.
      p. cm.
   Includes bibliographical references.
   ISBN 978-1-938905-06-3 (alk. paper) -- ISBN 1-938905-06-7 (alk. paper)
   1. Swindlers and swindling--United States--History--19th century. 2. Diamond mines and
mining--United States--History--19th century. 3. Hoaxes--United States--History--19th
century. I. Title.
   HV6698.Z9D534 2012
   364.16'3--dc23
                                          2012030845

First Printing: 2013
Printed in the United States of America
10 9 8 7 6 5 4 3 2 1

This publication was produced using available information.
The publisher regrets it cannot assume responsibility for errors or omissions.

Contents

Preface

Many years ago, I saw a televised interview in which a famous novelist discussed the differences between fiction and nonfiction. One of the points he made was that, as there are as many similarities as differences, the line often becomes somewhat blurred. While that is true, the main issue is that in writing fiction, one gets to make up the facts. Still, there are rules. Once something becomes a fact, even if the writer simply made it so, for the duration of that work it must remain a fact. If the woman's eyes are blue and her hair is blond, for example, the eyes must remain blue, whatever she does with her hair. The most important rule, perhaps, is that even created "facts" must be feasible. Every novelist knows that a reader will not stick with a story if the "facts" are too improbable to be believed.

Well, then, what does one do with a true story wherein the actual historical facts are indeed too far-fetched to be believed? All I can do is report the facts as I found them, stick an endnote on it to provide a trail to the source and assure the reader that throughout this entire narrative, other than the conversation, I made up nothing. Although the history herein is offered as accurate, many times through the context of this book you'll sit back and ask, "How could that have possibly happened? Is that a product of imagination?" As the author, I feel obligated to answer the readers' questions, but with this story I can only tell you that I don't know how these things happened, only that they did happen. Or, at least one of the people involved said they did happen. While I cannot say that some of the events are not a product of Philip Arnold's or Asbury Harpending's imagination, I can promise that I didn't make them up.

One of the things I can explain is how Philip Arnold managed to make investors believe that he'd actually found an "American El Dorado." The idea was not as fantastic in 1870 as it sounds to you and me. In the first place, who knew there was gold in California until it showed up at Sutter's Mill in 1848? Who knew there was silver in Nevada until the Comstock Lode was discovered a decade later? So, then in 1870, who was to say that there were not diamonds to be found somewhere in the largely unexplored American West? And, if such a place did exist, human nature being what it is, everyone who was offered the opportunity would certainly want to be in on the ground floor. Add in the fact that Arnold had taken the trouble to have a San Francisco jeweler certify that his sample consisted of real diamonds, and he was off and running. From there, the "great diamond hoax" became a viable concern, sustained by its own momentum.

Two aspects of the story that struck me as most interesting are worth a mention here. I agree with Asbury Harpending that if Philip Arnold had elected to go on the stage, he would have without question been one of the greatest actors of the nineteenth century. He played his part perfectly every step of the process, educated himself sufficiently to locate a feasible diamond field, acceded to the investors' demands when proper and made his own demands when he could get away with it. The other accomplishment, even more remarkable, is how he managed to keep a straight face through some of the events, such as when Mr. Tiffany produced his evaluation of the diamond sample he examined at $150,000. By extension, that meant that the last haul from the diamond field was worth $1,500,000! It would take a great actor to swallow that while knowing he'd invested only about $8,000 in the entire package.

As usual, I owe many debts. The Hardin County Clerk, Mr. Kenny Tabb, and his staff, most notably Susan McCrobie and Meranda Caswell, were helpful beyond expression. Likewise, Walter Bowman and David Kirkpartick of the Kentucky State Archives went above and beyond the call in helping me locate valuable documents. I am also indebted to Patricia Labounty of the Union Pacific Railroad Museum for the map of the track in the involved area. A tip of the cap also goes to the staff at the Bancroft Library at the University of California, Berkeley, Elizabethtown attorney John Scott and Asbury Harpending's great-grandson, Ron Pavellas. Again, as usual, the folks at Acclaim Press, Doug Sikes and Monica Burnett, contributed greatly to my efforts. John Snell, through his photographic wizardry and friendship, and my wife, Carol, provided support, as Dave Ramsay says, "better than I deserve."

So, here's the story of the great diamond hoax. Enjoy it as you shake your head and observe, along with Shakespeare's Puck, "What fools these mortals be!"

Many things are too strange to be believed,
but nothing is too strange to have happened.

– Thomas Hardy

AMERICAN EL DORADO

THE GREAT DIAMOND HOAX of 1872

Chapter One

Wednesday, November 30, 1870[1]
San Francisco, California

San Francisco's famous fog crept slowly up from the bay, first filling the low spots, then obscuring the mud, then enveloping the board sidewalks and eventually swallowing the buildings and the entire landscape. Through the swirling mist and rain, two huddled figures walked east on California Street.

"I hate bein' in town," said the shorter man. "It stinks."

"Well, you don't smell none too pretty yourself," commented the other. Unconsciously, he patted the bulge beneath his coat to insure himself that his precious cargo was still there. After a few steps, he added, "I agree with you though, John. I 'specially hate this town – you can't tell if it's winter or summer around here. I can stand fog and I can stand rain, but the two of 'em together is almost too much."

The other man grunted. "Wanna go back to Kentucky, Cousin?"

Again he patted the lump at his waist. "If my plan works out, we'll be home again soon enough." They walked a few steps in silence before he added, "And in grand style too."

"'Do you really think they'll go for it, Phil? These California investment boys didn't get to be as rich as they are by bein' fools, you know."

"You're right, they ain't fools. But George Roberts did get to be a millionaire by recognizin' an opportunity when he sees one and not bein' slow to jump in. Besides, greed is one of mankind's great motivators and I'm sure that how many ever millions he's got ain't enough. In addition, I've gone to some trouble to make sure that what we've been out in the wilds doin' ain't no big secret."

"As grubby as we smell and look, it'd be hard to keep anybody from suspectin' that we've been out prospectin'. Why did you have to wait 'til this time of night? A man could get robbed, you know." John Slack glanced anxiously around into the mist.

"Yeah," Phil agreed, again checking the package inside his coat. "Just leave it to me – I'll do all the talking. You just sit there and try to look like you don't approve of the whole thing. If Roberts asks you anything directly, be as vague as you can. At any rate, don't tell him nothin'."

As the pair neared a street intersection, Arnold peered down the cross street. "This ain't it," he concluded, "we got another block to go."

"What makes you think he'll even be in his office this late? This ain't no time of night to be doin' business?"

"All part of the plan," Arnold assured. "I sent him a telegram yesterday tellin' him that we would be in town tonight with some important business and asked him to wait in his office for us. As I said, just leave it all to me. Hold it; this is the place."

The pair stepped off the board sidewalk into the deep mud of the street. Across the way, a weak beam of light from the gas jet penetrated a few feet out the window into the swirling mist. Arnold rattled the door knob. Finding the door locked, he knocked loudly.

"Who is it?" came from within.

"Philip Arnold and John Slack."

Immediately the bolt slid back and the door opened. The men blinked as the light seemed very bright in contrast to the drifting fog in which they had been walking. In the doorway stood George Roberts, a short chubby man dressed in a spotless business suit. His roundish belly pushed his plaid vest out so far that his white shirt was exposed at the waist. "Why, hello Phil." He beckoned them to enter. After shaking hands with Arnold, he turned to Slack. "Good to see you both again," he said without enthusiasm, eyeing their disheveled appearance and the rifle Slack carried in the crook of his arm. Moving behind his desk, he motioned to the chairs opposite. "So, what's all the excitement about?"

"Sorry to be so much trouble," Arnold began hesitantly, "but I knew it'd be too late to get to the bank by the time we got the ferry across the bay, and you're a man I trust."

Roberts smiled approvingly as he polished his glasses on a handkerchief. "Thanks, Phil, no trouble at all. Always happy to accommodate a friend. Besides, the three of us have had enough gold and silver mining adventures to satisfy me of your honesty and reputation." Replacing the spectacles on his nose, he leaned his elbows on the desk. "Now, what can I do for you?'

"Well," Arnold drew the word out as he exhaled, "I know you've got a strong safe in the office here...."

"Why certainly you're welcome to store your gold dust in my safe," Roberts broke in. He leaned back him his chair and waited, a little relieved that storing gold dust was all the prospectors wanted.

Arnold hesitated a long moment before he spoke. "It ain't exactly gold," he admitted.

Slack spoke his first words since they'd entered the office. "And it ain't silver, neither." He started to add something else, but a sharp look from Arnold cut him off.

The relief in Roberts' eyes vanished. Deeply intrigued now, he again leaned toward his two visitors. He studied Arnold's face and then Slack's but could discern no hint of their secret. Then he noticed Arnold once again checking the bundle beneath his coat. He decided to take a stab: "I've heard rumors that you boys have been out prospectin' for diamonds."

"Why, hell George," Arnold said with a disgusted grunt. "Ever'body knows there ain't no diamonds in this country." He tried to let the mention of the word "diamonds" show no change in his demeanor.

"I don't know that," Roberts exclaimed, while he studied Arnold's face for any sign. "But I do know that back in our gold minin' days up around Placerville – of course it was called 'Dry Diggings' in those days – we used to find a diamond now and then when we washed out the dirt[2]. Everybody knew that there wasn't any gold hereabouts, either, 'til that feller found it up at Sutter's Mill back in '48. Everybody knew there was no silver in Nevada 'til the Comstock Lode came in. Now, they's gold and silver aplenty around here right enough, isn't there? I was fortunate enough to make a bundle on the Comstock, so who's to say there ain't diamonds included in the West's mineral wealth?"

"Clarence King's United States Geological Survey, for one," Arnold said knowingly.

"Yeah, I read that report," Roberts said with a sigh. "But they admitted that they can't say for sure. There are locations around where the geology is similar to the diamond fields in South Africa. The government also said that while it might not pay a man to go out lookin' for diamonds, if he did happen to see one just layin' on the ground, it'd be worth his while to bend over and pick it up."

Arnold turned to stare at his partner as if seeking Slack's approval. Slack's expression did not change, nor did he even look at Arnold, seemingly mesmerized by the fog drifting by the window. After a moment, Arnold sighed as he snatched his hat from the floor and rose from his chair. "I'm sorry to have troubled you, Mr. Roberts" he said, motioning Slack to get up. "I reckon we'll just be getting' on."

"Hold on now!" Roberts shouted, jumping around the desk to grasp Arnold's arm. "You said you have something you want to store in my safe and you're perfectly welcome to do so." As Arnold took another step toward the door, Roberts added, "There are plenty of desperadoes hanging around here, you know. They think nothing of killing a man for whatever might be in his pockets."

Arnold stopped. Again he looked at Slack for a long moment. "Well," he began, then stepped purposely toward the door, "thank you kindly Mr. Roberts, but I suppose we'll just take our chances."

"Phil," Slack seemed to have to force himself to speak, "don't be a fool. Mr. Roberts is our friend, and he does have a point. I felt sure somebody was followin' us on the way over here."

Arnold glared disapprovingly at his partner. Then with a sigh, he slowly brought forth the buckskin parcel from beneath his muddy coat. "Would you hold this 'til I can get to Mr. Ralston's bank in the morning?" He made no offer to hand the package over to Roberts.

"Certainly, certainly," the investor gushed, reaching for the pouch. "Let's have a look at what you've got here."

"NO!" Arnold shouted, jerking away. "What's in it ain't none of your affair."

"I'm not just being nosey," Roberts said contritely, "but I got to know what it is. If you come back tomorrow and I have no idea what you left with me, you could claim that I stole half of your goods."

Realizing the truth of that observation, Arnold's attitude softened a bit. "You know I wouldn't do that, George, but I do see your point." He considered a moment before going on, "Tell you what, give me some that of ribbon you've got in the drawer and I'll wrap it in a way that I'll know if the package has been opened."

"All right," Roberts agreed, "fair enough." He opened a desk drawer and handed Arnold a length of yellow tape. "Wrap 'er any way you like with this."

Arnold sat again and made a show of tying an elaborate knot around the mouth of the buckskin pouch. "I guess that'll do," he announced handing the package to Roberts. "You keep it safe now, and we'll be back in the morning."

"You can rest easy tonight," Roberts assured, resting the package caringly in both hands. "It'll be right here for you whenever you want it."

"Thank you kindly, George," Arnold said shaking hands. "If you don't mind, I'd like a receipt."

"Why," Roberts exclaimed, stopping, "how can I give you a receipt when I don't even know what you've left here?"

"Just say 'a package of great value,'" Arnold instructed.

"Well, I guess I can do that." Roberts placed the pouch in the safe, banged the door closed and spun the dial. With a satisfied glance at his two visitors, he walked to the desk and scribbled on a sheet of paper. "Here you go," he said, offering the receipt to Arnold.

"We appreciate your help and good judgment. You got to promise you won't say nothin' about this," Arnold said and returned his smile. Slack also smiled as he shook the investor's hand.

"You may rely on my integrity and discretion," Roberts assured. "I'll see you tomorrow."

The pair of prospectors walked out the door into the drifting moisture outside. "That ribbon ain't gonna keep him out of our goods, " Slack opined.

"Hush up," Arnold hissed, grasping his partner's arm to hurry him up the street. When he determined they'd moved out of earshot, he said, "I'm countin' on the ribbon not keepin' him out. If I'm any judge of human nature, I'll lay odds that he's got that pouch busted open by now and the contents dumped out on his desk. Since we told him to keep it a secret, I'll also lay odds that he'll bust a gut to get over to the Bank of California and tell his buddy Ralston about it."

"You don't reckon he'll steal our goods?"

After a few hurried steps, Arnold answered, "No, he wouldn't do that," After a few more steps he gleefully added, "but I'd give a gold goose egg to see the sparkle in Roberts' greedy eyes right now as he tries to figure out how to cut hisself in on our find!"

Slack laughed. "Well, he promised not to look and not to tell, so how the hell is he gonna cut himself in on somethin' he don't even know exists?"[3]

Chapter Two

Thursday, February 6, 1868
Hardin County, Kentucky

"Now, Phil, you look here, you better think this thing over real serious." The speaker was John B. Shepherd, a prominent citizen of Elizabethtown and an old friend of the Arnold family. "You've been married, what is it now, ten, twelve years?"

"As a matter of fact, it was thirteen years last week."[4] Tall and thin with dark hair and dark eyes, the devilishly handsome Philip Arnold was accustomed to having his own way, especially with the ladies. Also accustomed to going and doing as the notion struck him, he was not enjoying the trend of this conversation, even if it was coming from a friend of his late father. Actually, he concluded, it was more of a "Dutch Uncle" talk. "And before you see fit to remind me, yes, by hell, I know we've got four children."

"Well, then it's high time you settled down some, ain't it? I happen to know for a fact that Mary is pretty damn sick of your traipisin' around all over creation. It all started when you run off for the War with Mexico. Then...."

Arnold interrupted. "Hold on there, John. That was 'way back in '47, long before me and her got hitched."

"Don't matter, we're just reviewing your record and, more importantly, all you've made the poor woman endure. Then you didn't even bother to come home when the war was over, but run off to California like a damn fool lookin' for gold.

"Yep, that's right," Arnold agreed. "I was a '49'er and they was a hell of a lot of us damn fools out there." He hurried on before Shepherd had time to point out that the majority of those who went west in the 1849 gold rush did turn out to be damn fools. "I'm bound to point out that I did all right, too. I made some money and a lot of good friends. I can't help it if I finally got a little homesick and come back here, can I?"

"I guess you can't, but you came back here as poor as a bed bug beat out of the tickin' in the spring. That was in '54 as I recall, and, that's exactly when Mary's troubles began, ain't it?"

Arnold took a little offense at the suggestion that her troubles began with their marriage. "I allow that's for her to say. Anyway, she was happy enough to marry me then."

"I guess she was, but then you got the itch again and drug her back to California soon's you was married."

"No, John, it wasn't right away – we stayed here a couple of years. Anyway you know what a sleepy little village Elizabethtown was then. There wasn't even a railroad or anything to give even the semblance of life and buoyancy.[5] Mary was a little bored, too. She wanted to go to San Francisco as much as I did."

At that moment, Mary Arnold came in from the kitchen carrying a wooden tray with three mugs of steaming coffee. "Yes, I wanted to go," she admitted.

"And how'd you like California?" Shepherd asked, accepting a mug.

"Oh, San Francisco was OK, but I sure didn't like livin' at Railroad Hill up in Yuba County."

"Up around Camptonville, that's where the gold was," Philip interjected, slamming down his coffee. "We went there to mine gold. We had to go where it was, didn't we?"

"What didn't you like about it?" Shepherd asked, ignoring Arnold's question.

"Well," Mary said with a small laugh, "I think the county name, 'Yuba,' is from the Latin; 'Yu' meaning mud and 'ba' meaning more mud. It was cold there, too."

Shepherd eyed the woman as she talked. She was small and delicate and the years had been kind to her. Her auburn hair was complimented by her green eyes, which sparkled as she spoke and the fact that she'd borne her husband four children had only slightly impacted her girlish figure. "Yeah?" he said, happy that her presence and manner had lightened the atmosphere. "I didn't think it ever got cold out there."

"Maybe not in Southern California, but let me tell you that up near Reno, where we was…. Well," she interrupted herself, "one mornin' I had me a pot of coffee boilin' on the stove and decided to go pour it out."

"Froze before you could get it poured out, did it?" Shepherd anticipated her story.

"Oh, yeah," she said, smiling broadly, "But that ain't the thing."

"What then?"

"When I came back in, as I sat the pot down, I noticed that it was still warm." With a huge, triumphant smile, she finished, "Yessir, that coffee froze so fast it didn't even have time to cool off." She sipped her coffee demurely as the men laughed.

As the laughter faded, she broke the ensuing awkward silence by asking, "What have you men been in here discussing so seriously?"

Her husband and the visitor eyed each other for a long moment before Philip spoke. "He's heard that I've got the bug to go back out west."

"I see." She apparently wanted to say something else, but the glare from her husband silenced her.

"Hold on a minute here," Arnold said. "Let's not overlook the fact that even if you didn't enjoy livin' in a minin' camp, I made some pretty fancy money doin' that hydraulic gold minin' up in Yuba County. Made some good friends, too.

"Yeah? And where are they now?" Shepherd inquired.

"Well," Arnold leaned back in his chair, sure that he had now gained the upper hand in the discussion. "Cousin John Slack is still minin' in Arizona. George Roberts is a millionaire in San Francisco, as is his partner, Bill Lent. William Ralston is also rich and is the head cashier of the Bank of California and, if his track record is any gauge, Asubry Harpending has made and lost three or four fortunes since I last saw him[6]. They're good friends and good men all. Also, keep in mind that when we come back here in '62, I had money enough to buy this farm and we've lived pretty good since then, ain't we?[7]"

"Then I reckon it's those friends that put the fool notion of going back in your head?"

"And why not?" Arnold nearly shouted. "The whole bunch of us did all right with the Lincoln Gold Mining Company the last time. And, they keep writin' tellin' me about all the mines bein' discovered ever' day and all the money they is to be made."

"Oh, yeah," Shepherd commented. "I forgot about that the Lincoln one. That's when you left your wife and children here for two years."

"Well," Mary interjected, "Philip has proposed that we sell our property here and go back out West."

"How do you feel about that?"

She shot an anxious glance at her husband before she answered. "I'm willin' to move to San Francisco, but I ain't goin' back to no minin' camp."

"I reckon I'm wastin' my time here then." Shepherd rose from his chair and retrieved his hat from the rack.

"Hold on, John," Mary exclaimed, rushing across the room to grasp his arm. As he reluctantly turned back, she went on, "Me and Philip have talked it all over and agreed to some things."

"Then why'd you ask me to be here? I thought you wanted me to try to talk him out of it."

Mary stared at the floor for a moment. "Well," she admitted, "I guess I did put that idea in your head. I didn't figure that you'd do any good – his mind is pretty well set. So, the fact is that I want you to set some things down in writin', legal-like."

"Why, I ain't much of a hand to write, you know that."

"You're a sight better at it than either of us. So here's the thing, Meredith Arthur has agreed to buy all our property, and I'm willin' to sell it to him and let Philip use the money for his prospectin' ventures. But, I'm afeared that he might get killed by Indians or fall down a mine shaft or who knows what else might become of him. I surely don't want to be left in a strange country with nothin'. Philip says that if I'll go with him, he'll give me all the extry money he can to do with as I see fit. So, I want you to set that down in writin' so I can keep the paper with his promises he's made me."

"Well, all right, if that's what you want. Got any paper?"

"Right here," she said, retrieving a sheet of lined paper from a desk drawer. She handed over the paper and a stub of a pencil. Mary folded her arms as she settled in to wait while he wrote.

"Like I said," he sighed, accepting the writing material, "I ain't much of a hand, but I'll do the best I can." After about fifteen minutes of laborious work with pencil and paper, he handed the result to Mary. "That's the best I can do," he said.

With her trembling hands shaking the paper, she read:

As Mary E. Arnold Philip Arnold wife agee with Him to sell out unto Meredith Arthur Hers and His interest in All the Richard May Lands who was hir Father which he has bought & She has got And go with him back to california And stay until he wants to move back heare He binds Him Self By this Riten Paper As he is to hav The use of All The Land Money to doo Biseness on in that cuntry To giv over to Hir All The Money he can Speare To Bee Hers out of his Buseness as he gets it to By Hir A nother Farm or Home heare and what else She wants And to dwo as she Pleases with so she can hav sumthing For hir support as well as hir children.

Febuary The 6 1868.[8]

Mary took the pencil from Shepherd and handed it to her husband. He looked intently at her for a long moment before wordlessly signing his name at the bottom of the page. Taking the pencil from his hand, she affixed her signature. Then, with an air of satisfaction, she folded the paper in half. Running her finger along the crease, she solemnly folded it in half again, walked over to the shelf and tucked it inside the family Bible.

"There's one other thing," she informed.

"What?" Phil asked.

"I want you to give me your power of attorney," she demanded, "and I want it done legal."

"Well," Phil said with a sigh, "all right, but we'll have to go to the court house for that." Noticing her glare, he added, "We'll do that the first thing in the mornin'."[9]

Mary sat in a rocker with an air of satisfaction. For the first time since she'd married Philip Arnold, she thought, she had finally gained a little security.

Chapter Three

Amid the breath-taking scenery high in the Pyramid Mountains in the southwest corner of New Mexico Teritory, Philip Arnold, Asbury Harpending, and James Cooper stopped to admire the view.[10] Far below, the grassy plains stretched away to the west into Arizona Territory while the snowcapped peak of the mountain hovered above. To the men's left, the stream they'd been following gave forth a thundering roar as the foaming water made its rush to the crystal clear blue lake below. "How much farther is it, Phil?" Harpending asked, shouting to make himself heard over the noise.

Arnold, who'd previously been led to the site they were seeking by the man who'd discovered the silver deposits in these mountains, leaned against his walking stick and mopped his brow with a red bandana. "It's not far, Mr. Harpending; another hour or so should put us there. It's early yet, so we can rest here for a spell if you like." As one who, in partnership with San Francisco investor George Roberts and banker William Ralston, had put up the money for this mining venture, Harpending, although ten years younger than Arnold, was entitled to be called "Mister."

Philip Arnold had prospered in several ways in the two and a half years since his return to the West. Back in April, following an announcement of a silver strike in Arizona, Harpending and Roberts had hired him and his cousin John Slack to lead a prospecting party to that Territory. After fruitlessly searching in the vicinity of Tucson for more than two months, the pair returned to San Francisco empty handed.[11] Although they had made no money for their backers, each man, Arnold in particular, solidified his reputation as an honest and reliable person who knew his way around mines. Between mining ventures, he'd obtained a job as bookkeeper James Cooper's assistant at the Diamond Drilling Company in San Francisco. Cooper, along on this trip as an assayer, was employed at the drill company on much the same basis – the job kept them occupied during bad weather and provided a more steady income than they could expect from prospecting. Although over the past two years Arnold had given a lot of money to his wife – in accordance with their agreement – most of the money obtained from selling their Kentucky properties was still safely lodged in Mr. Ralston's bank.

Immediately upon Arnold and Slack's return from the Arizona prospecting trip, Ralston, the "man who made the city" (San Francisco[12]) informed them that a man named W.D. Brown, who had been in Arizona as a part of government survey party, had branched out to do a little prospecting on his own. In these Pyramid Mountains, he'd located a rich silver deposit. Despite his samples, Brown, unable to gain any financial backing in California, had disappeared before Ralston heard about the discovery. When a report from Arizona Territory's Surveyor General confirmed the presence of silver at Brown's site, Ralston and his partner Harpending employed Arnold to locate Brown. Harpending and Ralston were quick to buy out Brown, form the Mountains of Silver Mining Company, file the claim and employ Arnold as the superintendent of the mine. Along with Brown, Arnold and Slack were dispatched to the site to collect samples. Slack remained behind when Arnold returned to San Francisco in August. Within days, word spread all over town that the samples assayed as rich. These developments were key in Harpending's deciding to visit the site in person and organizing the present expedition.

"I hear," Arnold said as he sat on a rock, "that you're building a town near the mine."

"That's right," Harpending replied, leaning his massive frame against the sheer rock cliff opposite the stream. "There's been a single building there for a long time. The Butterfield Stage line used it as a way station until the war. A couple of years ago, the National Mail and Transportation Company started using it as a mail stop. I take it you've been in touch with your cousin Slack?"

"Yeah. We had a letter from him a few weeks ago. He says that he's selling lots in the town about as fast as they can get 'em laid out."

"Well, the miners have to live someplace," Harpending commented. "The Mail Company renamed the place 'Grant' after the president. It'll probably soon be the next boom town,[13]" he added thoughtfully.

"Ever'body always wants to be in on 'The Next Big Thing,' don't they?" Arnold said with a laugh.

"Yes. And that includes me and you, doesn't it?" Harpending returned his smile.

"I reckon it does. We've done all right for ourselves, ain't we?"

"Oh, I suppose we've managed to keep ourselves occupied and have a little fun while earning an honest dollar." Looking up the stream, he asked, "Are you ready to move on?"

"Anytime you are," Arnold said, standing.

"Are you sure of where we're going?" Harpending asked, falling in behind the other two men.

"All we got to do is follow this creek here," Arnold replied. "The spring that's its source is near the mine." As he had predicted, about another hour of climbing brought them to the entrance to the mine. Spiraling smoke betrayed the location of the tents comprising the town of Grant, visible in a swale just beyond.

❧

A week spent moving in and out of the mine digging out ore had convinced Asbury Harpending that the mine would pay them handsomely. Exploration of the surrounding country had yielded no other interesting prospects, so he was ready to go home and report to his partners. At Harpending's invitation, Philip Arnold, John Slack and James Cooper were gathered in the old stage stop, the one permanent building in town, for a farewell dinner.

"Mighty nice feed you're puttin' on here," Cooper commented, stuffing a biscuit in his mouth.

"Sure is," John Slack agreed. "Damned nice of you, Mr. Harpending."

"You all deserve it," Asbury Harpending said, smiling. "We've all worked pretty hard the last week." Addressing Cooper, he added, "You, James, have done a fine job of assaying the samples." Then turning to Slack, "And you, John, are making a regular town out of this dust bowl. This mine will pay off in the long run. We'll all get a nice pay day from it, no doubt."

"You ain't exactly been layin' around doing nothin', either," Arnold observed. "I know, of course, that you've been around gold mines, but how'd you become so knowledgeable about silver mines?"

Barrel-chested and broad, Harpending was a big man in every sense of the word. He brushed his black hair to the left, creating an unsymmetrical look that was offset by his even facial features. His blue eyes sparkled as he spoke. "Oh," Harpending said with a laugh, leaning back with a coffee mug in his hand, "the fact is that I once made a fortune silver minin' in Mexico."

"Yeah?" The other men said nearly in unison. "Would you mind tellin' us about it?" Arnold spoke for the group.

"Well, if you don't mind some ancient history, it is a kinda interesting story, although how I lost that fortune is more interesting than how I got it. Let me see," he began, sipping his coffee, "it was back just after I'd come to California, before the war...."

"Where'd you come from?" Slack interrupted.

"Kentucky."

"No!" Slack exclaimed. "Whereabouts? Me and Phil are from Hardin County, you know."

"Yes, I know," Asbury said. "I was born near Princeton, in Caldwell County[14], in western Kentucky pretty close to the Ohio River. As a matter of fact, that river is probably where I ought to start, if you boys really are interested."

"I'm all ears," Arnold said. "I've heard a little about your adventures, but know nothin' of your early life before you got to Railroad Hill. Please tell all you want to."

"All right. As a boy, looking across that river, I saw a land of enchantment and adventure – the plains, the mountains, the unbroken solitudes, the wild Indians, the buffaloes, and the Golden State on the shore of the Pacific.[15]

"What red-blooded American boy wouldn't go? Leaving out a few details, I ended up in San Francicso early in '57. As you know, I was lucky enough to make a lot of money on those hydraulic mines up around Placerville. I had a lot of money in Ralston's bank before my seventeenth birthday."

"What about the Mexican silver?" Slack asked.

"Well, after the gold played out, casting around for something to do, I began to hear a lot of talk about the land of Montezuma. I'd seen the coast, of course, coming 'round the horn to California, but all I knew about the interior was that there was plenty of riches to be had there, but a man would risk life and limb to get at them. I decided to take the risk, outfitted a trading vessel, hired a crew, stocked the boat with trade goods and set out. Again skipping a few details, I met a Mexican gentleman who happened to be broke at the moment – not an unusual state for Mexican gentlemen, I might add. He said that he owned an extremely rich silver mine inland in the mountains of Durango and he'd be happy to go into partnership with me if I would finance the operation.

"I was skeptical, of course, but he guaranteed me of the richness of his mine. He also assured me that the dangers were greatly exaggerated. So I bought all the supplies we'd need and we set out. Well, my partner hadn't lied about his mine, in fact, he hadn't told half the truth. We had us a time, mined and sold the silver and within a couple of years, I had a quarter of a million dollars in the bank and my two-thirds of the silver mine was worth a million more.[16] So, that's how I learned about silver mining, from my Mexican partner." He reached for the coffee pot on the stove and refilled his mug.

The other men sat in enthralled silence for a long moment. Finally, Cooper spoke, "You said the losing of your money was even more interesting? Please go on."

"Well," Harpending laughed, "I gave it all to Uncle Sam."

"What? How's that?" Arnold broke in. "I thought you were the quintessential unreconstructed Rebel."

"Well, 'give' might not be exactly the proper word, but I'll explain. I returned to San Francisco for a visit, as I thought, right about the time Lincoln was elected president in the fall of 1860. You boys all know how hot emotions were running then. Most of the residents of California were southerners, like us, or else foreigners who didn't care about states' rights and slavery one way or the other. I would have worked to have California join the Confederacy, but there were too many powerful men on the other side. Being young and hot-headed – I was just 21 – I got involved in a plot to take over the state by military force. That sounds silly now, but at the time, I assure you, it was well within our grasp. The ties to the federal government in far away Washington were not very strong. There were only about 200 Federal soldiers at Fort Point, less than a hundred at Alcatraz and a handful at Mare Island and the arsenal at Benicia. All were under the command of another Kentucky boy, Albert Sidney Johnston! We could have done it easily, and by January of '61, our plans were laid and we were ready."

"You mean to tell me that they had less than 100 men guarding the arsenal at Alcatraz?" Cooper interjected. "Incredible."

"Washington was not really concerned about California in those days," Harpending informed.

"Well, what happened?" Arnold was fascinated. "Did you figure that General Johnston would help you take over the government's property?"

"I thought that he at least wouldn't put up much resistance. It turns out that I didn't know that gentleman very well. I was appointed to a three man committee to visit the general and sort of feel him out on the matter. When we were ushered into his office, I beheld a blond giant of a man with a mass of heavy yellow hair. He had the nobility of bearing that marks a great leader of men, and it seemed to my youthful imagination that I was in the presence of some superman of ancient history, like Hannibal or Caesar, come to life again.

"He greeted us as politely as you can imagine. Then, in a matter-of-fact offhand way, he said, 'Before we go further, there is something I want to mention. I have heard foolish talk about an attempt to seize the government strongholds under my charge. Knowing this, I have prepared for emergencies, and will defend the property of the United States with every resource at my command, and the last drop of blood in my body. Tell that to your southern friends.'"[17]

"I reckon that took the wind out of your sails," Slack laughed. All were enjoying Harpending's story.

"You might say that," the big man answered with just a hint of annoyance. "Our little band of secessionists quickly melted away." Pulling a tobacco pouch from his pocket, Harpending began methodically packing his pipe.

Fearing that the story would end, Arnold spoke up. "You said you gave your fortune to Uncle Sam?" he prodded.

"Well," Harpending answered, blowing a puff of smoke, "like I said, 'give' might not be exactly the right word."

"What happened?" Cooper leaned forward in his chair.

"Being young and brash as I was," Harpending tilted his chair against the wall and hooked his heels over the rail, "I began to cast about for another way to serve the southern cause. I finally came up with a plot to cut off the flow of gold from California to the federal government. So, I managed to run the Union blockade, made my way to the Confederate capital at Richmond and had an interview with Jefferson Davis.

"I sorta sketched out my plan for the President, and he readily saw the importance of shutting off the flow of gold from California to Washington City. In due course, I received a commission as a captain in the Confederate Navy."

"Ha!" Arnold hooted. "What did you know about sailing?"

"Not a damned thing," Harpending retorted before adding, "and that was my undoing. I made my way overland back to California. That trip was not without event, but that's another story." Pausing to relight his pipe, he took delight in noting that his listeners were listening with rapt attention.

Through a cloud of blue smoke, he resumed. "I arrived back in San Francisco about, oh, July 1862, I guess it was, all set to equip a privateer and intercept the next Pacific Mail steamer, seize it and send its cargo of gold to the Confederacy. My navy commission would ensure my treatment as a prisoner of war rather than as a pirate should we be caught.

"Since I said 'we,' I might as well explain. As already noted, I needed help. I previously knew, of course, many men of like sentiment, and some of them volunteered their services and money. I was also lucky enough to run across an English gentleman named Alfred Rubery who, while he cared naught about the cause, craved the adventure of the thing as much as I.

"Well, we purchased a deep water ship named *Chapman* and loaded her with all sorts of arms in boxes labeled 'machinery.' The plan was, once we were at sea, to break out the 'machinery,' arm *Chapman* to the teeth and wait for the next Mail ship. We also employed a navigator, a man named Law, who was to meet us at a certain place on a certain night." Again he interrupted his narrative to ascertain that he retained the others' attention.

Noting their captivated impatience, he went on. "Well, the appointed time to meet the navigator came and went. Rubery and I waited, but Law did not show. Everything else was perfect – the night was dark, the sky was overcast and the winds were favorable, but, as we could not sail without a navigator, we were necessarily delayed. Even though I suspected treachery, there was no option but to board the *Chapman* and wait. By and by, the rocking motion of the ship lulled me to sleep."

"Well, hell fire man!" Arnold broke in. "What happened?"

Harpending hesitated a long dramatic moment. "I was rudely awakened by the lookout's shout of an approaching Federal gunboat. I knew in an instant that Law had betrayed us. Well, despite my feeble claim of being a Confederate sailor, we were arrested and taken to Alcatraz." Here the big man allowed himself a devious smile. "According to the newspaper accounts, Rubery and I were the most bloodthirsty pirates who ever slit a throat or scuttled a ship. Rubery, being an Englishman, was soon let go, but they lodged me in San Francisco's Broadway Jail to await trial. I'm satisfied that I am the only treasonous prisoner ever incarcerated in a county jail! It took the jury all of four minutes to find me guilty of high treason and sentence me to ten years' imprisonment and a fine of $10,000."

"You said you lost it all. A little ole $10,000 didn't break you, did it?" Slack asked.

"No," Harpending answered, "that was just to add insult to injury. Seein' as how they'd already confiscated all my property, they knew I could not pay the fine." He smacked his pipe against his palm, emptying the ashes. "Well, boys it's getting' late and I need to get an early start, so I think I'll turn in."

"Hold on now," Arnold pleaded, "you ain't gonna leave us there, are you?"

"We all figure to spend a lot of time together, so perhaps we'll resume another time. Suffice it for now to say that the government soon softened its posture on the treason – seein' as how I really hadn't accomplished anything – and decided to let me go. Not before taking every last dime I had, though. Well, good night all." With that, he walked out the door, leaving the others in a stunned silence.[18]

In a little while, Cooper spoke up. "They've got a new whore at the house up the street, what say we go check it out?"

"Good idea," Slack said, jumping to his feet. "Let's go, Phil."

"You know I don't go in for that kind of stuff," Arnold replied.

"I saw you talkin' to that new girl yesterday," Cooper observed.

"You may have seen *her* talkin' to *me*. You boys go ahead if you want. I have the feelin' that Mary wouldn't approve."

"Hell," Slack spat, "she ain't here to know the difference, is she?"

"I'd know," was Arnold's comment.

Another busy week wrapped up their business at the mine site, so, in mid-September, Arnold, Slack and Cooper gathered their supplies and set out for California, surveys and plats in hand. The late afternoon sun was a huge orange ball on the horizon as they entered a village near the Arizona border. Although the temperature was warm, the northern sky threatened snow.

"What is this place?" Awe, laced with a healthy dose of apprehension, filled James Cooper's voice as he viewed his surroundings.

"It's called Fort Defiance,[19]" his partner answered.

"Strange name," Cooper observed. "Why do they call it that?"

"This was once valuable grazin' land. The Indians put up quite a fuss when the government took it over." While Slack spoke, Cooper glanced around nervously. "What are you worried about, Jim?"

Glancing apprehensively around while wiping his brow, Cooper whispered, "Look at all these damned Indians. There's dozens of 'em."

"They're Navajo, Jim. They're peaceful now," Slack assured. Having been in the Arizona Territory during the years his cousin Phil was in Kentucky, the man knew a lot about the area and its inhabitants.

"Let's find some place to eat," Arnold suggested, "I'm damned tired of Slack's beans."

After the trio made their arrangements at the livery stable and asked about a restaurant, they started in the direction the operator had indicated when one of the Navajo approached. Cooper fearfully cowered behind his companions as the native stopped them.

With well practiced motions, he indicated that he wanted tobacco for his pipe. "What have you got to trade?" Arnold asked.

"Hell, Phil, he don't understand white man talk," Slack said stepping forward. Using the sign language he learned during his stint in this country during the war, he indicated that a swap might be affected if the red man had any possessions of interest.

The native opened his buckskin shirt to reveal a necklace, a rawhide strand festooned with quarter-inch cylindrical beads. The bright beads, alternating a deep red and a pale green, sparkled in the low-angled sunlight. The old man removed the string from his neck and offered it to Slack. "Let me see that," Cooper shouted, any fear of the native now gone. "Those are garnets and emeralds," he said to Arnold, examining the stones. "Hell, give him all the tobacco we've got."

Arnold produced a pouch and handed it to the native. Turning to Cooper, he asked, "You know about gemstones, do you?"

"Yes, I do." Cooper answered. "Ever since I've been working around all those diamonds at the drill company, and that's been six years now, I've been interested, so I've read up on the subject." Running the beads through his fingers, he opined, "These are worth some money."

"Find out if he's got any more of these gems," Arnold instructed his cousin.

While Slack carried on a gesturing conversation with the Navajo, Arnold asked, "Say, Jim, where would you suppose he got these stones?"

"Well, some of them might be found around here – these Indians know a lot of things the white man doesn't. To my knowledge, there's never been any emeralds found in this country, but the geology is about right, so who's to say? These boys do a lot of tradin', too. It could be that he got 'em off some Mexican."

Slack interrupted the conversation. "He says he got a whole sack full of these colored stones that he'll trade for a quart of whiskey."

Slack was quickly dispatched to get the whiskey. He returned with a jug at the same time the old native appeared, carrying a buckskin pouch. When the whiskey was passed over, Cooper greedily grapped the pouch and opened the drawstring. "Well?" Arnold demanded.

"My God," Cooper shouted, "there's rubies and sapphires in here in addition to garnets and emeralds." The three men spent quite a time inspecting the stones, their hunger forgotten.

Later, at supper, Arnold gazed across the table at Cooper. "You, know, Jim, I'd prefer to think these gemstones occur naturally around these parts," he said absentmindedly. The glazed look in his eyes betrayed a racing mind.

"It could be," Cooper commented.

"Would you be willin' to teach me about diamonds and emeralds and garnets and such when we get back?"

"Sure," Jim Cooper said. "I've got some books in the office I'll loan you. Soon's we get back to the drillin' company, you can read 'em to your heart's content."

Chapter Four

Ensconced in the privacy of the bookkeeper's office at the Diamond Drilling Company, James Cooper and his assistant, Philip Arnold, were enjoying a slow afternoon. As the lengthening shadows crept across the floor, Cooper slapped his accounts book closed, propped his feet up on his desk and broached a subject that had long been on his mind. "Say, Phil, have you read those books I loaned you?"

"'Read' don't exactly get it," Arnold answered. "Try 'studied' or 'pored over.'"

"Well, what have you learned about diamonds?"

"A lot about what they look like in their natural state and after they've been cut, how much they're worth and the kind of geology where one can expect to find 'em." After a pause, he added, "Nothin' you don't already know, and thanks, by the way, for the loan and all your teaching."

"Think nothin' of it," Cooper said, with a dismissive wave of his hand. "I read the same books, so you're probably right. You also learned that the chips left over from cutting good stones and some of the ones that cannot be cut into jewelry quality are what we use in the drills we have around here."

"Of course," Arnold answered. "Goodness knows I've seen enough of the industrial quality in the office here."

"Ever consider buying any of 'em from the company?

"What? Why?" Arnold was stunned. "They ain't worth much, in fact ain't good for nothin' except the drills. Why would a man want to buy any of what we've got here?"

"Oh, I don't know," Cooper said, shifting in his chair. "I just thought that since you're in the chips now, you might be castin' around for the 'Next Big Thing.'"

"If you're talkin' about the $25,000 I got from Roberts for my interest in the Mountains of Silver Mine, I had to split that with my wife, so I wouldn't exactly call my situation rich."

"By the way," Cooper said, letting his feet drop to the floor. "I heard that Roberts sold a part of what he got from you for double what you got."[20]

"I heard that, too," Arnold replied, his eyes flashing. "More power to 'im. I figure that venture is gonna fail, what's why I sold out."

"What makes you think that it's gonna fail? You and I both know it's a rich mine. Obviously Harpending and Roberts think it's a big thing. Harpending went to London to sell shares in it over there. They wouldn't have done that unless they thought they could make a pot full of money."

"I suppose you're right about that," Arnold agreed, "but you know how hard-headed Harpending can be. There ain't no tellin' what kind of trouble he and his old buddy Rubery are liable to stir up.[21] And, there's rumors to the effect that something ain't exactly right about the legal claims they filed over in New Mexico." He paused to stare out the window for a long moment before adding, "Besides, I hear tell that the Apaches are on the war path over in the territories.[22] Well, it's Harpending and Roberts' problem. I'm glad I'm out of it."

Cooper waited a moment before he spoke. "As for me, I guess I'm just as well off to have been a hired hand in that adventure, even if I didn't get the big money you did."

"Well, I can tell ya that cousin Slack feels the same way." Arnold started to add something but stopped short, studying the dusty floor at his feet for several minutes. He leaned toward Cooper, his elbows on the desk. "Say, Jim what was that you said about the 'Next Big Thing?'"

Cooper stared intently across the room. "Oh," he began, trying to sound offhand, "hangin' around with the rich folk like you and Harpending and Roberts and Ralston sorta gives a man a hankerin' to at least have a share in the next millions to be made."

"I certainly wouldn't put me in the same class with those boys. It would seem to me that you and I have as good a chance as anybody of bein' in on the next big thing, though, whatever it is. Somebody will discover another gold or silver lode any day now. All you gotta do is join in the rush and hope to be among the first to get there."

Rising from his chair, Cooper walked to the window and idly watched the ships in the bay. "No, I don't expect that the next big thing is gonna be gold or silver – we've had plenty of those already, so nobody would get too excited about that."

Arnold sat up straight in his chair. "Well, what then?" he demanded.

The other man turned from the window. "Did you ever think about creatin' the next big thing rather than waitin' for it to happen?"

"What the hell are you talkin' about? If it ain't gonna be gold or silver, what could it be?

Cooper took a single step toward the other man. "Did it ever occur to you that there might be diamonds to be found somewhere in this country?"

"What?" Arnold was incredulous. "There ain't any diamonds in this country."

"How do you know that? Ain't it a fact that some were found years ago in the hydraulic minin' up north of here?"

"Yeah," Arnold admitted, "but only just a few."

"How many diamonds were washed out and thrown away because nobody recognized what they were?"

A long silence ensued while each man considered. "So," Arnold said at length, "what are you sayin'?"

"I'm just askin'," Cooper replied, returning to his desk. "We got them garnets and emeralds over in New Mexico, didn't we? Who is to say that there ain't some diamonds over in there some place too?"[23]

"Well, now that you mention it, what I read about the geology of the county where the diamond fields in South Africa are ain't that different from what I've seen over in the territories. You're right, who is to say just what the limits of riches in the American West are?"

"Have you ever heard of El Dorado?" Cooper asked with a sly grin.

"I know that Placerville is in El Dorado County," Arnold replied, "but I don't know what it is."

"It ain't a what, but a where. It's a mythical land where the streets are paved with gold coins and there's diamonds and other precious stones just laying around waiting to be picked up."

"There really ain't no such place, though, right?"

"Well," Cooper said, "the Spanish and other explorers put in a heap of time look in' for it."

"But they didn't find it?"

"No," Cooper admitted, "they didn't find it, but that doesn't mean it doesn't exist. As we said, who is to say that El Dorado ain't over in some unexplored section of Arizona or Utah or someplace?"

Arnold laughed. "You know the old mountain man Jim Bridger claimed that he'd seen a place where everything had been instantly petrified. He said there were "peetrified" birds singing "peetrified" songs, and the bushes bear the most beautiful fruit – diamonds, rubies, sapphires and emeralds big as black walnuts!"[24]

"Yeah," Cooper returned the laugh, "I imagine that Jim Bridger knew about as much about diamonds as a pig does about Sunday. Anyway, I've heard some of Bridger's tall tales. He claimed there's a river out there somewhere that's ice cold where it bubbles out of a spring at the top of a mountain and boiling hot at the bottom.[25] My favorite, though, is the time a pack of wolves chased him up a tree. Bridger said wolves are smart."

"How so?"

"Well, he said that after several hours of them snappin' and growling around the base of the tree, three of the wolves took off, leavin' only two of them there to keep an eye on him."

"What?" Cooper was incredulous.

"Yep. Bridger said he thought he might get away, but before he could make a break for it, the other three came back." Arnold paused before delivering the punch line, "They brought four beavers with 'em to gnaw the tree down so they could get at ole Jim."[26]

When the laughter subsided, Arnold said, with a little hesitation in his voice, "I got me an idea."

"Yeah?" Cooper's interest was piqued.

"What if we was to get some of the industrial diamonds we've got around here and mix 'em in with the stones we got off that old Navajo?"

"What if we did? Then what?"

"Well, if a fellow was to claim he found all the gems someplace," all hesitation was gone from his voice now as he hurried on, "you know how crazy about diamonds the folks around here are. Why, a man ain't nobody at all in San Francisco society if he doesn't have a diamond stick pin in his shirt, and no self-respecting lady would dare be caught without a pair of diamond earrings."

"There's a big difference between industrial diamonds and chips and gem quality stones," Cooper pointed out.

"I know that and you know that, but how many people could even tell the difference between a raw diamond and a hunk of glass? It just might work." Arnold's voice was thoughtful.

"Hold on now, Phil. Are you gonna try to convince somebody that you found diamonds, sapphires, rubies and emeralds all in the same location? Nobody is gonna be gullible enough to believe that."

'Oh, don't be so sure about that," Arnold said thoughtfully. "Like you said, ever'body wants to be in on the next big thing. Can you see a man like Roberts or Ralston or even Harpending, for that matter, passin' up a chance to be in on a diamond strike?"

"Well, you might be on to somethin' there. Greed is a powerful motivator." After a moment's thought he added, "You'd have to convince 'em that the stones were real, though."

"Hmmm," Arnold mused. "I could take the bag of stones over to Fontrier, Bellmere and Company Jewelers and get them to certify that they're genuine."[27]

"What makes you think the jewelers would certify them as real?"

"Because," Arnold shouted, "for a fact, they are real!"

The two men fell silent, each lost in his own thoughts. Finally, Arnold broke the spell. "I think I see what you meant about creatin' the next big thing instead of just sittin' around waitin' for it."

"Well," Cooper commented, "that's fun to think about, and perhaps a slick talker like you might pull it off, but I wouldn't have the balls to actually try such a thing, even if I thought anybody would actually fall for it, which I don't."

Arnold made no reply as he stared out the window lost in thought.

Chapter Five

Wednesday, November 30, 1870
San Francisco, California

George Roberts did not bother to ask who was knocking on his office door. Hurrying across the room, he flung the door open to reveal, as he knew it would, the Bank of California's William C. Ralston. "Get in here," he whispered, pulling his millionaire friend into the room.

"What the hell's the matter with you, George? I was about ready to go to bed when your man arrived insisting that I get over here right away. What's going on?"

"Keep your voice down," Roberts advised, poking his head out the door to glance up and down the street. Satisfied that Ralston had not been followed, he closed the door, threw the bolt and turned to his visitor. "You're not gonna believe it," he began.

"Believe what? What's so all-fired important as to drag a man out on a night like this?" The impatience in his voice was obvious.

Roberts made no reply, instead opening his desk drawer to extract a buckskin pouch. The mouth of the bag was open; a length of yellow tape dangled from one corner. Fixing his eyes on Ralston, he wordlessly up-ended the bag, dumping the contents onto the green ink blotter covering his desk. Out tumbled about 50 gem stones, most colorless, some blue, some pale green, some medium red and some a deeper red. Amid the sparkling pebbles lay a folded sheet of paper. Ralston gasped as he took in the glittering spectacle. "What are they?" His voice betrayed no hint of impatience now.

Picking up one of each color, Roberts said, "Well, this is a garnet, this one is a sapphire, this green one is an emerald and these red ones are rubies and this," he announced, grandly displaying one of the larger colorless stones, "is a diamond!"

"Are they real?" Ralston asked, holding one of the red ones up to the light.

"Yep." Rotating the gem so that it flashed red and blue and pink in the gas light, he proclaimed, "This here is a gen-u-wine American diamond."

"How do you know? I know you're familiar with gold and silver, but you don't know any more about rubies or diamonds than I do. You wouldn't know a genuine diamond from a buffalo chip." Ralston did not take his eyes from the glittering pebble in Roberts' hand.

"Have a look at this," Roberts replied, retrieving the paper that had fallen from the pouch onto the desk. Wordlessly unfolding it, he handed it over to the banker.

Ralston reluctantly laid the gem he'd been examining aside. Turning his attention to the document, his eyes widening with each word he read. He had to clear his throat before he trusted himself to speak. "This is a jeweler's certification that these are genuine gemstones."

"I know. You'll notice that it also says they're worth perhaps $125,000."[28]

"I'm no one to dispute that," Ralston opined, "but I doubt that the jeweler knows much about uncut diamonds. Anyway, where did you get 'em?" he asked, scooping up a handful of the scintillating nuggets.

"A couple of prospectors found 'em," he replied. "You know the men – Phil Arnold and John Slack."

"I know Arnold," Ralston said, examining the stones. "He's a good man." He took his eye off the stones long enough to stare at Roberts. "They just turned all this loot over to you, did they?"

"No, of course not. They just brought the bag to me for safe keeping. They would have put it in your bank had they gotten to town in time. As it is, they said they'd be back in the morning to retrieve the package and deposit the whole lot with you. They swore me to secrecy, by the way."

Ralston laughed. "So, naturally, the first thing you did was send for me."

"Well, no," Roberts smiled. "The *first* thing I did was open the pouch as I'd promised not to do. Then, seeing what it was, the second thing I did was send a runner to get you and then find out where Arnold and Slack went."

"Arnold's got a home with a wife and children here in town, doesn't he? I'd guess he went home."

"Yeah, I think he owns a small house. You can guess again, though, about where they went. As we speak, he and Slack are playing poker over at the Red Dog saloon."[29]

"Where did they find these?" Once again, the stones riveted his attention.

"I don't know. As I didn't know what was in the pouch, I didn't ask. But, I do know, as you do, that they've spent a lot of time in the over territories, so I'd guess they got this booty somewhere over in Arizona or New Mexico."

Ralston studied each of the dazzling objects in his hand. "So, you promised not to tell and not to peek, so as far as you're concerned, you don't know that these exist, not to mention me knowing about them."

"I reckon that's about it. Would you figure we can buy these from them, Bill?"

Ralston considered a moment before he answered. "Maybe." He started to add something, but decided to hold it.

"Well, then, let's get on over to the Red Dog and make 'em a proposition."

"Hold on there, George. Let's think this thing through."

"Oh, yeah. I forgot that I don't know what it is they left with me." He seemed a bit crestfallen.

"Never mind that," the banker commented. "They'll get over that quickly enough if we make a good enough offer."

"Well, the jeweler says they're worth $125,000, and that's in the raw." Roberts was excited once again. "You know how crazy these San Franciscans are about diamonds! Lord only knows what these stones would be worth once they're cut. Hell, let's go make 'em an offer." He jumped to his feet.

"Sit down, George," Ralston ordered. "This is a big deal, maybe too big for just you and me to handle. There's more to it than just this little bag of sparklers. I'd better send a cable to Harpending and see what he thinks and get him involved." As if thinking aloud, he went on, "The first thing we need to do is find out where they found these goods. Besides, as I said, I have no faith in this jeweler's opinion. Getting to the source would be a world better than simply owning this little bag of gems."

"Why, they wouldn't tell. And I don't blame, 'em. If I found such a place, I sure as hell wouldn't tell anybody where they came from."

"They will if we offer enough. Put this back in your safe," Ralston ordered, pouring the stones back into the bag. "When they come back in the morning, you just send 'em to me."

☙

William Ralston was entertaining a visitor in his luxurious office at the Bank of California. Anyone observing through the spotless glass windows above the gleaming polished walnut half-walls would simply have seem two impeccably caparisoned business associates engrossed in an earnest discussion.

A clerk knocked before opening the door a crack. "Excuse me, sir. There's a couple of men here to see you."

Ralston looked up expectantly. "Philip Arnold and John Slack?"

"The one doin' the talkin' did say his name was Arnold, yes."

"Ask them to come in." As he spoke, Ralston shot a knowing glance at his guest.

"Come right in, we've been waiting for you," Ralston greeted when the two men appeared at his office door. At their hesitation, he urged, "Come in. Please come on in. Close the door."

The two men complied, but only entered the room far enough to allow the door to close. As the two men clung to the office's back wall, Slack studied the plush green carpet while Arnold glared at the banker. "Damnit, I thought our business was private," he growled.

"It is. I assure you it is," Ralston tried to sound reassuring. "I don't believe you gentlemen have met. Mr. Arnold, Mr. Slack, this is our friend Mr. Bill Lent." Ralston's visitor rose and extended his hand with a smile. Neither Arnold nor Slack made any move to acknowledge him. "Uh," Ralston went on, covering the awkward silence, "Mr. Lent is as interested in our project as I am. Please take a seat."

Arnold and Slack, both considerably cleaner and better dressed than when they'd arrived at Robert's office the previous evening, slowly moved forward and sat in the chairs facing Ralston's desk. Lent was standing behind and to the left of the two visitors. "Roberts promised not to tell anybody," Arnold said, his voice gruff. "First thing I know not only has he inspected our goods, but told you about it. Now, you've brought in this man," he jerked his thumb over his shoulder before turning to glare at Lent. "Why not just take out a full page ad in the newspaper?" he roared, returning his attention to Ralston.

40

"It's all in the family, Phil." Ralston said soothingly. George and Bill here and I are partners in many enterprises. You'll have to admit that we do all right." He prudently made no mention of his communications with Harpending.

Arnold again looked disapprovingly over his shoulder at Lent. "Would you mind gettin' over here where I can keep an eye on you?" It was more of a demand than a request.

Ralston inclined his head to indicate a chair against the wall behind his desk. Lent obligingly moved to it and sat. "Now then, how's that Phil?"

"Where the hell's our goods?" Arnold demanded. "Roberts said you had 'em."

"Yes, that's so," Ralston said. "George brought your, uh, package here for safe keeping, as I understand you yourself intended to do had the hour of your arrival last night not been so late." Seeing Arnold's attitude soften by a nearly imperceptible amount at the truth of that comment, he went on, "I assure you that your merchandise is as safe as a babe in its mother's arms."

"That may be so," Arnold said, his voice slightly less harsh, "but I'd feel a damn sight better with that babe in my own arms. How 'bout puttin' it there right now?"

"Certainly, certainly," Ralston said cheerfully. "I'll have to leave you for a few moments, though. I'm the only one, you see, who has access to our most secure vault." He pushed a button on his desk and almost instantly a clerk appeared at the door. "Would you see if these gentlemen require anything, please, Mr. Watkins?" Then, turning to Arnold and Slack, "Please excuse me for a moment. Mr. Watkins will get you anything you want."

After Ralston left the room, Watkins said, "Coffee, gentlemen?"

John Slack started to say something, but Arnold's hand on his knee froze the words in his mouth. "No, thank you," Arnold said.

The two prospectors eyed Lent suspiciously. Sensing the distrust, he offered, "I hear you men had a little luck, where was it, over in Arizona Territory?"

"Ain't none of your business where it was," Arnold growled.

"Well, that's just what we're here to discuss," Ralston said, re-entering the room at that moment. He placed the buckskin pouch in Arnold's hand. "There you go, safe and secure."

Arnold seemed to relax a bit now that he had the package in his hand. He pulled the mouth open to inspect the contents. "Well, I ain't tellin' you where they came from," he countered. "Only thing you need to know is me and John here found 'em and they's plenty more where these came from." He jerked the rawhide string to close the pouch and gave it a reassuring pat.

"George and Bill and I have plenty of money to invest." Ralston put on his best banker's voice. "Now we have no intent of doing you men out of anything; we just want to make a simple business proposition."

"We ain't interested in no business proposition," Arnold said, not unpleasantly. "Nor any other kind, either," he added.

"Well, it won't cost you anything to hear us out," Lent interjected. "Wherever your find may be located, there'll be expenses involved in travel and mining, not to mention the costs involved in obtaining a legal claim to the land."

Slack, who had been mute the entire time spoke up. "There ain't very much diggin' to be done."

"Shut up, Cousin," Arnold hissed. "You just let me do the talkin'." Cowered, Slack dropped his eyes back to the floor.

"I reckon you have a point about the travel and filin' fees," Arnold admitted. "I was figurin' on selling what we've already got to raise the money necessary for filin' and then us workin' the claim ourselves."

"That's exactly why you need men like us involved," Ralston said triumphantly. "Why if you offered to sell the goods you've got, word would spread all over this town faster than wildfire. You wouldn't be able to go to the outhouse without a dozen men following you. They'd monitor every move you made."

An awe-struck look covered Arnold's face. His countenance made obvious that he had not considered that aspect of the situation. Saying nothing, he began to rub his temple as if he had a headache.

Sensing the upper hand, Ralston rushed on. "Now, Phil, if you'd consider selling us a part of your interest, we'll pay you handsomely. Additionally, we'll furnish all the money needed for supplies and transportation, we'll hire any necessary labor and take care of the legal aspects. All you'll have to do is lead us to the location of the, uh, goods, and you'll be set. You men won't even have to pick up a shovel."

"No!" Arnold shouted. "I ain't interested in sellin' my interest to anybody at any price!" Then, more calmly he added, "How 'bout loanin' me the money with the goods we've already got as collateral?" He held up the pouch containing the gems.

Ralston allowed himself a smug smile. "Now surely, Phil, you don't expect me to loan out my depositor's money on such a risky venture, do you? Despite the jeweler's assessment, I don't know the value of these good or if there's any more where these came from or even where that is. No, I'm afraid a loan is out of the question." The banker leaned back in his chair as if to indicate that having reached a stalemate, the conversation was over.

"Now hold on, Bill," Lent said, standing. "Mr. Arnold, he's right, of course, about the bank's money, but what we're offering is out of our own pockets. George and Bill and I are willing to take whatever the risks are ourselves."

Arnold seemed to consider briefly. Then, abruptly, he stood. "Nope," he said, "I will not sell any part of my interest to anybody at any time for any price."[30] He picked up his hat from the desk and clamped it on his head.

"But you haven't even heard our offer," Bill Ralston said, standing and obviously trying to contain his frustration.

"Did you not understand me? No part, nobody and at no price you could name. Come on, John, let's go."

Slack made no move to get up, but did maintain his hang-dog look. "John, let's go," Arnold repeated, louder.

Slack raised his eyes from the floor, looked rapidly from Arnold to Lent to Ralston and then back at his cousin. Suddenly, a determined look came into his eyes and his gaze shifted to the banker. "I might be willin' to sell my interest," he said, a note of defiance in his voice.

જી

Asbury Harpending and his old friend from the *Chapman* adventure of Civil War days, Alfred Rubery, were enjoying an afternoon of rare English sunshine strolling in London's Hyde Park. The weather was cool, but Harpending, homesick for anything American, could not help himself. Anything that reminded him of home, even something as simple as sunshine, was irresistible. "It's good to get out of the office for a while," Harpending observed as a nanny pushing a pram rolled by. "I'm pretty sick of this whole business."

"Why don't you just chuck it and go home then? Let *The Times* and its financial editor, what's his name, Samson, go to blazes."

"Don't think I haven't considered it," Harpending said with a sigh. "But I do have partners who are depending on me; several people have invested in good faith and I've engaged offices here for several years."

"Not to mention that you're too bloody hard-headed to let them beat you with words."

"Well, there is that too," Harpending said with a wry laugh. "That bastard Samson seems to think he's more powerful than the Queen."

"He may very well be," Rubery observed. "If the *London Times* publishes a favorable review from him, that ensures success, and a bad report is the equivalent of a death warrant for any business enterprise, especially American mining ventures."

"Don't I know it?" Harpending snorted. "That's why he and I got into it over my trying to attract investors for the Mountains of Silver business. You know, he's so adamant about it being a scam that I'm beginning to think that Samson is on the take somehow."[31]

Rubery was about to make some observation when a clerk from Harpending's office approached. "Yes, Bently, what is it?"

"Sorry to disturb you, sir. A huge cablegram for you has arrived from America. It's marked 'Urgent' in big, bold red letters."

Standing, he made his apologies to Rubery and hurried along with the clerk to his offices. He had only just gotten seated at his desk before the clerk laid a two-inch thick stack of paper before him. As advertised, the top sheet proclaimed the message to be "URGENT." "This isn't a cablegram, it's a letter," Harpending mused to himself.

"Very good, sir. Anything else?" The clerk appeared anxious to leave his boss to his work.

"No, thanks Bently. Go on about your business."

Harpending dove into the stack of paper, observing right away that the communication was from his friend and fellow speculator, William Ralston. He also noted that the fee for sending the cablegram was more than $1,100.[32] "Must be very important for Ralston to have spent that much of his own money," he mumbled under his breath.

As he read the sheets of thin paper, he found himself reading faster with each page. Ralston's cable told of a vast diamond field located somewhere in a remote section of the United States. He did not know the actual location yet, but he did know that the find was worth, as a conservative estimate, $50,000,000 and that Ralston and George Roberts had complete control of the proposition.[33] Ralston also insisted that Harpending drop everything and rush to California to take over as general manager of the company they would form. "The man's clearly lost his mind," Harpending mused to himself.

The ensuing days flew by. Harpending cabled Ralston that he could not possibly leave London at the present time and hoped that would be the end of his involvement with the diamond business. He tried to attend to his current business – attracting British investors for his American gold and silver mining properties, dealing with the press and reassuring his partners. Ralston, however, was far from satisfied and exhibited his discontent by sending a daily cable, each more insistent than the last that Harpending rush to California. Although Harpending responded in the negative every day, little by little his resolve began to erode and give way to excitement. "Ralston's captured a fifty million dollar financial circus and badly wants me to become the ringmaster," he told an aide.

One afternoon as Harpending sat in his office composing his latest half-hearted refusal to Ralston's demands, an aide knocked on the door. "A gentleman to see you, sir."

"Who is it?," Harpending asked with a sigh, half relieved and half irritated at being interrupted.

"Baron Rothschild, sir," the aide replied laconically.

"Hell, man" Harpending shouted, "show him in." Somehow rumors of an American diamond field had made their way "across the pond," and London's financial district was rife with them. Many of Britain's leading financiers had sought an audience with Harpending, but an office call from the most aristocratic banker in the nation was well above all the others in importance and prestige.

"Come in, please come right in sir," Harpending cooed, affecting his most British manner.

"Good afternoon, sir," the refined gentleman greeted, removing his kid glove before offering his hand.

"I'm honored," Harpending said, shaking hands. "Please have a seat." He pushed away the usual visitor's hard chair in favor of the luxurious seat kept in the corner especially for occasions such as this. "Would you like some coffee or tea?" Detecting a slight hint of annoyance on the Baron's face, he added, "or something stronger?"

"No, thank you, no," the Baron replied, crossing his legs and leaning back into the plush cushions. "I have another engagement shortly, so I'd prefer to get right to it, if you don't mind." He placed his silk hat on Harpending's desk.

"Yes. Yes, of course," Harpending said, leaning forward to place his elbows on the desk. He assumed that Rothschild's visit had something to do with Ralston's diamonds, but considered asking if the Baron perchance had interest in any of his gold mining properties. He would have intended that as a joke, of course, but had failed at jokes often enough to know that most Englishmen did not appreciate his sense of humor. "What can I do for you, sir?"

The nobleman shifted in his chair. "Well, I have heard the rumors of Mr. Ralston, who is our mutual associate, having access to a vast American diamond field. I desire to know if there is any truth in these wild claims making the rounds of our financial district."

Harpending hesitated only a moment before pulling Ralston's cables from his desk drawer. "Here," he said, passing them across the desk, "You can see for yourself what Mr. Ralston has to say."

Rothschild briefly purused the documents. "Would you allow me to study these?" His manner was, as always, extremely polite and disarmingly unassuming, characteristics of his breeding and hallmarks of his success.

"There's an empty office next door," Harpending said, indicating the room to his left. "You may take them over there and study as long as you like."

In less than an hour, Baron Rothschild returned to Harpending's office and handed the cables back. "These communications are very interesting. Mr. Ralston seems sold on the truth of the matter," he said, resuming his seat. "May I ask your feelings on the subject?"

"Well," Harpending sighed, "while I do have the utmost faith in William Ralston and I do know first-hand that some diamonds have been found in America, I must tell you that I have serious doubts as to the existence of such an abundance of diamonds in the American West. Personally, I think that this bubble will eventually burst."

"I see," said the Baron after a brief pause to consider Harpending's words.

"Do not be so sure about that. America is a very large country. It has furnished the world with many surprises already. Perhaps it may have others in store. At any rate," he added, retrieving his hat and gloves, "if you find cause to change your opinion, kindly let me know."[34]

After the Baron made his exit with Harpending's assurances that he would be notified should any such change occur, Asbury Harpending engaged in some soul-searching. He had good and sufficient reasons to ignore Ralston's pleas, but if such a knowledgeable and successful personage as Baron Rothschild was willing to look into the possibility of an American diamond field, perhaps he'd better rethink his position.

The next few days were again punctuated by a daily, more insistent, cable from Ralston. Finally, late on a Friday afternoon, Alfred Rubery poked his head into Harpending's office. "So, how goes the hunt for diamonds, old bean?"

"Ralston assures me that we're dealing in facts, not hopes," Harpending sighed, laying his work aside. "He also says that not only is this diamond field real, it's within his control. Today's cable begs me to come if only for a brief stay – 60 or 90 days."

"What's the problem?" Rubery asked, taking a chair. "Go."

"Well, Alfie, you know damned well what the problems are. I see a future of activity and wealth for me in what I'm doing right here. I'd hate to be distracted from that even briefly. But…." He finished the sentence with a sigh.

"Look here, old chum," Rubery said. "Once you get to America, it will be quite easy for you to find out the truth of the situation. If the truth happens to correspond with Mr. Ralston's statements, everything else in the world in the way of business or enterprise will seem commonplace and cheap. Otherwise, you can just come back here and pick up where you left off." His earnestness impressed his friend.

"Well," Harpending admitted," Baron Rothschild's interest got my attention. I must confess that I'm beginning to get the urge to go."

"I'm surprised at your reluctance," Rubery said with a confident air. " Make up your mind to go to California and find out what all this cable correspondence means." The visitor paused, thoughtfully stroking his reddish-brown mustache. "Personally, I'm bored to death, just pining for a bit of excitement." He slapped his hands on the arms of the chair as he leapt to his feet. "I will go along with you, and we will stir up things again in the Far West."[35]

Chapter Six

From the outside, the Arnold home was the very picture of contentment and tranquility. The grass lawn was manicured, the walkway was smooth and spotless, the clapboard siding a gleaming white and the shutters and gingerbread trim were a harmoniously contrasting forest green. The flowerbeds lining the walkway and the shrubbery flanking the porch reflected the thoughtfulness and attention to detail of the owner's personality. Inside, the atmosphere was not quite so serene.

Indeed, much turmoil had occurred between Philip and Mary Arnold in the six months since the husband had returned from the Arizona Territory. As agreed, he had forked over $12,000 as her share of the proceeds for the sale of his Mountains of Silver interest – money that ensured the orderliness of the house and surrounds, the neat appearance of the well-dressed children and the abundance of food in the icebox. However, to Mary's dismay, when Philip returned from the mine, he stayed home only long enough to bathe, shave and eat a few meals before he was gone again.

Unknown to Mary Arnold, the reason for his latest absence was that Ralston, Lent and Roberts had refused to invest any money in the diamond venture without further information.

On the other side, Arnold and Slack continued to flatly refuse to disclose the location of the diamond field, although they did say it was 500 miles or so to the east and hinted that it might be somewhere in Arizona or New Mexico. So, a compromise was struck. The prospectors agreed to conduct an agent chosen by the investors to the diamond location and let him inspect to his satisfaction. Arnold's only proviso was that the man should be blindfolded, coming and going.[36]

Banker Ralston appointed David G. Colton, a San Francisco man he knew to be particularly level-headed, honest and of diverse background. At Oakland, Arnold, Slack and Colton boarded a Central Pacific train bound for a destination unknown to Colton, the latter being blindfolded any time the train approached a station. Upon leaving the train, the trio meandered around through a desolate country, Colton again being blindfolded much of the time. They returned to California with about 60 pounds of rough diamonds, rubies and other valuable gems and reported to Roberts, Lent, Ralston and Harpending, that gentleman having returned from England in April. According to Arnold, "We found diamonds plentiful, but not over a very large extent of country. We made two other discoveries about 100 miles south of our first discovery, which I am satisfied will pay to work."[37] By some process unknown to Arnold and Slack, the investors determined the value of this haul to be $600,000.[38]

Harpending, despite his reluctance to leave England, was apparently all in by now, as he was quite upset that Roberts had brought Lent in the fold. Nonetheless, the investors agreed to pay Slack $100,000 for his share of the claim. Arnold still flatly refused to be bought out at any price. This deal was struck: the investors would advance Slack a down payment of $50,000; the prospectors would make another trip to the diamond field and return with a couple of million dollars worth of stones as evidence of good faith. If all was in order at that point, Slack would receive the remaining $50,000.[39]

Controversy was brewing, once again, on this Sunday morning in the Arnold household. "You're going where?" Mary Arnold's anger was reflected by both the volume and tenor of her voice. Still an attractive woman, Mary Arnold was careful about her appearance even on days like today when she had no plan to leave the house. Her housedress was new and her strawberry blonde hair was neatly piled atop her head.

"England, I said," her husband replied as calmly as he could manage under the circumstances. Phil had not imagined that she would take kindly to this news, but he had not anticipated this degree of anger, frustration and hostility either. Phil was his usual dapper self, having spent his ritual half hour preening before the mirror earlier in the morning.

"You've been gone more than you've been home in the last six months," she declared. "Did it ever cross your mind that perhaps I could use a little help around here?"

"Now, you know that ain't so, Mary. I've been home plenty." He knew she spoke the truth, but thought denying it would perhaps convince her.

No such luck. "Well all right, let's see. It was November last year when you and your cousin come back here from silver minin' Arizona and had them gems with you, right?"

"Yes, that's right. And I also had $25,000 with me. I gave you half the money to spend however you saw fit, didn't I?"

"I'm not disputin' that," she spat. "We'll discuss the money later. Right now we're talkin' about how you spend your time. Then it was in February that you and John and that other man went traipsin' off to Lord knows where and was gone for nearly two months."

Phil, sensing an opening, said, "I thought we were discussin' **where** I spend my time, now how. "Anyway," he hurried on, "you know I had to convince Mr. Roberts and Mr. Ralston that there were more gemstones where the ones we had came from, didn't I?"

"Well," she retorted, frustrated that he was again trying to divert the discussion, "we'll also talk about what you spend your time doin' all the times you're gone from here another day. What I do know is that you left me here with a house and four children to tend to."

"By hell, woman," he shouted, "what do you think I spend my time doin'? Ain't I a good enough provider?"

"Yes, you are," she had to admit. "But don't think for a minute that I don't know what kind of women hang around those minin' camps, and I've seen 'em lookin' at you, too."

"Well, yes, there's whores in the camps, and I can't help what they look at. But, let me assure you, they ain't no whores – nor nobody else, except a few hostile redskins, for that matter – where me and John and Colton went. And now that you mention it, how do I know what you've been doin' while I'm out workin'? I've seen men eyeballin' you, too, you know."

Greatly annoyed, she spat, "You just go look at the children playing in the back yard and you'll plainly see what I spend my time on." Taking a moment for her anger to dissipate, she moved across the kitchen to the table where her coffee had gone cold. Refreshing the mug, she sat. "Anyway, why do you want to go to England?"

"It's a business trip," he answered enigmatically. "Cousin John is goin' with me. If anybody should happen to ask where we're at, you just say you don't know. It is very important that nobody, and I mean nobody, finds out where we've gone."

"How long'll you be gone this time?" she sighed, stirring a spoonful of sugar into her coffee.

"I ain't sure," he replied, sitting opposite her. Reaching across the table, he took her hand in his. "I promised Ralston and the others, and now I'm promisin' you, that I'll be back just as soon as humanly possible." He paused to squeeze her hand before adding, "And soon – very soon – after I get back, we'll be richer than you ever dreamed."

℘

Phil Arnold and John Slack stepped down from the train at London's Victoria Station, more travel-worn than from even the most arduous of their prospecting journeys. To ensure that no one would suspect what they were up to, they had taken a circuitous route, eventually boarding a steam ship in Halifax and arriving in England nearly a month after their departure.[40] Their total expenses so far had taken only a small bite out of Slack's $50,000, so they had plenty of money for their mission.

"And you thought San Francisco smells bad," Arnold laughed, inhaling deeply. "How do you like the odor of jolly old England in July?"

"I thought you said this country was civilized," Slack commented, faking a cough.

"Well, I guess we'd consider it about as civilized as they consider us. They think Americans, especially westerners like us, are all Buffalo Bill. Let's go find our luggage."

A short time later, the carriage delivered them at the front door of The Carlton City Club, newest of the West End's gentlemen's clubs. Ordinarily, Americans would not be admitted to the restricted membership establishment, but the $20,000 letter of credit they carried bearing the backing of London's prestigious financial firm, Smith, Payne and Stewart Company,[41] cut through the myriad barriers. "Now remember," Phil admonished, "you're Mr. Burchem and I'm Mr. Aundle. Don't be signin' your real name on the register."

"I reckon I can remember that my middle name is my last name for the duration of this trip. Say, did I ever tell you about the Hardin County, Kentucky, boy who went off to Cincinnati one time?"

"What about it?" "Aundle" bit, bracing himself for one of John's jokes.

"When he got to the hotel, he signed his name with an "X," then thought about it, went back and drew a circle around the X. When the clerk asked him why he did that, he said that bein' off in the big city and all, he didn't want to give his right name." Slack laughed heartily at his own joke.

"Well, you just remember to do the same, Hardin County boy. And, while you're at it, try to remember that you and I are both well-heeled California gentlemen now."

The pair paid off the taxi and turned to face an imposing set of polished marble steps leading to the massive oak door. In the lobby the furnishings were all Philippine mahogany, shining brass and spotless glass. The walls were papered with a French velveteen covering, the shade of which was an exact match for the plush carpet on the floor. Phil stepped forward as they approached the desk. "Mr. Aundle and Mr. Burchem," he announced.

The clerk raised an eyebrow. "Americans?" Phil did not care for the condescending tone.

"We have reservations," he declared, trying to match the Englishman's patronizing tenor.

"We shall see about that," the clerk intoned, his patronizing inflection unaltered. Checking the ledger, his eyes widened as he read whatever the manager had written about the expected American guests. "Yes, I see that you do have a reservation." As his eyes rose to meet the American's gaze, he added, "Sir." His glance fell once again to the ledger. "You gentlemen are in the Prime Minister Suite." A more subservient note dominated his voice now.

"Very good," Aundle said as he signed the register and moved aside to allow his partner access to the ledger.

"We shall require a bottle of your finest brandy." Burchem ordered, trying to affect a British air.

The clerk slapped the bell on the desk. When the bellboy appeared, he commanded, "Show these gentlemen to the Prime Minister and see that you step lively."

෴

"The offices of Leopold Keller Company, if you please," Aundle directed the cabbie.[42]

"Right, Guv," the man replied, clucking the horse into motion. After they traveled a few blocks, the driver glanced over his shoulder at the passengers. "Wantin' some fine jewelry, are you?"

Even though the Americans realized that the man was just making conversation, they were not inclined to disclose anything concerning their mission. "Just doin' some shopping," Burchem mumbled.

"Well, you've made a bloody good choice," the driver said amicably. "One of London's finest establishments, this is." The carriage rolled to a stop in front of the jeweler's showroom door.

The two Americans quickly paid off the driver and walked through the glass door into the brightly lit interior of the jeweler's shop.

"Mr. Aundle and Mr. Burchem to see Mr. Keller," Phil informed the clerk who greeted them at the counter.

"We have an appointment," Burchem added, attempting to impart a tinge of importance to his voice.

The Americans had only a moment to take in the glamour of the jewelry on display in the glass cases surrounding them before a short man with a bushy black moustache hurriedly approached. "Welcome, welcome gentlemen," he enthused. "I am Mr. Keller and our entire company is at your service. Mr. Aundle, I presume?" Mr. Keller extended his hand in a stiff gesture.

"This is Mr. Burchem," Phil said, taking the jeweler's hand.

"Please come into my office," Keller invited, shaking hands with Burchem. "I am in receipt of your letter of credit and most eager to conduct business with you." The three men walked to the rear of the store and into a lushly furnished office. "What are your requirements?" Keller motioned the visitors to the chairs facing his desk.

"We desire to purchase some uncut diamonds," Aundle announced.

"Very well," Keller replied, a look of slight perplexity covering his face. "What quality do you desire?"

"Oh," Aundle drew the word out as he glanced at his partner out of the corner of his eye, "we're actually more interested in quantity than quality."

"Very well," Keller repeated, his bafflement increasing. "How many, then?"

"A lot," Burchem interjected.

"I see," Keller said, his bewilderment deepening further. Taking another tack, he asked, "How much did you desire to spend?"

Aundle squirmed a bit in his chair. He did not care to disclose the amount of money at his disposal at this time, despite the jeweler's knowledge of the $20,000 letter of credit. Also noting the uncertainty on the Englishman's face, he redoubled his resolve not to say anything about what they intended to do with the diamonds. "Well," he said, noncommittally, let's see what you have on hand and then we'll see where it goes from there."

"Very well," Keller repeated. "You gentlemen make yourselves comfortable. I'll return straightaway. Can I offer you any refreshment?"

"No, we're fine," Aundle replied, a bit testily, eager to conclude this transaction and get on with the next phase of their mission.

In only a moment, Keller returned, a small green velvet bag in his hand. "Here you are, gentlemen," he announced, dumping the contents onto a red velvet display mat on his desk.

Aundle quickly counted about 50 stones. "It's a start," he commented as he and his partner leaned forward to examine the diamonds. Neither man noted that the office lights were arranged to produce the best effects from the glittering gems.

"This is approximately," Keller hesitated a moment, calculating in his head, "$2,000 worth."

"These are fine," Burchem said, "but we need many more than this." He waited expectantly for a moment, then slammed his palm on the desk. "Many more!"

"I have others, but they would be of an additional, uh, excellence compared to these."

"Well, you might throw in a couple of better quality," Aundle commented. "No more of this kind?"

"These are all I have on hand," Keller admitted with a sigh, "but I can get more if you gentlemen can give me a day or two."

"We can do that," Aundle said. "Do you have any rubies?"

"Certainly," Keller perked up. "Shall I get some from the showcases?"

"No. No," Aundle quickly responded. "We want uncut stones. Only uncut."

Keller's curiosity overcame his wish not to endanger the large sale. "I see," he said, then added, "May I ask if you intend to have us cut the gems for you?"

"No, we do not."

Keller waited for elaboration. Seeing that none was forthcoming, he asked, "Some other firm then? Perhaps someone in New York?" Now the jeweler waited expectantly.

"What we plan on doing with the merchandise is none of your affair, sir." Now it was the American who offered a condescending tone.

"Yes. Yes, of course. It's just that someone buying uncut stones, especially in the quantity you desire, is highly unusual. I just wondered...."

"If our money ain't good enough for you," Burchem cut him off, "they's other shops around here." He glared hard at Keller who seemed at a loss for words.

Scowling, Aundle asked, "When will you have more diamonds, and can you get us some uncut rubies?"

"Certainly. The day after tomorrow should be time enough," Keller said, trying to hide his exasperation.

"See you then," Aundle announced, standing. "Let's go, John."

Three days later, the two Americans were aboard a steamship bound for a Canadian port. Hundreds of gems worth more than $20,000 were concealed in their luggage. They had departed from North America at Halifax in an attempt to cover their tracks; return via Canada would hopefully make it easier to smuggle the hoard of uncut gems into the United States.

❧

Totally oblivious to the bustle in the lobby of the Bank of California, Asbury Harpending made a beeline for the head cashier's office. Ignoring the clerk posted outside Ralston's inner sanctum, he burst through the door, the clerk hard on his heels.

Startled at the interruption, the four men huddled around the banker's desk looked up, the meeting suspended. "I'm sorry, sir," the clerk stammered, "I tried...."

"Never mind," Ralston said, waving the clerk away. "Hello Asbury," Ralston greeted his partner. "You know George Roberts and Bill Lent, of course. Have you met General George S. Dodge?"

Harpending, ignoring the gentleman's proffered hand, raised his hand, displaying a yellow sheet of Western Union telegram paper. "I need to see you, William," he said.

"OK. Go ahead," Ralston replied. Noting Harpending's stare at the General, he assured, "It's all right, General Dodge is Bill Lent's partner in many mining enterprises; he's fully aware of our, uh, gemstone, venture if that's what's on your mind."

"It is," Harpending answered noncommittally. "Nevertheless, could I see you alone?"

"Certainly." Ralston's voice was as cheerful as usual. "Gentlemen, you would please excuse us?"

After Lent, Dodge and Roberts filed out of the room, Ralston said, "Now, Asbury, please sit down. What's all the excitement?"

"I got a telegram here from Arnold and Slack," he said, handing the yellow slip to the banker. "As you can see, they've returned from the diamond field and want somebody to meet 'em over at Lathrop."[43]

"This telegram was sent from Reno," Ralston observed. "Why do they want somebody to meet them?"

"I don't know," Harpending snorted. "I suppose to share the heavy burden of the responsibility of a million dollars worth of diamonds if they have accomplished the mission they agreed to."

"That's a reasonable assumption and a reasonable request," Ralston said, with a nod of his head. "Will you agree to go?"

"Me?"

"Why not. It's got to be me or you or Roberts or Lent or General Dodge. You know neither George nor I can go, so...."

"Who the hell is this Dodge fellow anyhow? What's he doing in this deal?" Harpending seemed angry.

"As I told you, he's Bill Lent's partner. As you know, now that we've bought out Slack, we plan to buy out Arnold. That will leave us free to reap the entire benefits of the find. The simple fact is that Lent feels that we need Dodge's expertise, not to mention his money."[44]

"Well, I don't like it," Harpending roared. "There's too damned many fingers in this pie. I'm gonna have a talk with Roberts – he's the one who brought Lent in on the deal – and now this other man. I don't like it at all."

"We can take that up later," Ralston tried to sound soothing. "How about you go to Lathrop, meet our intrepid prospectors and escort them home? I'm eager to see what they've brought from the diamond fields."

"So am I," Harpending said, calmer now. "I'll leave first thing in the morning."

Chapter Seven

The fact that the town is located in the beautiful San Joaquin Valley and is the junction point for the Central Pacific's west-bound trains is about all that Asbury Harpending could see that the town of Lathrop had going for it. He had waited in the sweltering heat for a seeming eternity for the overland train to arrive.

Extracting a red bandana from his pocket, he wiped the sweat from his forehead with one hand while lifting his gold pocket watch by its chain with the other. He observed that all of four minutes had elapsed since he'd last checked the time. Impatiently snapping the watch case closed, he considered going back inside the station building to wait, but decided that he preferred the open air, hot as it was, to the stifling, malodorous interior where several other people were waiting. Stepping into the shade of the building, he took a seat on the bench along the wall. With his feet stretched before him, despite the heat he had nodded off into a shallow sleep when a shriek from the steam whistle jolted him wide awake.

With a hiss of steam and a screech of brakes, the train slid to a stop opposite the station's platform. The first man out of the passenger car, the conductor, hopped to the boards shouting, "Thirty minute rest stop, folks. You might want to find something to eat. There's a diner just down the street." Harpending anxiously scanned each face as the passengers descended the single iron step to the platform. After a dozen or so people came down, he waited an additional few minutes before it became obvious that no one else was exiting. Harpending mounted the stair and entered the passenger car's musty interior.

At the extreme rear of the car, Philip Arnold sat in an aisle seat, a glazed look in his eyes. Next to him, his head leaning against the window, John Slack was sound asleep. Both were travel-stained and weather-beaten, bespeaking much hardship on their journey. Arnold stared straight ahead at nothing, as dazed as a combat veteran. If he saw Harpending, he took no notice. As Harpending approached, he noted the rifle between Arnold's knees and a bulky, heavily wrapped package resting on his lap.[45] His right hand grasped the rifle as tightly as if he expected someone to try to wrest it away.

"Phil?" Harpending touched his shoulder.

The weary traveler did not move for a moment, then slowly shifted his gaze to Harpending's face as his forehead wrinkled. "Oh. Hello, Asbury," he said, his voice lacking any emotion.

Harpending took a seat opposite the two men. Slack still slept. "We've got a few minutes here; do you want to get off and stretch, perhaps get a bite to eat?"

Arnold seemed not to understand at first, then shook his head as comprehension crept into his befuddled mind. "No, I'm more than ready to turn this responsibility over to you," he patted the bundle on his lap, "and get home for some rest."

"Very well," Harpending agreed. "Tell me about your trip." He leaned closer as Arnold shook his partner awake.

Slack stared at his partner while the cobwebs cleared his head. Arnold jerked his thumb to indicate that they had a visitor. "Oh, hello, Harpending."

"Howdy, John. You boys look like you've had some adventure," he prompted, hoping to draw the story of their journey from them.

"Indeed we have," Arnold whispered as he glanced around at the few passengers remaining in the car. "Wait 'til the train gets in motion; then we'll have some noise to cover our conversation."

Harpending nodded. The trio made idle chatter about the weather and the drought until the bell rang, the other passengers filed back in and the train lurched into motion. As the car filled with the noise of the rattle and clatter of the wheels on the track, Harpending leaned in close. "Well?" His voice was anxious.

"You wouldn't believe it. We found a spot even richer in stones than what we'd seen before," Arnold whispered just loud enough to be heard above the din. "Even the anthills were covered in diamonds and rubies. We picked up, oh, I'd guess a couple of million dollars worth and did 'em up in two packages, one for each of us to carry."

Slack noticed Harpending eyes fall to the bundle on Arnold's lap. "By then we'd about used up all our supplies, so we packed up, covered our tracks and lit out. We'd traveled a couple of days when we came to a river swollen out of its banks," he explained. "The ford was washed out, so we had to build a raft to get across. The current was so swift we lost control and nearly got upset. As it was, one of the bags full of gems fell into the water and was lost." Slack told the story breathlessly and earnestly.

Harpending thought the tale lurid, yet not improbable.[46] He was also impressed with the prospectors' sincerity and obvious travel-weariness. "Go on," Harpending urged, finding himself getting excited.

"That's about it," Arnold said, relieved that the tale was told. "We figure this collection here," again he patted the bundle on his lap, "is worth about a million or so." Then he added, "I think the one we lost was probably worth a little more, but, at any rate, we've kept our end of the bargain."

Harpending resisted the urge to snatch the package from Arnold's lap, rip it open and have a look. Instead, he continued to question the two men until the conductor announced the stop at Oakland. When the train screeched to a halt, all three men moved to the station's platform. "Well," Arnold announced, "I reckon this is where we turn the responsibility over to you." As Harpending extended his hands to accept the package, Arnold drew it back. "I'd like a receipt," he growled. After Harpending scribbled on a slip of paper, Arnold smiled and shook his hand. "We're gonna go find a bath and some food before we go home. Mary wouldn't let me in the house lookin' and smellin' like this."

"We will be in touch," Harpending assured, shaking hands with Slack. As soon as the two men were out of sight, he hefted the bundle and dashed inside the station. Trying to contain his excitement, he instructed the telegraph operator to send a quick note to William Ralston at the Bank of California. Taking the telegraph pad to a table, he looked over his shoulder to ensure no one was watching before hunching low over the pad and writing: "Have expected goods STOP Arrange carriage to meet ferry STOP Have interested parties gather at my house STOP Harpending."

℀

The evening fog was just beginning to creep in over the water as the ferry approached San Francisco's Embarcadero. Asbury Harpending peered anxiously through the gathering dusk to see if his carriage would be waiting as he'd requested. Heaving a sigh of relief when he spotted it waiting, he thought he was beginning to understand the burden that Arnold and Slack had borne as they transported the package now resting in his lap from wherever they gathered the contents.

"Good evening, sir," his driver greeted him. "May I take the package?"

"No!" Harpending replied, a little more sharply than necessary. "Just get me home as quickly as you can."

As the horse clip-clopped along, Harpending was glad that the home he'd recently purchased from his friend Ralston was only a short distance away up Rincon Hill. The bundle on his lap seemed to grow heavier by the minute, and his eagerness to see the contents also increased with every revolution of the wheels. When the carriage pulled up into the circular drive in front of his house, he jumped to the ground, sped up the walk on foot and through the front door.

Mrs. Harpending knew from experience that the set look in her husband's eye meant there was no time for conversation. The determination in his tread told her that there would not even be a greeting although he'd been away from her and their three daughters for three days. "They're in the billiards room," she advised as he trekked through the sitting room with scarcely a glance at her.

Assembled in chairs around the perimeter of the room sat William Ralston, Bill Lent, George Roberts, Alfred Rubery and General Dodge. Each man leapt to his feet and moved instinctively to the billiard table in the center of the room as Harpending entered the room. Wordlessly and without ceremony, Harpending cut the elaborate fastenings. Grasping the lower corners, he dumped the contents onto the green felt surface. A gasp escaped each throat as a couple of hundred gems tumbled into the light. Like so many twinkling stars, the colorless, red, green and blue stones reflected and refracted the soft glow from the gas jets lighting the room.[47]

After a long moment of silence, Ralston was the first to find his voice. "My God," he sighed, "there must be a fortune here."

"Arnold said he thought this was about a million dollars worth," Harpending informed, holding one of the larger colorless stones to the light. As each man picked up one of the gems, nobody thought to wonder just how Arnold had arrived at that evaluation.

Harpending related the "lurid" story that Arnold and Slack had told about the rigors of their journey and the lost bag of jewels. He also told Ralston of his feelings transporting the package on the ferry, and that he now understood why Arnold had asked for someone to meet them. While he was speaking, each man rolled the stones on the table under his hand, often picking one to examine more closely and watching for his neighbor's reaction. Whatever differences of opinion that had separated these men's ideas were gone now; they were of one mind. At length, George Roberts suggested that a business meeting was in order. As all agreed, Harpending gathered the stones back into the bag from which they'd been dumped. "I'll place this in my vault for safe keeping," he offered.

Noting that Bill Lent was about to voice an objection, William Ralston cut him off. "Bill," he said, "as you know, I had this house built to my personal specifications. The vault here was installed by the same company that furnished the one for my bank. I assure all of you that the goods will be perfectly safe here."

These men all knew each other well. Each had an impeccable business reputation and they were long-time business associates, the very cream of San Francisco's business community. Yet, somehow, being in the presence of all these jewels created a faint air of suspicion, if not outright distrust. The entire group insisted on watching Harpending place the package in the vault. After he slammed the heavy door and spun the dial, several of the party stepped forward to try the handle just to be sure the goods were safely locked away.

"Gentlemen," Roberts began when everyone found a seat in Harpending's office, "it would appear that there is definitely some diamond mining to be done. It is obvious that the goods we just examined are worth several times the money we've already invested, and there is every indication that there's plenty more where these came from." Several of the men, most notably General Dodge, had previously had doubts about the venture, but no one voiced any disagreement or uncertainty now. Every man puffed his cigar and waited, lost in individual thoughts. "Very well, then, if we're all in agreement, I suggest we rough out some plans to form a company, the intent of which will be to mine and market whatever diamonds and other gems may come into our possession." Murmurs of agreement went through the room. "Is it understood that Mr. Harpending, Mr. Lent, Mr. Ralston and I, by virtue of monies already advanced and other sums already agreed to, own three quarters of the diamond property?"[48]

"Yes," Ralston agreed. "Philip Arnold owns the other one-quarter."

"What about Slack?" General Dodge asked.

"We owe him $50,000 and he's out," Ralston advised. "Now, we have many plans...."

"How much would it take to buy Arnold out?" Dodge interrupted, a sharp note in his voice.

Harpending answered, "I broached that issue with him on the train from Lathrop. He said that he would not sell any portion of his interest to anybody at any price."

"He's been adamant about that all along," Roberts added.

"Well, I want in," Dodge nearly shouted. "If I can't buy out Arnold, are any of you willing to sell me a share?"

"Calm down, General. We'll work something out," Ralston resumed. "There's riches enough here to go around. Now, as George was saying, as a first step, I nominate Bill Lent to be the president of our proposed company."

Through the clouds of smoke, everyone looked at the others. "There being no disagreement, then so be it," Ralston said after it became obvious that no one would speak.

Bill Lent got to his feet. "I'm honored, gentlemen. May I nominate Asbury Harpending to be the general manager?"[49] Again, no one voiced any objection. "Very well, then, so be it." Exhaling a cloud of blue smoke, he thought aloud, "Let me see, what's to be the first order of business?"

"We need to get a definitive valuation of the goods in the vault," Harpending ventured.

"Yes," Ralston agreed, "and I know just where to get that done." In response to the questioning looks, he said, "Mr. Charles Tiffany of New York City is the most knowledgeable jeweler in the country and owns the finest lapidary in the world."

"That's so," Roberts agreed. "Let's send him a sample of our goods for his valuation."

"No, not send," Rubery interjected, "We'll take a representative sample to New York and put them in his hand." As Rubery had invested no money in the venture and hence had no standing, his comment drew some questioning looks from the others.

"I take it you want to go, Alfie?" Harpending was only half joking, attempting to lighten the mood.

"You're bloody damned right. If you're going, I'll be happy to keep you company."

"As president, you should go along too, Bill," Harpending addressed Lent.

"Yes, and I'd like my partner, General Dodge to go along."

"Very well," Harpending said, "I'll contact Tiffany's and make arrangements for the four of us to take a large sample of the gems to New York as soon as possible."

"All right," Lent had taken charge of the meeting. "The next item we should deal with...."

"Hold on a minute, Bill," Ralston broke in, "I think Arnold and Slack should be included in this trip to Tiffany's."

"Why?" Lent seemed surprised. "As we said, Slack is out as soon as we put the money in his hand."

"Let's not forget that none of us has the faintest idea of where the diamond field is," Ralston advised. "On that basis alone, not to mention our integrity, we cannot afford to alienate Mr. Arnold."

"I guess you're right about that, but what about Slack? I see no reason why we need him." Lent was upset.

"Well," Harpending stepped in, "he and Arnold are partners and cousins, and he does know where the mine is. I say we make an effort to keep him happy until we get this thing off the ground."

"I agree," Roberts said, "but, as he's already sold out, he has no say about anything."

Harpending thought for a moment. "Then we'll hire him to keep him involved."

"Great idea," Ralston commented.

"All right. Now, then," Lent resumed, "we need to find out where this diamond field is and send somebody who knows what he's doing out there to have a look and report on the possibilities."

Philip Arnold. Arnold was the silver-tongued perpetrator of the Great Diamond Hoax. Courtesy of Hardin County Historical Society.

Asbury Harpending. According to his version of events, he was one of the men who lost heaviest in the hoax. Courtesy of Union Bank.

George Roberts. He and Harpending were in on the diamond venture from the beginning. Courtesy of Union Bank.

William Lent. He was the only man who took legal action against Philip Arnold attempting to recover hoax money. Courtesy of Union Bank.

Mr. Charles Lewis Tiffany. The founder of the famous jewelry company, he certified Arnold's diamonds as genuine and incredibly valuable. Courtesy of Library of Congress.

William Ralston. He is shown here later in life. Courtesy of Union Bank.

William Ralston. Shown here in the 1860s, the San Francisco Banker and financier put up much of the diamond hoax money. Courtesy of Union Bank.

General George McClellan. For a short interval, the famed Civil War figure was willing to lend his name and prestige to the diamond venture. Courtesy of Library of Congress.

Clarence King. Head of the Government's Fortieth Parallel Survey, he is the man who exposed the diamond hoax. Courtesy of Library of Congress.

Some members of the Fortieth Parallel Survey. James Gardiner standing with a rifle, Clarence King standing at right. Courtesy of U.S. Geological Survey.

Benjamin Butler. As a Senator from Massachusetts, the "Beast of New Orleans" was instrumental in helping the San Francisco and New York Mining and Commercial Company gain title to the diamond field lands. Courtesy of Library of Congress.

Samuel Emmons. A member of the Fortieth Parallel Survey, he helped his boss expose the diamond scam. Courtesy of Library of Congress.

George Armstrong Custer. While stationed in Elizabethtown, the flamboyant boy general amused himself by writing and wearing a different outrageous costume every day. Courtesy of Library of Congress.

Horace Greeley. The famous New York newspaperman stood ready to provide the positive publicity the company would need to sell stock in the diamond venture.

Marriage License.

#774

THE COMMONWEALTH OF KENTUCKY,

To any Minister of the Gospel, or other Person, legally authorized to solemnize Matrimony.

You are permitted to solemnize the Rites of Matrimony between (Mr. Philip Arnold) and (Miss Mary E May) the requirements of the law having been complied with.

Witness, William T. Samuels, Clerk of the Hardin County Court, at Elizabethtown, this 3d day of January 1855

Wm T Samuels, clk

Morton & Griswold, Printers, Louisville.

Certificate of Marriage.

This is to Certify, That on the 30th day of January 1855 the Rites of Marriage were legally solemnized by me, between Mr. Philip Arnold and Miss Mary E May at Elizabethtown in the County of Hardin in the presence of Eliza LaRue, and Rebecca Helm and others

Signed Jno. Ⱥ. Yeaman

(Note—The Statute requires the names of at least two Witnesses to be inserted in the foregoing Certificate.)

Morton & Griswold, Printers—Louisville.

Philip Arnold and Mary May's marriage certificate from 1855. Courtesy of Hardin County Clerk.

Philip Arnold assigned his power of attorney to his wife before again departing for California in 1864. Courtesy of Hardin County Clerk.

I Mary E Arnold Pillip
Arnold wife goe with
Him to fell out venkere:
Meradeth to ther Hers & His
ihtrest in all the
Richard May Lands who was
his father which he has
Bought & She has got
And go with Him Back to
Califonia And stay untill
he wants to Mou Back heare
he Binds Him self By this
Riten Paper And He is to Hav
the use af All the Land Money
To dea Bisenes on in that
cuntry to giv over to His
All the Money He can spare
To Bee Hers out of His Bagnes
As He gets it to By His it
rather Farm or Home heare
And what else She wants
And to dou as She pleases
with so She can Hav somthing
for Hir Sport as well
As His children

February the 6 1868

witness

J B Shepherd

C R May

Philip Arnold

Mary E Arnold

The agreement Mary Arnold extracted from her husband before she agreed to return to California with him in 1868. Courtesy of Kentucky State Archives.

Elizabethtown, Ky. May 3rd 1875.

Dear Sir: "Confidential"

I herewith send you a little information, which I think may be useful to your Office in Louisville

Mess Arnold & Polk, Bankers, at this place went to protest in New York for $150 last week, for lack of funds, this we think very strange, and coupled with this, they have not discounted any paper for the last sixty days, but are rediscount-ing their paper in Louisville, and to a customer of ours, who is one of the best men in the Co who applied for a loan at their Bank for $50 to day - they said they could not discount for the next month, or two.

I would like you to make a note of this, as I cannot say what the result may be - Arnold is the

Page 1 of the letter which spawned the trouble between Longshaw and Holdsworth and Arnold and Polk. Courtesy of Kentucky State Archives.

wealthy man of the concern, but
I think, he will not last long –
Polk has not one dollar in the
world, and is actually nothing
more than Arnold's clerk –
Arnold made what money he had
by salting mines in Arizona with
diamonds and selling them (the
mines) at great profit – for this
little speculation he was arrested
and laid in jail for some time
but was released on some small
technicality, & has since then
been enjoying his ill gotten gains
This I give you in
strict confidence which you
can use at your discretion
Hoping you are
quite well
I am yours
very respectfully

Chas Bird Esq
Cincinnati, Ohio

Page 2 of the letter. According to Longshaw's court testimony, obscuring the signature was common business practice. Courtesy of Kentucky State Archives.

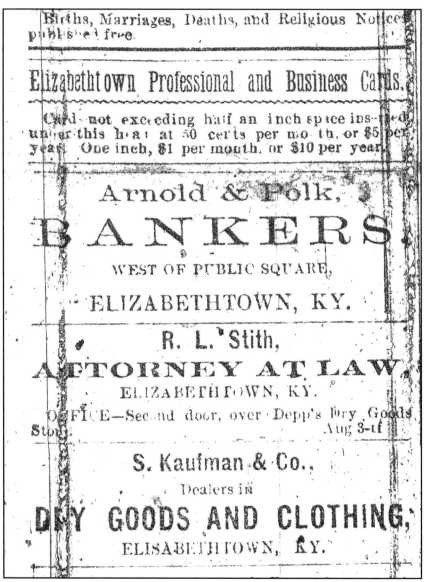

Births, Marriages, Deaths, and Religious Notice published free.

Elizabethtown Professional and Business Cards.

Card not exceeding half an inch space inserted under this head at 50 cents per month, or $5 per year. One inch, $1 per month, or $10 per year.

Arnold & Polk,
BANKERS.
WEST OF PUBLIC SQUARE,
ELIZABETHTOWN, KY.

R. L. Stith,
ATTORNEY AT LAW,
ELIZABETHTOWN, KY.
OFFICE—Second door, over Depp's Dry Goods Store. Aug 3-tf

S. Kaufman & Co.,
Dealers in
DRY GOODS AND CLOTHING,
ELISABETHTOWN, KY.

Newspaper advertisement for the banking firm of Arnold and Polk. The advertising rates in 1872 give some indication of the value of the vast sum Arnold's diamond venture paid him. Courtesy of Hardin County Historical Society.

Hardin Circuit Court

Wm M Lent plaintiff

vs _____ In Equity

Philip Arnold &c Defendants.

The following are the contents of the iron
safe seized by the Sheriff under the attachment in
this case and which by consent of parties
were taken from said safe by the Sheriff and placed in
his hands as Sheriff subject to the order of the Court herein
viz:

✓	Currency	$260.50
✓	Neck lace & ear rings of unknown value.	
✓	3. Rings Fingers " "	
✓	Jewelled cross in leather case value unknown	
✓	1 pair ear rings in " " " "	
✓	1 Gold watch & chain in case " "	
✓	14. twenty dollars pieces gold	280,
✓	4 Tens " "	40.
✓	2 Fives " "	10,
✓	2 two½ " "	5,
✓	Mc Cracken County bonds.	

Mch 1. 1869 No 1049. denom. $100.00 , Coupons 8 — 40. incl

" " " 1050 " " " " "

" " " 1051 " " " " "

" " " 1052 " " " " "

" " " 1053 " " " " "

" " " 1054 " " " " "

" " " 1055 " " " " No "

Hardin County Sheriff Wood listed the contents of Arnold's safe. Courtesy of Kentucky State Archives.

Also in the safe was this note signed by San Francisco investor George D. Roberts. Note that it has been assigned payable to Mary Arnold. Courtesy of Kentucky State Archives.

Lent managed to gain an attachment against all of Arnold's property, up to and including the bales of hay in the barn. Courtesy of Kentucky State Archives.

The object of this suit (among other things) is to attack any property of the defendant and any moneys that may be due to Deft Philip Arnold by McCracken County and especially any claim or interest that said Arnold may have in the bonds and coupons thereof issued by McCracken County which bonds are numbered and are as follows viz; the certain McCracken County bonds and coupons thereof issued in aid of the E&P. R.R. dated March 1st 1869. payable Twenty years after date to bearer with 7.% interest per annum payable semi-annually March & Sept 1st respectively in each year at the Bank of America in New York City on presentation of the proper coupons. Each of said bonds being signed by G.A. Flournoy County Judge and J.S.Spence County Clerk the coupons attached to each of said bonds being numbered from 8 — 40 inclusive.

Forty three of said bonds are of the denomination of $1000.00 each and are numbered both on the bonds and on the coupons attached to each as follows viz; No's. 151 — 169 inclusive and No's. 171. 172. 176. 267. 268 and No's. 274 — 292. inclusive.

Twenty five of said bonds are of the denomination of $100.00 each and are numbered both on the bonds and on the coupons attached to each as follows viz: No's. 1042 — 1060. inclusive and No's. 83. 84. 85. 86. 87. & 90. ————

John M Harlan
Atty for Plff.

Determined to get at everything Arnold owned, Lent's attorney (John Marshall Harlan) went after Arnold's McCracken County bonds. Courtesy of Kentucky State Archives.

Circuit Court of the United States
District of Kentucky, At Louisville

William M. Lent
vs.
Philip Arnold, et.al.

Monday March 24th. 1873.

This day came the parties by their Attorneys, and by consent of all parties, the attachment herein is dismissed as settled and agreed, and this action and the cross suit of May E. Arnold are dismissed agreed and settled each party paying his own costs, as per agreement in possession of parties.

W. D. Wood late Sheriff of Hardin County is ordered to deliver the attached property to Philip Arnold & May E. Arnold, And then came said Philip Arnold and May E. Arnold, and acknowledged the receipt of all the attached property, and said Sheriff and his sureties are discharged, by consent of parties from all further responsibility in reference thereto.

By consent of parties, It is ordered that either party may withdraw from the files any original paper filed by them upon leaving a certified copy of such paper in lieu of the original

Lent and Arnold came to this settlement after the case was moved to Federal Court. Courtesy of Kentucky State Archives.

In active pursuance of their lawsuit, Longshaw and Holdsworth attempted (unsuccessfully) to get depositions from Clarence King and New York attorney Samuel Barlow. Courtesy of Kentucky State Archives.

Longshaw and Holdsworth are summoned to court in their suit with Arnold and Polk before resorting to gunfire to settle the dispute. Courtesy of Kentucky State Archives.

"Yes," Ralston agreed. "Of necessity, we'll have to include our prospector friends in that trip. In fact, I'd like to see if for myself. I'll arrange to leave the bank for a few days."

"Of course Arnold and Slack will have to guide us; we don't know where it is," Harpending advised. "But it is getting late in the season. I'll go too, but I have no desire to be out in the wilds someplace when the snow flies and the thermometer drops through the floor."

After some discussion, agreement was reached to employ a mining engineer of impeccable reputation to accompany Lent, Ralston, Roberts, Dodge, Harpending and Arnold and Slack to the diamond site. The trip would have to wait, of course, until the weather improved in the spring. Upon arrival, the engineer would make a thorough examination of the site and reach conclusions concerning the worth of minerals and gems to be found there and the feasibility of establishing a mine.

"Before we go on," Harpending suggested, "we're overlooking one small detail." Every face turned to him, waiting. "How do we know that out prospector friends will agree to all of this?"

The room fell silent. These men had been so wrapped up in their own ideas and dreams that no one had even considered what Arnold and Slack might want or have to say. Finally, Roberts spoke up. "As I'm the one they first approached with the diamonds, I appoint myself to speak with Phil about it. He's knee deep into this project, so I'm pretty sure he'll agree."

"And Slack?" Ralston asked. "As soon as we pay what we owe him, he'll be fairly prosperous. He might not be interested in further adventure."

"Well," Harpending boomed, "if so, more power to him. As long as Arnold is in, we really don't need Slack."

"Now," Lent resumed, "as several of us know, there will be legal issues to be addressed. Without any evidence other than what I've been able to gather from Arnold's vague hints, I assume that this diamond property is somewhere in Arizona or New Mexico, so it's probably on government land."

"I've come to the same conclusion," Ralston said. The others nodded agreement.

"Well, then," Lent continued, "we will need a lawyer to draw up papers of incorporation for us, and we may well require an ally in Congress to help us gain mining rights on the property."

"As we'll be going to New York City anyway," Ralston chimed in, "I suggest we contact my old friend Samuel Barlow while we're there. You know him, don't you, Asbury?"

"I do," Harpending answered. "He'll be an excellent choice. Not only is he one of today's foremost attorneys, he is an expert in business affairs, well connected socially and has a lot of influence with important political figures."

"That's right. I've known Sam for twenty years and have found him to be top drawer in every respect." Ralston paused to study the group. Again, there was no disagreement. "One of those political figures Sam knows is no less than General George Brinton McClellan." With a dramatic pause for effect, he added, "They don't come any bigger than that."

Astonishment showed on every face. "Barlow has influence with 'Little Mac?'" General Dodge asked, clearly impressed. Evidently, he alone realized the irony of the diminutive McClellan being "big" in politics.

"Sam was a major figure in McClellan's campaign when he ran for the presidency against Lincoln back in '64," Ralston informed. "So, yes, I happen to know that he still retains a few markers he can redeem whenever he sees fit."[50]

"Well, then," said Lent, "let's hope we can make him see fit to work with us."

"I don't think there'll be a problem," Ralston said. "Sam's always been an avid supporter of every public enterprise and not one to pass up an opportunity such as this."

"What can McClellan bring to the table?" Rubery, the Englishman, asked.

"Window dressing, my dear Alfie, window dressing," Harpending answered. "The object of the game here will be to sell stock in our company. The more attractive we can make the enterprise to investors, the more readily they will open their pocketbooks to our enterprise."

"Very well then, gentlemen, I think that'll about wrap it up for tonight," Lent concluded. "Quite an exciting evening, eh?"

"Hold on," Ralston spoke. "There's one more detail I'd like to suggest."

Everyone who had left his chair stopped. "What's that?" Lent asked for the group.

"I think it would be a good idea to display some of these stones in front of the public before we take them to Tiffany's," Ralston said. "That will certainly put the town abuzz and drum up interest in our venture."

There was no immediate reaction as each man considered the idea. "People will naturally want to know where they came from," Roberts advised.

"Of course they will; that's part of the goal," Ralston pointed out. "There's no danger of us revealing the location, because we don't know it. That will allow us to be mysterious about the site, and that will add more fuel to the public discussion. I'll display some of them at the bank."

"I like it," Roberts said. "I'll display some at my office, too."

"Count me in," Lent added, "I'll take some to my office."

"I don't care for the idea of having our goods just lying around loose," Harpending said. "I'll get some display cases."[51]

With that, the meeting broke up. After the others left, Rubery and Harpending went into the study for a night cap. "What are you going to tell people when they ask where these stones came from, and who owns the site?" Rubery inquired, sipping his brandy.

Harpending laughed. "I'll just say they came from my diamond mine," he roared with laughter.

"And as to the location of said mine?"

"It's somewhere within 1,000 miles east of here," Harpending said with a grin.

The Englishman shook his head. "That takes in a lot of territory, doesn't it, old chap?"

Chapter Eight

Thursday, October 5, 1871
New York, New York

The dazzling array of diamonds, rubies, sapphires and emeralds on public display at the various venues around San Francisco had, indeed, produced the desired effect. The entire city, business and social, was abuzz with the news of an American diamond field having been discovered. Everybody, as anticipated, clamored to know exactly where this "American El Dorado" was located. That clamor was exceeded only by the bellowing from men wanting to invest early in the diamond mining venture so as to be in on the ground floor. By agreement, and despite the mounting pressure, Roberts, Ralston, Arnold, Harpending, Lent and Dodge, who had purchased an interest from Roberts (the money helped pay off Slack's remaining $50,000), steadfastly refused to sell any interest at any price until they had organized their diamond mining company.

Toward that end, Bill Lent, General George Dodge, Asbury Harpending and his pal Alfred Rubery had traveled to New York City to contact a lawyer, get Tiffany's evaluation of the stones they carried and perhaps make some political connections. On the train traveling east, the men had been somewhat surprised to learn that the buzz of excitement was not limited to California. At every stop, in every station and every restaurant, they had been approached with a proposition for some local group to buy in. The same had proven true in New York City; they were approached by prospective investors at every turn. Still, every offer was refused, although all concerned felt that the time to "go public" was rapidly approaching.

Philip Arnold had agreed to all the as yet unnamed company's plans without hesitation. He did not even blink an eye before agreeing to lead an inspection party to the location of his diamond find as soon as the weather allowed. His only difficulty in the entire affair had been the two day squabble he'd had with his wife about going off on another trip. She screamed that she had grown weary of his excusing his absences with promises of future riches. In exasperation, he had finally just packed a bag and walked out, leaving an end of the discussion to another time. Arnold, perhaps beginning to feel a little intimidated by all the excitement, insisted on keeping the bag of gems in his possession. The canvas bag, which did not escape his grip the entire trip, contained only ten percent of the collection he and Slack had brought to California from their last excursion.[52] His cousin, John Slack, now an employee of the company, had also agreed, and they both were along on this evaluation and organization trip to New York.

The law offices of Samuel Latham Mitchill Barlow were as lavish as any business office Phil Arnold had ever seen. From the name stenciled in gold leaf on the glass door to the lacquered walnut woodwork, plush leather-upholstered chairs and the deep red carpet, every fixture spoke to Barlow's success as a businessman and corporate attorney. When the group was ushered into his inner sanctum, Barlow, a man of medium height with a shock of coarse black hair and a bushy black mustache, rose to greet them. "Asbury Harpending," he enthused, shaking hands, "how many fortunes have you made and lost since I saw you last?"

"I'm working on the third," Harpending laughed while introducing the other men. After an exchange of pleasantries all around, the business meeting began in earnest. "There's no need for me to ask why you gentlemen are here," Barlow began. "Everybody from here to San Francisco knows what you boys are up to."

"It goes east from here, too," Bill Lent informed. "Some folks in England, including Baron Rothschild, are interested."

"All right, then," Barlow said, "I'm flattered that you gentlemen would come all the way across the country to me. I'll do all I can for you in every way. So, what's on the top of your list?"

"We want you to draw up articles of incorporation for us," Lent advised. Barlow hurridly scribbled notes on a pad.

At the end of the lengthy ensuing discussion, the decisions had been made that the company would be incorporated in California, have its principal offices in San Francisco and the capitalization of $10,000,000 would be divided into 100,000 shares at $100 per share.[53] The men had already agreed that Phil Arnold, as the man who'd found the bonanza, owned one-fourth of the stock, Bill Lent and General Dodge each owned one-eighth and Asbury Harpending, William Ralston and George Roberts each owned one-sixth. [54] "What's the intent of the company?" Barlow asked.

"To secure our discovery," Harpending answered. "If we can attract several influential men – names the public would recognize – to invest in our company, we will have a much better chance of holding on to our claim than if we try to restrict the stock to three or four individuals."

"I'll write it up so that you'll own all the lands, discoveries, reservations, lodes, claims, rights locations, minerals, metals and allotments made or to be made, found or to be found, gathered or obtained by any of the parties."[55] His hand moved as rapidly over the pad as the words tumbled from his mouth.

"I hope we're not gonna have to pay you by the word," Lent joked.

"Well, you hired me so we don't miss anything," Barlow said, unruffled. "Have you thought of a corporate name?"

"We were thinking 'San Francisco Mining and Commercial Company,'" General Dodge suggested.

"You don't want to incorporate the word 'diamonds' in the name?"

"Absolutely not," Harpending roared. "When it comes to the legalities of the thing, we want to keep our intent as obscure as possible."

"I see. Well, the suggested name certainly conveys the intent," Barlow observed, "but I was under the impression that you gentlemen intended to drum up some interest here in New York City."

"Indeed we do," Harpending agreed. "That's one of the reasons we came to you. We would also hope to establish an office here if we can find – that is if you can help us find – the right men."

"As I said, I am completely at your disposal. All right then, if that's the case, how about 'The San Francisco and New York Mining and Commercial Company?'"[56]

"That's it," Harpending and Lent said, nearly in unison.

"Very well," Barlow said, a satisfied smile on his face. He poised his pen above the pad. "What's next?"

"Well," Harpending began slowly, "we need to contact Tiffany's to arrange an evaluation of the goods we brought."

"You brought some of the diamonds with you? Where are they?" For the first time, a note of excitement tinged the attorney's voice.

Phil Arnold spoke up for the first time since he'd said "hello." "They're in a safe place," he said. Unknown to the others, he'd rejected the suggestion to place the stones in the hotel safe. As the weather was very cool, all the men were wearing overcoats, and Arnold had secreted the bag of gems in the lining of the coat now draped across his lap. "I will produce them when necessary."

"All right. As it happens, I know Mr. Charles Lewis Tiffany personally, and I also happen to know that he's aware of your presence in this city and your mission." Almost as an aside, he added, "Mr. Tiffany doesn't miss much in the world of gems. I am sure that I can arrange a meeting with him."

"Splendid!" Lent cried. "Now, Sam, there's a little more ticklish issue."

"I'm all ears," Barlow replied.

With a glance at Arnold and Slack, Lent said, "The lands we'll need access to are on government property. We're going to have to find some way to ensure that Congress amends the laws necessary to allow us to have exclusive rights to the properties."

"Hmmm," Barlow mused, stroking his mustache, "We'll need an influential congressman involved then, won't we?" He hesitated a moment, then added, "I think General Butler just might be interested. He's a Representative from Massachusetts, you know."[57]

Asbury Harpending jumped to his feet, the secessionist blood still coursing in his veins instantly coming to a boil. "Benjamin Butler? The Beast of New Orleans? I will not work with that Yankee son of a bitch!" While he was Union commandant of New Orleans during the war, Butler had secured his reputation with all Southerners when they felt that he implied that the ladies of that city were no better than common prostitutes.

All present were shocked by this outburst, Arnold and Slack, being fellow Kentuckians, less so than the others. Barlow spoke up calmly, "Hold on, Asbury, we'll need him, and I think I can promise that you'll like him once you get to know him a little."

Harpending was far from convinced, but did realize that they would need any ally in Congress. If Butler was in Barlow's pocket, he would have to do.

"I suppose so," he mumbled aloud. Hardly content, he leaned close to Arnold and whispered, "President Davis labeled Butler 'a felon, an outlaw, an enemy of mankind, and ordered that if captured, he ought to be hung!'[58] Despite what Mr. Barlow says, I don't think I shall care to be associated with him. No sir, not at all."

"I'll arrange for him to meet with us, too," Barlow confidently stated, ignoring Harpending's aside. 'What else?"

"Mr. Arnold and Mr. Slack are the men who discovered the diamond field," Harpending advised. "As such, they are, at this time, the only persons who know the actual location. However, they have agreed to lead a party, including a knowledgeable mining engineer, to the site come spring. We'll require a man of impeccable reputation, one whose appraisal of our property will carry great weight with prospective investors. If you…."

"Say no more," Barlow interrupted. "I know just the man, and, as it happens, he's in New York just now. His name is Henry Janin. He's examined more than 600 mining properties without a single mistake, certainly without ever having caused a client to lose even one dollar because of poor judgment on his part."[59]

"Sounds like just the man," Dodge said.

"He is," Barlow assured. "If he has any failing at all, it is that he takes no chances. Why, he's been known to turn down a good mine simply to strengthen the confidence of investors in other properties. I assure you that Janin's OK, if you get it, will guarantee the reputation of your property in every market."

"Will he be available when spring arrives?" Harpending inquired.

"We'll have to ask him about that," Barlow said. "He doesn't work cheap, but he's the man you want, all right."

"Well, Sam," Bill Lent said, "you get what you pay for. Speaking of which, assuming we get – ah – the laws arranged as we need, will that require some money?"

"Yes, we should also allocate some funds for acquiring land titles," Barlow informed, hedging the issue of how they'd get the laws "arranged." "I'd think $100,000 should be sufficient."

"While on the subject of money, I suppose we'd better discuss your fees," Harpending commented, having calmed somewhat from his outburst at the mention of General Butler.

"Well, let me see," Barlow said, thoughtfully stroking his mustache. "In view of all the valuable services I'm providing, I think $500,000 would be a reasonable compensation."[60]

If that figure shocked anyone, the faces betrayed nothing. "Would you be willing to take at least some of that in company stock?" Lent asked.

"Certainly," Barlow said through a smile, "I'm convinced this project will pay us all handsomely." Rising to his feet, he added, "Give me the afternoon to arrange things, gentlemen. I will be in touch at your hotel in the morning."

The meeting broke up with Philip Arnold having said one sentence while John Slack and Alfred Rubery, members of non-standing, had uttered not one word. Arnold was not upset – he was content to let the money boys do the talking. For now.

಄

While the men were at breakfast the next morning, a messenger arrived and put a note in Bill Lent's hand. Opening it, he announced that Barlow had indeed arranged a meeting and that they were to be at the lawyer's home at seven this evening. Thus being at loose ends for the day, Phil Arnold did consent to place the bag of precious stones in the hotel safe while he and Cousin Slack went shopping. The rift with his wife over the continued absences still on his mind, Arnold was in hopes that a nice gift from one of New York City's famous stores might repair some of the damage he'd done when he just walked out.

The hired carriage rolled to a stop in front of the fashionable home on the corner of Twenty-Third Street and Madison Avenue promptly at seven p.m. This late in the fall, full darkness had nearly descended, and the house was brightly lit, ready to receive visitors. The westerners piled out, Phil Arnold tightly clinging to the bag containing the gems. A smartly turned out valet answered the bell, took their coats and ushered them into the library where several men waited. As the introductions went around, they met General George McClellan, the former Union Army commander and presidential candidate, Benjamin "Beast" Butler; Horace Greeley, publisher of the New York *Tribune*; Mr. Charles Lewis Tiffany of the famous jewelry firm bearing his name and a Mr. Duncan of the banking firm of Duncan, Sherman and Company. Despite the auspicious company, Asbury Harpending, by his own admission an unreconstructed rebel, could not resist joking to Phil Arnold that if the Sherman who was Duncan's partner happened to be General William Tecumseh Sherman of "marching through Georgia" fame, his evening would be totally complete.

General McClellan, better known as "Little Mac," was exactly what the southerners understood him to be: short in physical stature, but long on ego; dark and handsome; dapper; arrogant and filled with self-confidence. An aura of personal superiority enveloped him like an indestructible bubble.

Benjamin F. "Beast" Butler also presented the anticipated image. He was bald on top; gray hair hung low on the back of his neck, running over his shirt collar. Having seen his image in the newspaper many times during the war, Harpending observed that the General was heavier and grayer than in his soldier days. Corpulent and sloppy, he presented the quintessential image of a corrupt politician. In consideration of all Butler was and had been, Harpending had to force himself to shake the man's hand.

Horace Greeley, the publisher, looked much the same as Butler: bald on top with gray locks flowing over his collar. His wire-rimmed spectacles and watery eyes, however, presented a more scholarly countenance. His presence at the meeting gave Harpending pause. "I hope you understand, sir, that our business here is private."

"Of course," Greeley responded. "I simply have a nose for news and like to be present when it happens."

"My point exactly," Harpending said, louder than necessary. "I should not care to read an account of tonight's meeting in your newspaper tomorrow morning." His attitude was just a bit challenging.

"Mr. Greeley is here as my guest," Barlow pointed out. "I understand your point, Asbury, and assure you that Mr. Greeley will print nothing until you give him our approval to do so."

"I assume the time will come – when your stock becomes available – when you will welcome publicity," Greeley said soothingly. As Harpending and Lent nodded agreement, he concluded, "When that time arrives, I – and my newspaper – shall be at your service."

Apparently satisfied, Harpending turned to their host. "Mr. Barlow, when you said you could get the attention of important men, you did not exaggerate, sir."

"I could not agree more," Lent said. "My compliments, sir." For emphasis, he made a show of making a deep bow from the waist.

"Happy to be of service, my friends." Observing the expectant faces around the room, he added, "Well, gentlemen, we all know why we're here. Let's get to the business at hand. Mr. Harpending?"

Harpending extended his hand to Arnold who reluctantly handed over the bag of stones. With a flourish, Harpending grasped the lower corners of the bag and let the contents tumble to the surface of the heavy oak table that had been moved to the center of the room directly beneath the gas light chandelier. An audible gasp escaped several mouths as the rough, but nonetheless sparkling, jewels bounced on the table top. For a few long moments, the hiss of the gas was the only sound in the room. Then, as if on command, the New Yorkers converged on the gems, rolled them in their fingers, held some up to the light and just let them rest in the palms of their hands as if some magical power would seep out of the jewel and soak through the skin.

The westerners stood back to let the New York men drink in the aura of the glittering stones. After long minutes of this random examination, Mr. Tiffany took over. He looked at individual stones gravely, sorted them into little heaps and held some up to the light, looking every whit the great and knowledgeable connoisseur that the world knew him to be. Slowly, he examined each of the perhaps fifty gems he'd arranged by type, rubies here, sapphires there and a large of pile of diamonds in the center. Finally, he stood erect and rubbed his chin. Philip Arnold held his breath as Tiffany began to speak. "Gentlemen," he said softly, "these are beyond question precious stones of enormous value. But, before I can give you an exact appraisement, I must submit them to my lapidary and will report to you further in two days."[61] As Mr. Tiffany smiled in self-satisfaction, Arnold exhaled as if a great weight had been lifted from his diaphragm.

The valet appeared with bottles of bourbon, brandy and cigars. As ice tinkled in the crystal glasses and laughter filled the room, Arnold noticed that Harpending and Lent had literally cornered General McClellan and the three of them engaged in solemn conversation. Arnold wandered in that direction, hoping to overhear, but their quiet tones left him wondering about the topic of their discussion.

Before the meeting broke up, the California men accepted Tiffany's receipt for the stones and agreed that after his examination, Tiffany would deposit the gems with Mr. Duncan's firm for safekeeping.

Philip Arnold rose early on Saturday morning. After getting dressed as quietly as possible so as not to disturb his roommate cousin, he took the elevator to the lobby and entered the restaurant. Just as he'd hoped, Asbury Harpending sat alone reading Mr. Greeley's newspaper and sipping coffee. "Good morning," he greeted.

"Why, hello, Phil," Harpending said, smiling as he lay the newspaper aside. "You're up early."

"I need to talk to you, Asbury," Arnold said, a note of supplication in his voice.

Although Arnold was ten years senior to Harpending, their relationship was not unlike Harpending was the father and Arnold the son. This arrangement was due to the fact that throughout all their business dealings in gold and silver mining, Harpending had been the one who put up the money, while Arnold generally served as the intermediary with those who performed the physical labor. "Of course," Harpending said, "whatever I can do for you. Would you like some coffee?" A wave of his hand signaled for the waiter.

"I've got a little problem with all these goings-on," Arnold began, taking a seat opposite the other. "As you know, I've agreed to lead a party to the diamond field."

"Yes, I do know. You have been vested in the company stock despite the fact that you have not risked a cent, so why is that a problem?"

"Well," Arnold began, "in the first place, ninety percent of my gems are in Mr. Ralston's bank in California." He started to go on, but paused as a waiter approached with a coffee pot. Both men waited patiently while the man poured coffee into both their cups. When the waiter walked away, he resumed, "the other ten percent is in some New York vault, either Tiffany's or Duncan's."

"All perfectly safe, I assure you," Harpending said. He'd noted that Arnold had referred to the gems as "mine," rather than "ours" but decided to let it pass for the moment.

"I must confess I'm a bit surprised that you trust all these damn Yankees. I don't. Anyway, however secure the goods may be," Arnold continued, "I've placed my property at the mercy of others without proper security and the considerations I've received, you will agree, are a mere trifle compared with the value of what I've agreed to disclose."

"I see," Harpending said, no commitment in his tone. "Don't forget about that 108 carat diamond we own back in California. We've been offered $96,000 for it. Your share of that would be, let me see, a little more than $30,000."

"Pie in the sky!" Arnold retorted. "I want some cold cash as a guarantee of good faith," he announced without hesitation. Studying Harpending's face for a reaction, he went on, "But, I'm willing to leave that money in escrow until we get Tiffany's evaluation. Then we'll get Janin's – if that's who we hire to examine the site – report. Suppose we go in the spring and the man says the ground is not what I have represented; my secret is known. On the other hand, the property might be worth more and be even richer than I've represented."[62]

Harpending considered what Arnold had said. "What would make you comfortable?"

"I want $100,000 as a down payment, or else I'll go get the bag of stones – they're mine – and go home." Encouraged by the look of agreement on Harpending's face, he added, "And, after I lead you to the diamond field, if it's as I've represented and the inspector's report is satisfactory, I want an additional $150,000."

"Sounds fair to me," Harpending agreed. "I'll discuss it with our partners."

While waiting for Tiffany's report, telegraphic exchanges concerning Arnold's demand flew thick and fast among Ralston, Lent and Harpending.

☙

Late on Sunday afternoon, Barlow sent word for the men to assemble at his office at nine a.m. on Monday. When they arrived, Charles Tiffany was seated behind the desk with Mr. Barlow, a huge grin on his face. As soon as the door closed behind then, Tiffany announced, "Gentlemen, your precious stones are safe in Mr. Duncan's vault. I am happy to inform you that my firm has fixed the value of the gems we examined at $150,000."[63]

As Tiffany sat back with an air of satisfaction, Philip Arnold, unable to restrain his amazement, had to turn his face to the wall.

As the men started to file out of the lawyer's office, Barlow said, "Mr. Arnold, would you stay a moment, please?"

Arnold tried to wipe any hint of his feelings from his face before he turned back. A little curious and slightly concerned, he noted that Bill Lent remained in his chair. "Close the door," Barlow directed.

"What is it?" Arnold asked, closing the door, his heart in his throat.

Barlow did not speak, but merely pulled open a desk drawer. Extracting a stack of bills, he methodically counted out the crisp $1,000 bills. When the pile reached 100, Lent spoke up. "Now there, Arnold, is the $100,000 you wanted."

"Now let's be clear," Barlow said. "This money guarantees that you will not sell any gems to anybody, and you will not reveal the location of our diamond field to anybody outside our company. Is that understood?"

Arnold began stuffing the bills inside his shirt.[64] "Yes. What about the mining engineer we're gonna hire?"

"He will be considered a member of the company," Lent snorted.

As Arnold rose to leave, Barlow stopped him. "One more thing. All concerned feel that this transaction, while not exactly conforming to the agreed program, is entirely business-like and does not hinder the goals of the San Francisco and New York Mining and Commercial Company in any way."[65]

"OK," Arnold said. As soon as his back was to the desk, a huge grin reappeared on his face.

Although Tiffany's report was not intended for public consumption, the news somehow leaked and was common knowledge in speculative circles before the Californians left New York. If "bombarded" would describe the spate of offers to buy in on the way east, only "assaulted" would adequately express the action of prospective investors at every stop on the journey back to California.

On the westbound train heading home, Arnold and Slack sat apart from the other men. "The gems we brought to New York were only a tenth of the collection you and I delivered to San Francisco," Slack whispered, although no one was within earshot.

"Yes, that's right," Arnold said.

"Well, if Tiffany's said they are worth $150,000, then the whole lot is worth $1,500,000!" John Slack shook his head. "Phil, we only paid $20,000 for the whole kit and caboodle, including that big one that we've been offered $96,000 for! I'm scared, Phil. This thing is gettin' way out of hand."

"Well, John," Arnold said, "you've got your money, so there's nothing for you to worry about."

Slack, neither as glib nor brazen nor as mentally quick as his cousin, slowly realized the truth of that observation. His mood considerably lightened, he asked, "How the hell can somebody who supposedly knows what he's talkin' about come up with a value of a million and a half?"

Arnold simply smiled. "I'm damned if I know, Cousin." He turned to look out the window at the passing landscape a moment. Turning back, he added, "I'm damned if I know, but I'll take it."

Chapter Nine

Mary Arnold was so angry that the veins carrying the blood beneath her translucent skin stood out in bold relief in her neck and forehead. "Again?" she screamed. "You no more than got home from New York and now you're talking about going overseas again?"

Her husband quickly realized that all the good will he had created by bringing her a nice gift from New York was undone the instant he mentioned that he would be returning to England. The ruby and diamond bracelet from Tiffany's was beautiful and expensive and she'd liked it. The fact that her husband considered it a kind of inside joke, being unknown to her, made no difference. "Well, I'll be here for a week or so before I go," he muttered, knowing it was a weak rejoinder.

"Well, that's something," she admitted, "but you'll miss Christmas with the children." Her plaintive tone made that as much of a plea as an observation.

"Can't be helped," he asserted. Then he paused to gather his thoughts and took the initiative. "How 'bout the $50,000 I gave you?" he asked. "That's something, too, wouldn't you say?"

"That's a different question," Mary said, making a visible effort to calm herself. They both realized that money was no longer an issue. Hence, she no longer had tiring of the promise of future riches in her arsenal of arguments. His promises were coming to fruition, and her bank account showed it. She took a seat at the kitchen table, realizing that many wives would be happy to have no more problems than she.

"What?" Phil was confused.

"The fact that I have a husband that's never at home is a big concern," she said with a sigh. "Where that money came from is another worry." She hesitated to bring what was really on her mind. "Phil, just what are you up to?"

"Oh, it's just business," he said, trying to sound dismissive. Joining her at the table, he added, "Nothing for you to concern yourself about."

Mary Arnold had heard his "now don't you worry your pretty little head" attitude before and did not like it. "For all I know," she said, "whatever it is you're doing may be illegal. Maybe you'll end up doing twenty to life in prison and then I won't have to worry about when you'll be coming home." He could not decide whether her tone conveyed anger, concern or frustration.

"I'm not going to prison," he assured. "Mary," he said, trying to sound sincere, "if all goes as planned, sometime before next year is out, we'll be fixed with all the money we can ever spend and then I'll be around so much that you'll be wishing I'd go someplace. You'll be trying to find ways to get me out from under foot." He smiled as he patted her hand soothingly.

"What am I supposed to tell the children when they ask where their Daddy is?" He heard a note of resignation in her voice.

"Tell them that I'm out earning the money that puts food in their mouths and clothes on their backs."

"Can't you tell me what you're involved in? I worry."

"I can tell you this much," he sighed. "I'm in partnership with Asbury Harpending, George Roberts, Bill Lent and William Ralston. You know all of them and you know that they are the most upstanding citizens of this town. I hope knowing that will ease your mind."

She hated to admit it, but she did feel better knowing that whatever it was he was doing involved those honorable and honest men. "Well, if you say it will be over within a year, there must be a schedule. Can't you at least give me that much?"

"All right," Phil said. "It's all approximate, but I'm to go to England and meet Harpending and Lent there. My business there will take only a week or so, and then I'll be back in New York by the end of January. After that, I have to meet Cousin John on the way home. I'll spend a couple of weeks with him before I come home, probably toward the end of February or early March."

"John's not going to England? Where will you meet him?"

"No, he's got work to do here. We'll meet up somewhere between here and New York," he said, being as vague as possible before rushing on. "Then I'll be here 'til spring hits. The whole bunch of us will take a little trip as soon as the weather allows – April or May, I guess – and soon after that, we'll be on easy street. I promise."

✑

Asbury Harpending and Alfred Rubery were huddled over the desk in Harpending's office, more or less just socializing. As soon as the meetings with Barlow and Tiffany were concluded, the diamond business was on hold until spring, so Harpending had returned directly to London. He was eager to resume the business he'd interrupted six months ago at Ralston's insistence. Rubery had, as usual, just tagged along.

Harpending found everything pretty much as he'd left it, so he dove right back into trying to attract British investors to the American gold and silver mining interests of which he was a part. The battles with the British financial press had resumed as well, so he was busy juggling those issues. Hence, the diamond fields, while never entirely out of his mind, were on the back burner.

"A gentleman to see you, sir," the clerk said, gently rapping on the jamb of the open door.

"Show him in," Harpending replied, not knowing who to expect since he had no appointments. He was much surprised when a well dressed Phil Arnold appeared in his office doorway.

"What the hell are you doing on this side of the pond?" Harpending shouted, rising to shake hands. "You remember Alfie, of course?"

"Yes, I do," Arnold replied, shaking hands with both men.

"Well, sit," Harpending commanded, "and tell me what brings you here."

Arnold shucked his overcoat and took a chair. "Well," he began, "I just got tired of hanging around San Francisco, and I knew you were here, killin' time the same as me, so I just thought I'd check in."

"I see, a holiday then," Harpending said, not at all satisfied with that explanation. He knew Mr. Arnold well enough to realize that he seldom did anything without a definite purpose. "Did you bring your family along?"

"No," Arnold squirmed a bit in his seat. "It's just a quick trip. How are you boys doing?"

"Oh, just mucking through, as the English say. I have lots on my plate here."

"I know you do," Arnold said, "I read the papers. "Do you plan to have everything wrapped up in time to go to the diamond fields with me come spring?"

"Oh yes, indeed," Harpending chimed. "I'm fully invested in that project, not only in money but in interest and excitement as well. I'm really looking forward to it. By the way, did you know that our partner Bill Lent is in town?"

"Yes, he told me before I left New York he'd be coming over.[66] I suppose he keeps in close touch with you?"

"He does," Harpending agreed. "Sometimes he helps me field some of the inquiries, particularly about the diamonds. The Rothschilds, among others, are still quite keen on our diamond project, don't you know?"

"Tiffany's appraisal caused quite a stir, didn't it?" Arnold allowed himself a smug smile.

"Sure did." Harpending let that soak for a moment, then changed direction. "How long have you been here?"

"Oh, just a few days. I was in hopes the weather would be better."

"About average for this time of year," Harpending informed. "How long do you plan to stay?"

"I'm not sure; I guess until I've seen all the sights – Westminster Abbey, Windsor Castle all that, you know. " He started to add something else, but stopped short.

An awkward silence ensured as the three men tried to think of something to say. At length Arnold said, "Well, I guess I'd better be gettin' on so you two can get back to work." He stood and donned his coat.

Harpending got up and shook hands. "Well, don't be a stranger," he said through a smile. "We must have dinner one evening at my club."

"I'd like that," Arnold said as he walked out the door.

As soon as he was gone, Rubery turned to his friend. "What the bloody hell was that all about?"

"As you British say," Harpending shook his head, "I haven't a clue."

Knowing that Lent and Harpending were around and perhaps watching his every move, Arnold had made special arrangements with the Leopold

Keller Jewelers to conduct his business late in the evening when it was nearly dark at this time of year. His thinking was that the other men would already be at the club or otherwise occupied before settling in for the evening. Nonetheless, he looked carefully both ways up and down the street before ringing Keller's bell.

"Mr. Aundle," Keller greeted, "you're very prompt. Please come right in."

"Good evening," Aundle said. Foregoing the pleasantries, he got right down to business. "Have you got the goods I asked for?"

"Indeed, I have," Keller smiled. Please come into my office." In the back room, Keller opened the vault and produced a small velvet bag. Dumping the contents onto a display mat revealed about 100 rubies in the rough. "Just in from our Paris office," he informed.

"Very good," Aundle said, rolling the stones under his fingers. "How much?"

"These will be $3,515 American dollars."

"OK. So what does that make I owe you all together?"

"Let me see," Keller mused, consulting the ledger on his desk. "With the $5,060 you've already received in diamonds, it comes to a total of $8,575."[67]

"That's the exact figure I had," Aundle said, producing a stack of bills. "I think you'll find this to be correct." He handed the money to Keller. "That concludes our business, I believe."

"Ah," Keller said hesitantly, "I assume you do not want any of these gems cut or polished? I assure you that our…."

"You assume correctly," Aundle cut him off. "Good bye, sir."

☙

Having given up its struggle against the cold and dark for the day, the weak winter sun slunk behind the mountains to the west as the train chugged into the Union Pacific's Denver terminal. Philip Arnold, cold, tired and covered with soot, was more than ready to end this phase of his mission. His journey from London had not been easy, either physically or mentally. The seas had been rough and the possibility of having his secret cargo discovered was a constant worry. Many anxious moments were had in sneaking the diamonds and rubies through the Canadian port and having made it this far gave him only slight opportunity to breathe easier. When the car screeched to a halt, he pulled his coat tightly around him and walked to the exit. As he stepped down, he was relieved to see John Slack, huddled under a huge buffalo robe, waiting on the platform.

Slack hurried over through the swirling snow. "Welcome home, Cousin," he said, taking Arnold's carpetbag. "Happy to have you in sunny Colorado. How was the trip?"

"No fun. And you are not nearly as happy to see me as I am to be here," Arnold commented. "We're nearly to the end." The two men walked through the crowded station to where Slack had a taxi waiting. "Did you arrange everything as I asked?"

"Well, I got you a room at the hotel," Slack said sheepishly.

"What about the exploring I wanted you to do?" Arnold was tired and impatient.

"This ain't exactly the kind of weather I like to go campin' in," Slack exploded as the carriage began to roll. "I can't even remember the last time the temperature was above freezin'."

"Did you at least you look at the geological surveys I gave you?"

"Yeah, I did. And I talked to some old sourdoughs who know all there is to know about prospectin' in this part of the...."

"What! I told you to keep your mouth shut."

"I didn't tell 'em nothin'," Slack said defensively. "It was just shop talk around the stove amongst us old prospectors. I've seen you do the same thing yourself many a winter's evenin'."

The carriage arrived at the hotel. In the lobby, Slack advised, "You're tired, Phil. Get a good night's sleep and I'll fill you in on what I found in the morning."

"At least tell me you brought the goods from our previous trip abroad," Arnold demanded as he scribbled his name on the register. Accepting the key and turning his back to the clerk, he added, "We're gonna need those stones."

"Yeah, I brought 'em," Slack replied testily. He too was weary, tired of being badgered and treated like a second class citizen.

The next morning Slack was drinking coffee in the restaurant when Arnold came down. "Good morning, Phil," he said, pouring coffee into another mug. "Did you sleep well?" He slid the steaming mug across the table.

"Only because I was too tired to worry," he grumbled, accepting the coffee. "What did you tell the prospectors, and what did you find out?" He took a seat opposite and stirred sugar into his coffee.

"As I said, I didn't tell 'em nothin', but I found out plenty." He paused to sip from his cup.

"That's good. I'm sorry I was so grouchy last night. It was a hard trip." He waited a moment for Slack to answer. After watching John contently sipping his coffee for a moment, he demanded, "Well, what did you find out?"

"We discussed the geography – I didn't say much about the geology – of these parts pretty thoroughly, and they put me on to several locations which might meet our needs." Ignoring Arnold's impatient body language, he paused again fussing over his coffee. "Then I matched the sites with the criteria you gave me on the surveys, and I think I've found the perfect locale."

"Is that so? Where."

"It's in the northwest corner of Colorado, just south of the Wyoming border and a little east of Utah. There ain't a damned thing there except sage brush and jackrabbits, but the geology is nearly perfect. In fact, one of the prospectors , who'd found a diamond or two years ago in California, told me that the place seemed so likely that he himself had once looked for diamonds there."

"You asked him about diamonds, you fool?"

"No, damnit, I didn't ask; he volunteered that information. I made out like I wasn't interested when he said it, too. Like I told you, just some old men killin' time swappin' tales around the stove."

Arnold pictured the location on a map in his mind. "I'd think that would be perfect from a weather standpoint. I'm sure they have howlin' blizzards at this time of year and it's unbearably hot in the summer."

Slack laughed. "Hot! One of the old sourdoughs told me that he was out there sittin' in the shade of a big rock one day – there ain't no trees, you know – when he seen a coyote go by chasing a jackrabbit."

"So? Nothin' unusual about that."

"Nothin', 'cept he said it was so hot that they was both walkin'."

Arnold laughed with him for a moment. "That's hot," he allowed. Then, "How far is this place from the railroad?" Finally, Arnold seemed pleased with his partner's work.

"Well, we'll have to go there to pick out the exact spot we want, of course, but there's a little spot on the tracks just barely into Wyoming at Rawlins Springs that is within 30 miles or so."[68]

Phil Arnold spent the rest of the day poring over the geological surveys and maps. By supper time, he announced to himself that he was pleasantly surprised by the work his cousin had done. The site's features matched very closely the geological resources of the venues in South Africa where diamonds had been found. This location in the United States, subject to blizzards of snow in the winter and airless droughts in the summer would be ideal as visitation would be limited to a few short weeks in the spring and a like period in the fall. That, along with the fact that the site was also remotely located, would keep nosy people away and limit the time anyone could actually spend on the ground. Add in the fact that it was Indian country and they'd still been known to take to the warpath, yes, this location would suit his purposes quite nicely.

Phil sat back to review the situation. Adding the gems he'd brought to the ones held out from the previous trip gave him nearly $10,000 worth of stones – plenty for the purpose at hand. The money boys were deeply hooked and even now were gathering in New York to employ an engineer to inspect the diamond fields. Slack had done excellent leg work, and so he'd soon be ready for the engineer's inspection. With a satisfied smile, he thought that all in all, everything was going according to plan.

Now, if only he could catch a break in the weather.

༺༻

Green buds were beginning to populate the ends of the branches of the maple trees along New York City's streets when Asbury Harpending, William Lent and General George Dodge convened in Samuel Barlow's office to discuss the employment of a mining engineer.

"I tell you this man Benjamin is the best engineer in California," Dodge declared.

"However that may be, General, I had a telegram from William Ralston last night saying that Benjamin was in Montana and out of touch," Harpending informed.

"Well, he'll be back won't he?" Dodge was insistent.

"Perhaps, but who knows when?" Lent asked.

"Whenever it is," Harpending interjected, "it'll be too late. We simply do not have time to wait. We need to get this trip organized and underway within the next couple of weeks."

"That's right," Barlow said. "Anyway, we've previously pretty much settled on Henry Janin, haven't we? I'm told that he's a keen observer with a critical mind and decided business sense and ability. My friends say he does not get carried away by his feelings and is too sagacious to be caught in the traps that mine sellers usually prepare for the inspecting engineer."[69] He stopped to let that thought take effect. Seeing Harpending and Lent nodding agreement, he went on, "Janin's the man, and he's right here in the city at the New York Hotel."

"I'll go over there and make an appointment with him," Lent said. "We'll see what his terms are."

"All right," Barlow pressed on to the next topic, "I have news from Washington."

All present leaned toward the attorney's desk. "From Butler?"

"From Congress," Barlow corrected, even though all present knew that the money they had funneled through Barlow to the congressman from Massachusetts (in the form of stock) was behind the news. "Congress passed 'An Act to Promote the Development of Mining Resources in the United States,' a fancy title for just what we wanted."

"What does it say?" Harpending asked.

Barlow picked a paper from his desk. "How's this sound?" he asked. He read aloud:

> *That all valuable mineral deposits in lands belonging to the United States, both surveyed and unsurveyed are hereby declared to be free and open to exploration and purchase, and the lands in which they are found to occupation and purchase by citizens of the United States and those who have declared their intention to become such, under regulations prescribed by law and according to the local customs or rules of miners in the several mining districts, so far as the same are applicable and not inconsistent with the laws of the United States.*[70]

"Well, I suppose I'll have to admit that old 'Beast' Butler did his job," Harpending said.

"He ought to," Lent commented, "We paid him right enough. But that leaves an important question unanswered," he pointed out. As the others turned to him, he asked, "Does 'mineral deposits' include diamonds?"

"General Butler has been instructed to ensure that, if and when it becomes necessary, the Attorney General opines that it does," Barlow said.

The meeting adjourned with Lent's promise to meet with Janin and report back in the morning. When they reconvened, Lent was crestfallen. "I met with Janin last night," he announced. "I offered him $1,000 and the right to purchase 1,000 shares of stock at $40 per share."

"What'd he say?" Barlow asked.

"He said he'd have to think about it."

Asbury Harpending cleared his throat. "Well, as it happens, gentlemen, I had dinner with Mr. Janin last night. He took some convincing, but he agreed to accompany us to the diamond field and give us his report, provided that the whole affair would take no longer than a month of his time."

"What are the terms?" Lent angrily demanded.

"We're to pay him $2,500 cash, pay all his expenses and allow him to purchase 1,000 shares of stock." Here Harpending hesitated a moment and shot a sidelong glance at Lent, "at $10 per share." [71]

"What?" Lent exploded. "That's ridiculous! I made the man a fair offer, and I will not pay him more."

"Those terms seem reasonable enough to me," Barlow said.

"I paid $40 a share for my stock," Lent roared. "Why the hell should we let him buy in so much cheaper? I won't have it, I tell you!"

"Because we need his approval before the stock is worth anything, that's why," Harpending reasoned.

"Well," Barlow said, "General Dodge, it looks as if you have the deciding vote. What say you?"

The General looked at Harpending for a long moment and then at Lent for an equal amount of time before he spoke. Clearing his throat, he said, "I think all of us, including Mr. Janin, had better make preparations to go on a trip."

Seeing that his objections had been overridden, Lent reluctantly agreed. The decision was made that Harpending, Rubery, Lent, Dodge and Janin would depart as soon as arrangements could be made and the weather broke and meet up with Arnold and Slack at Denver.

Chapter Ten

Saturday, May 24, 1872
Denver, Colorado Territory

How ironic, Phil Arnold thought, that on this, his last trip away from home, he really had been sorry to leave. The late winter/early spring interlude with Mary in San Francisco had been entirely pleasant: the weather was fine, his plans were going well, the project was nearing fruition and Mary seemed happy. From all he could see, she had accepted his promise that this trip would be the last. They'd agreed that upon his return, they'd sell out and return to Kentucky. That had long been one of her goals and, while he said nothing to her about it, he assumed that once this little adventure was over, the sooner he got the hell out of town, the better for all concerned.

His cousin John Slack, now totally a hired hand of the California and New York Mining and Commercial Company, had appeared on schedule and now that all else was in readiness, they were awaiting the arrival of the New York contingent, including the expert mining engineer, Henry Janin. As the easterners' train was expected on Monday evening, he'd asked Slack to arrive today just to give them a chance to work out any last minute kinks which might arise and to rehearse their roles in the drama about to be played out. The two prospectors were sitting in the restaurant in their hotel enjoying a leisurely dinner. "There is still one thing that worries me," Slack said, slathering a biscuit with butter.

"What's that? Looks to me as if we're all set."

"This engineer they've hired, this Janin, I'd guess he's no fool," Slack said around a mouthful of biscuit.

"No, I'm sure he isn't," Arnold opined, thoughtfully swirling the ice in his glass. "That's exactly why they hired him to inspect the site."

"Well, ain't he gonna see right off that something's not right?"

"What would make you think that?" Arnold smiled as if he found Slack's concerns amusing.

"For one thing, no more'n I know about such things, I'd be very surprised if diamonds and rubies and emeralds and sapphires actually were all found in the same location. Nature just don't work like that."

Arnold chuckled. "You know this for a fact?"

Slack stopped a fork load of steak halfway to his mouth. "Of course I don't. Like I just said, I don't know nothing about it, but then I ain't no high priced mine inspector, either."

"Just eat your dinner and relax, Cousin. Let me worry about the inspector." Perfectly at ease, Arnold leaned back in his chair.

"Yeah, Phil, I know you know what you're doing, but I just can't see how you're gonna pull the wool over his eyes. Talkin' about something in a New York office is one thing, but to actually take them – and him an expert – to the site. Well, I'm scared."

"It'll be fine," Arnold assured. "Like I've been tellin' you all along, greed is a powerful motivator. Tiffany valued the first lot we had at $1,500,000 didn't he? You just play your part as we've discussed and leave Mr. Henry Janin and his report to me."

Slack was prepared to protest further when a Western Union messenger entered the room calling, "Mr. Arnold, Mr. Philip Arnold, telegram. Telegram for Philip Arnold."

"Here!" Arnold shouted, raising his hand. He accepted the small brown envelope and handed the boy a tip. "You expectin' to hear from somebody?" Slack's anxiety was ratcheting up again.

"No," Phil said, ripping the envelope open. His companion's concern went up another notch as Arnold's face reddened. "By God, I will not have it!" His voice was much too loud for the surroundings.

"What? What does it say?"

He slammed his fist on the table, rattling the chinaware. "It says there's a party coming from San Francisco – representatives of Ralston, Roberts and Dodge – are comin' to meet us so we can lead 'em to the diamond fields. I will not do it!"[72]

"What's the problem?" Slack asked, "You've already agreed to lead the party comin' from the east."

"Yes, and that's enough people to take there. Aside from Janin, those are men who have money invested. I'll not take anybody else." With that he jumped to his feet.

"Where are you goin"?

"I'm going to the telegraph office. I'm gonna notify Harpending's party – there're at St. Louis – that if this California bunch shows up, the whole deal is off!"

A furious exchange of telegrams among Harpending, Roberts, Ralston, Lent and Arnold flew back and forth over Sunday afternoon with the result that all the New York party except Lent would hold at St. Louis while he went on to Denver to meet with Arnold. Lent's hope was that he could convince Arnold to allow the San Franciscans to accompany the New York investors to the diamond field.

Advised of Lent's arrival, Phil Arnold was waiting at the station when Lent's train puffed in late on Monday evening. "Why, hello Arnold," Lent chirped, totally ignorant of how adamant Arnold was.

"Don't howdy-do me, damn you," Arnold growled. "You wire those California folks to go back right now or we'll all just forget the whole thing and go home.

"Now Phil, you know we can't do that; there's already too much money and...."

"If you think I can't, you just stand over there and watch. I've already checked; the next train west leaves in about an hour. I'll just buy me a ticket and go back to California."

"Aw, come on," Lent pleaded. "What's your big objection?"

"It's clearly a departure from all the plans we made and everything I agreed to," Arnold roared. "Now you listen to me. I've kept every agreement I've made, done everything I've been asked to do, attended every meeting and met every obligation. I flatly refuse to expose my secret to the entire world!"

After several minutes of heated argument, seeing that further discussion was useless, Lent proposed that Arnold wait while he telegraphed Harpending in St. Louis. Arnold agreed and walked into the waiting room and took a seat, his face set in determination. Lent went to the telegraph office. In about fifteen minutes, he returned, a telegram in his hand and a downcast look on his face. "Well," he announced, "I'm out-voted again. Harpending and Dodge agree with you.[73] I've already bought a ticket west. I'm to meet the Roberts' party at Salt Lake and return to San Francisco with them."

Having won that round, Arnold suppressed a satisfied smile as he stood to shake Bill Lent's hand.

ℛ

With mining engineer Henry Janin in tow, George Dodge, Asbury Harpending and Alfred Rubery arrived in Denver on Wednesday afternoon. Phil Arnold was all smiles when he met them at the station and ushered the New York party to the hotel. Although they were travel weary from the long trek, they were also eager to get a look Arnold's diamond fields. As Arnold had already reserved rooms, and with his assurance that the good weather was expected to hold, the decision was made to rest up until Saturday. For those two days, the entire group relaxed in the hotel, attended the theater, ate in the best restaurants in town, drank in the best saloons, generally enjoyed themselves and, in quiet moments, dreamed of the riches awaiting, now just a matter of mere days away.

At two a.m. on Saturday morning, Harpending was sleeping soundly when he was jolted awake by loud pounding on his door. Rousing himself, he crossed the room and opened the door to find an apprehensive Philip Arnold standing in the hall. "What the hell's going on?" he demanded.

"Get dressed," Arnold ordered, "our train leaves in an hour."

"An hour?" Harpending was confused. "Why the hell didn't you tell me earlier?"

Arnold glanced anxiously up and down the hall. "Because I didn't want anybody to know."

Harpending pulled him into the room and closed the door. "Damn it, man, I'm your partner. Didn't you think it'd be safe to tell me the plan?" He was now awake enough to be annoyed.

"I'm not worried about you," Arnold explained, "but I guarantee you that we're being watched. Ever since Tiffany's evaluation of our goods in New York, I've felt eyes on the back of my neck the whole time. I am also sure that every move you and Dodge and Lent have made is under observation, too. I'm sorry, but I thought not tellin' anybody was the best way to ensure that nobody would know our travel plans. We'll sneak out of here in the middle of the night unobserved. Neither you nor I wants anybody following us."

Harpending could not disagree. "An hour you say?"

"Actually," Arnold said consulting his pocket watch, "it's about an hour and a half. Slack is waking up Dodge right now. You get dressed while I'll go get Rubery up. We'll meet up in the lobby in thirty minutes."

By the time the five men assembled in the lobby, Arnold had a taxi waiting out front. Although the driver looked askance at the sleepy men, he kept his questions to himself as they drove to the Union Pacific's station. Arnold was delighted to note that, aside from his party, the station master was the only person in the building. On schedule, the train pulled out carrying the men northwest toward untold riches.

❧

At mid-morning, Sunday, June 1, 1872[74], the train delivered the diamond miners to the remote station at Rawlins Springs, Wyoming Territory.

"Where in the hell are we?" Harpending demanded. "This is the most desolate place I've ever been."

Arnold, still concerned about being followed, looked over his shoulder, as he had done a thousand times during the trip, once again and said, "You ain't seen nothin' yet. We've still got more than 100 miles to go; wait 'til you get a look at some of the country between here and where we're going. It'll make this place seem like the Garden of Eden."

"Say, old chap," Rubery spoke up, "all along, you've led us to believe the diamond fields were in Arizona or New Mexico, not this far north."

"I never said that," Arnold pointed out defensively.

"True," Harpending observed, "you never came right out and said that."

"What now?" Dodge asked.

"I've made all the arrangements," Arnold said. "You gentlemen just relax while John and I round up the mules and supplies. I've made sure that we'll have plenty to eat and tools to mine with."

An hour later, Arnold reappeared leading a horse for each man. Behind him came Slack leading pack mules loaded with picks, shovels, cooking implements and boxes of food.

"You boys ready for some adventure?" Arnold chirped.

Suddenly the burden of the long trip from New York melted away. The men eagerly climbed aboard the horses and looked expectantly at Arnold, who seemed a bit bewildered. Finally, Dodge impatiently said, "Well, let's go."

Making a show of consulting a compass he carried in his pack, Arnold ordered, "Follow me!" as he turned his horse to the south. With great enthusiasm, the others fell in behind.

Several hours, six changes of direction and eight dusty miles later, the enthusiasm was long gone when Arnold announced that they'd traveled far enough for the day. Although the men were tired, frivolity prevailed as they divided up the chores of caring for the animals, cooking and cleaning up. A pleasant evening passed swapping stories around the fire before each man went off to dreams of how he would be spending the vast wealth soon to be his.

After breakfast the next morning, Arnold climbed a nearby mesa to get his bearings. Again consulting his compass, he led the party off again, this time to the west. At midday, he turned to the northwest and they traveled in that direction until gathering dusk called a halt. As the men settled down for the evening, the companionship was not quite as jovial as it had been the previous night.

The next day brought a repeat. After checking his bearings, Arnold led off to the south. Harpending, who had been keeping up with the directions wondered why they changed course so often, seemingly at random. Rather than alarm anyone, he decided to keep his thoughts to himself for the present. By the time they made camp for the evening, everyone was fed up with wandering through the desolate country. Some minor squabbles were had when assigning the chores, and the evening meal passed virtually without conversation.[75]

Late that night, Harpending finally could hold his peace no longer. "Damn it, Arnold," he exploded, "how much farther is this place?"

Arnold stared into the fire for a long moment. "Well," he drew the word out, "I can't say for sure, but I reckon we'll be there sometime tomorrow."

"You're not sure?" Dodge demanded. "Several times today it looked like to me that you didn't have any more idea where you were going than some of these jack rabbits."

"I'm bloody tired of climbing up and down these inhospitable hills," Rubery commented. "It's difficult to imagine that this country, so devoid of everything else, could hold any riches."

Arnold seemed subdued. Once, during a lull in the argument, he started to speak, but evidently thought better of it.

"How 'bout you, Henry?" Harpending asked, addressing Janin.

"Makes no difference to me," Janin replied stoically. "I get paid no matter what."

Finally, Slack, who had been quiet during the entire journey, settled the issue for the day. "We'll be there tomorrow," he said, certainty in his voice.

Despite Slack's assurance, Harpending still had misgivings. As he lay on his back staring up into a star-filled sky such as is never seen around any town, he decided that if they didn't reach their destination the next day, he would turn back. The possible consequences of that action filled his thoughts as he drifted off into a fitful sleep.

Upon awakening the next morning, the men were in no better mood. In desperation, Arnold proposed, "I'll tell you what. You gentlemen just rest easy here this morning while I go out alone and make sure of our way. I think I can spot a landmark out this way," he said pointing north. "I'll be back as soon as I can and lead you to the diamond field."

"Absolutely not!" Dodge roared. "I'm damned if I'll let you go off and leave us sitting here with no idea of even where we're at, much less where we're going!"

After another argument boiled down, Harpending once again provided the voice of reason. "That's fine with me, Arnold," he said, "as long as your partner, Slack, stays here."

'That's sensible." Rubery agreed. "OK by you, General?"

"I suppose so," Dodge grumbled unhappily. Then turning to Arnold, he added, "You sure as hell better get back here. If you don't, I swear I'll track you down wherever you may hide and make you wish you'd done right."

"Nothing to worry about," Arnold assured. He saddled his horse and headed out alone, riding northwest.

The men literally sweated out a sweltering morning. At one point, Alfred Rubery's face clouded in concentration. "Did you hear that?" he asked Harpending.

"Hear what?"

"A train whistle. I swear I heard a train whistle."

"Alfie, we're four days away from the railroad," Harpending pointed out.

"Well, I heard a whistle. The way we've been wandering 'round, the railroad might be just over that hill right there for all we know."[76]

They were just preparing the noon meal when Arnold came whooping over the hill whipping his horse. "Everything's all right. We're nearly there," he shouted reining his horse. "Let's eat and then we'll head out."[77]

Spirits soared as they set out again. Everyone was excited, and the arid air was filled with energized chatter as they trekked along through the afternoon, seemingly uphill every step of the way. Finally, about four p.m., as they broke onto a perfectly level mesa, high above the surrounding valley on three sides while a sheer mountainside bounded on the north, Arnold called a halt. Climbing out of his saddle, he jumped to the ground and announced, "Well, boys, this is it. Welcome to El Dorado."

Chapter Eleven

Instantaneously following Arnold's announcement, all the hardships and petty grievances of the journey were forgotten. With each man pitching into the chores, the camp was set up and the stock were fed, watered and picketed in a flash. The men eagerly tore into the pack boxes to get picks, shovels and gold mining pans in their hands. The instant those duties were attended to, all eyes turned expectantly to Philip Arnold.

In answer to the unspoken request, he made a "follow me" motion and walked to the center of the mesa on which they were camped. The table-like surface, some forty acres in size, was littered with rocks of various sizes with a small stream running through the center. [78] Arnold was pleased to note that the winter weather had obliterated all signs of anyone having ever set foot on this ground before. He stopped at an outcrop of red-streaked sandstone jutting above the level surface for a length of 100 yards. "This is the area here where we initially found the gems," he announced. Kicking the sandstone, he advised, "You boys might want to look around the base of this." Immediately, Dodge, Rubery, and Harpending scattered off in different directions, each wielding a pick or shovel or knife, while Janin took Arnold's advice, crawling around the base of the outcropping. Within five minutes, Rubery jumped into the air shouting, "Yahoo! Alleluia! Look what I've got." The others rushed over to view the small diamond he'd dug up with his Bowie knife. The colorless bit in his hand sparkled in the fading sunlight, flashing red and blue and green as Rubery rotated it for all to see.

Everyone scattered to return to digging with renewed vigor. Arnold and

Slack just stood back, content and serene, occasionally making a suggestion as to what appeared to be a likely spot. Almost every time, their recommendation yielded a stone with just a little work. Within the first fifteen minutes, every man had found at least one stone and some had located several. By the time darkness called a halt to the hunting, everyone was exhausted, but still excited.

Unlike the previous evenings, no bickering accompanied the division of chores. The fire was built, supper cooked and consumed and the dishes washed without a cross word being exchanged. As everyone gathered around the camp fire, at last it was time to take stock: each man dumped the gems he'd collected into a common pile near the fire. Everybody was mesmerized by the dazzling display the accumulated gems made, sparkling in the fire light. "How many?" Janin wondered, wildly excited.

"I'd say about 500," Dodge guessed.

"And just to think that my name will forever be associated with such an astounding discovery," Janin gushed, obviously delighted.[79]

Arnold was somewhat offended that Janin took credit for what was clearly his discovery, but decided to let it pass. "Looks to me to be about three pounds of diamonds," he, as the diamond expert, said.

"That'd be about 400 carats," Janin advised.

"Yep, that's right," Rubery said. "What are they worth?"

Janin rubbed his chin thoughtfully. "Oh, the bigger ones are more valuable, but they should average about $10 per carat."

"So this pile we gathered in a couple of hours is worth $4,000?" Harpending let out a low whistle. "That ain't too shabby for an afternoon of grubbing in the dirt."

"That's just the diamonds," Arnold pointed out. "We've got a couple of pounds of rubies, emeralds and sapphires here, too."

"How much would they bring?" Rubery was as excited as anyone, even though he had no financial interest.

"Oh, Janin," said, "let's say maybe a half dollar per carat."

The men fell silent, each savoring the intoxicating sensation that accompanies the sudden acquisition of boundless wealth. At length, Arnold broke the spell. "In the morning," he said, "we'll start washing the gravel – that's the only way to really find diamonds.[80] What we've done so far has just scratched the surface." He was glad that, in the darkness, no one could see in his face the satisfaction he was deriving from his little pun.

"I hope someone wakes up early," Dodge said. "I'm eager to gather some more wealth. The more gems we come back with, the more the stock will be worth."

"That's right," Harpending agreed, "so I'll try to awake early."

"Did y'all ever hear about Jim Bridger's alarm clock?" Because John Slack rarely spoke, his question got everyone's attention.

"Jim Bridger?" Janin said. "I seriously doubt that he ever carried a clock into the wilds when he went exploring.

"Didn't have to carry it," Slack informed, "he found it somewhere out here."

"Bridger found a clock?" Rubery was skeptical.

"Well," Slack said, clearly enjoying stringing the others along, "strictly speaking, it wasn't rightly a clock. Actually it was a mountain which had a rock face that rose straight up from the ground, just perfect to bounce back an echo."

"Yeah? So, how do you get a clock out of that?" Harpending demanded.

"Bridger said," Slack continued, trying to draw out the story as long as he could, "that the mountain was so far away that it took the echo about six hours to get back." He paused for dramatic effect, before delivering the punch line. "So, when he was ready to call it a day, he'd yell out, 'Time to get up!' and six hours later, the echo would wake him up."

After the laughter subsided, Janin said, "I'd say that will just about do it for today. Gentlemen, we've had a great day. I bid you good night and an even better day tomorrow." He stood and picked up his blanket.

With that, the circle around the fire broke up, each man finding his own spot to roll up in a blanket. Soon all were asleep, visions of sugar plums, no doubt, dancing in each man's head.

☙

The fact that no one yelled, hence no echo came back to awake the camp, did not matter as the sun was barely over the horizon before all the men were astir. As before, no squabbles over the division of chores occurred; each man was willing to do his part cheerfully and efficiently so they could get back to the business at hand as soon as possible.

As Arnold and Slack were the only men present who had any experience at "hands-on" mining, theirs would be the responsibility of showing the others how to operate a gold pan in the stream. While the others were cleaning up after breakfast and tending to the stock, Arnold and Slack went off with shovels and buckets to collect some samples for washing. When they returned, each with a bucket full of the sandy soil and rocks, Arnold took everyone to the bank of the stream and called the class to order. "Fill your pan about two-thirds full," he instructed while Slack demonstrated. The others did as directed.

"Now, pick out the big rocks and pitch 'em away. While you're at," he added with a grin," if you happen to see a diamond or other gem, put that in your pocket.

"Dip the pan just under the surface of the water." Again, the others followed Slack's example. "Move the pan slowly back and forth across the water current, gently rocking it as you do. See how the water washes the dirt and silt away?" He walked up the bank observing each man, encouraging when necessary. "Diamonds are more dense than rocks," he said, "so this action will allow the diamonds to settle to the bottom of the pan. Keep working it until all the dirt is gone. That's it. Now, tip the pan down a bit and let the contents flow through your fingers."

He'd started to go on, but Janin interrupted him. "Whoopee!" he shouted, jumping into the air, "Look at this beauty!" In his hand was a yellow diamond about the size of a bean. "Ain't this a whopper?"

"I do believe that's the biggest one we've found so far," Harpending observed.

Seeing that, Dodge and Rubery hurriedly dumped their pans and refilled them with Arnold's dirt, determined not to miss out on the action. "Everybody OK?" Arnold asked. When nobody even looked up from their work, he said, "All right, Slack and I will go dig more samples while y'all wash."

As the sun rose in the sky, the men steadily washed the material as Arnold and Slack carried the soil-filled buckets to the stream. The only interruptions were when someone would let out a yell as he found a gem. By the time the sun was directly overhead, everyone was ready for a break. They walked back to the camp and deposited the morning's haul in a separate pile beside the one containing the pervious evening's accumulation of gems. The new pile was nearly half as large. "Not a bad morning's work," Rubery observed. The others heartily agreed as the excitement of the discovery had not abated in the least.

After a brief rest, the men started for the stream to resume work. Before starting for the stream, Arnold picked up a couple of pack boxes, now empty of provisions. Janin ran a few steps to walk beside him. "Say, Phil, how 'bout I do a little of the digging?"

"Help yourself," Arnold said, agreeably. "As a matter of fact, I've got another chore for myself, so if you want to keep the others in material to wash, I'll build the dam."

"OK. Any suggestions on where to dig?"

"You're the expert," Arnold pointed out. He turned away so that Janin would not see his face.

"Only on the feasibility of mining and possibility of mineral resources, not on how to dig up diamonds," Janin admitted.

"I wouldn't feel too bad about that," Arnold said. "Nobody in this country knows much about how to find diamonds or what they're worth." He did not point out that his entire scheme hinged on that fact.

"You and Slack seem to have done pretty well."

"Just lucky," Arnold said dismissively. While the others began filling their pans, Arnold handed Janin a shovel and a bucket. "Happy hunting." As Janin went off in search of rich diggings, Arnold walked a hundred yards or so downstream from where they were working. Kneeling, he began to break up the boxes. Using rocks as support, he fashioned the wooden boards into a rough, but effective, dam across the stream.

Engrossed in his work, he had not noticed that Harpending was standing behind, watching him work. He was startled when Harpending spoke, "What the hell are you doing?"

"Oh," Arnold jumped to his feet. "Hello, Asbury."

"Why are you doing that?" Harpending repeated.

"Well, since it's all we can do with the primitive equipment we have here, the method we're using to wash the dirt is how you pan for gold, not diamonds. So, as many stones as we find will probably get washed out of the pan along with the rocks. This dam will give us one more chance to catch those." His eyes fell to the newly constructed barrier. "As a matter of fact," he said reaching into the muck at the base of his dam, "look at this." He picked a good-sized diamond from the mire and held it up for Harpending to see.

"I'm damned glad we have a man like you along." Harpending took the gem from Arnold to examine it. "You certainly do know what you're doing." He handed the stone back.

"It's what they pay me for," Arnold said, again pleased at his little joke.

After supper that evening, everyone was relaxed and in an excellent mood. Lighting his pipe, Janin spoke his mind. "Gentlemen, there's little use in continuing to explore this field – it's rich beyond imagination; that's proven. The important thing now is to determine how much similar land is in the neighborhood and to seize everything we find. There is much to be done in the way of locating, surveying and securing the property, water rights and timber lands.

"Our provisions supplies will allow us to remain here much less time than I feel is necessary for this work and, besides, I know that General Dodge is ill and Mr. Harpending is anxious to get home as his wife may be ill, as well. So, I propose that I spend what time we have left here exploring and marking the surrounding country. I will require an assistant; the rest can stay here and continue to mine if anyone so desires.[81] If anyone so desires, he may accompany me."

"I've done all the tramping about in these parts I care to," Arnold commented. "So, if it's all the same, I'll stay here and guard our property."

"Me, too," Slack agreed.

So, the decision was made that Arnold and Slack would remain on the ground while the others explored the surrounding lands, marking and staking property which might prove, to use Harpending's word, "diamondiferous."

After three days, the exploration party returned late in the evening to find the two prospectors totally relaxed, smoking and resting on the ground. Janin was wildly enthusiastic about their discoveries. "We secured five streams," he explained, "being all we found on this side of the mountain. The one I named Arnold Creek, in your honor, Phil, and two others, which are larger, will suffice for all demands for power and washing for any amount of machinery and any number of tons of daily washing of gravel. We also secured 320 acres of prime timber land, ample for fencing and flumes – steam power will never be necessary. The streams are so situated that they can easily be carried to any part of the property. I'll tell you, gentlemen, without a doubt, what we've located here will control the gem market of the entire world!"[82]

"Well, then we'd better hurry back to New York and huddle with our lawyer to secure the claim," Harpending said.

"Yes, and the sooner the better," Dodge agreed.

"I'd like to stay longer and examine the lands more," Janin said, a tinge of pleading in his voice.

"Our food is about gone," Rubery pointed out.

"Well, I think we could stay another day, anyway," Janin insisited.

"I agree that we'd better go," Arnold said, "but now that we've all been here tramping around and diggin' in the ground, it wil be obvious to anyone who happens to wander by that some mining has been done here. We'd better not leave the property unguarded."

The others were stunned at not having thought of that possibility. "Yes, that's right," Harpending agreed.

"So somebody is gonna have to stay here, and whoever it is will have to eat," Arnold said.

"Yes," Harpending added, "so we'll have to leave enough food to last him until we can resupply."

"Who will stay?" Janin asked. "As much as I'd like to, I must file my report as soon as possible. Does everyone agree?" As all nodded in agreement, he said "So it's not me who'll stay."

"Nor Arnold nor Dodge nor me," Harpending opined. "We all have business to attend to."

"I'm willin' to stay," Slack volunteered.

As the men looked at each other, Arnold stated the obvious conclusion. "Well, that leaves only Rubery."

The looks on those two men's faces betrayed the truth: they did not like each other and clearly were unhappy with the decision. Despite the fact that the logic was perfect, Rubery protested, "Hey, what? I'm just along for the ride. This is merely a pleasure trip for me, you know. I certainly don't want to sit out here in the middle of nowhere until, and if, somebody decides to come relieve us."

"It's getting late. Let's sleep on it," Harpending suggested.

After the others were asleep, Dodge approached where Rubery was lying. "Alfie," he whispered, "are you awake?"

"Of course," Rubery answered, "how the bloody hell could I possibly sleep with the thought of having to stay here with that boorish Slack hanging over me?"

"Keep your voice down," the General ordered. "I'll make it worth your while to stay."

Whispering now, Rubery asked, "What do you have in mind?"

"I'll pay you $300 a week for as long as you have to stay here," Dodge said.[83]

Although that certainly got his attention, still Rubery did not immediately agree. "I'll think on it," he said.

In the morning, Harpending approached his friend. "Alfie, old boy, you know it's unthinkable to leave these vast riches unguarded," he said.

"Yes, I do realize that," Rubery said, deciding not to mention Dodge's offer or that he'd already decided to accept it. With a sigh, he added, "All right, old chum, as a personal favor to you, I'll stay."

"Good!" Harpending exclaimed.

"But you better make damned sure that relief party gets here." Rubery demanded. "And fast!"

Despite the money each was earning to stay, Rubery and Slack made a perfect picture of a dejected looking pair as they watched the others pack up and file away down the mesa headed for the railroad and civilization.

⚮

Asbury Harpending again thought that Philip Arnold was leading them "'round and 'round the mulberry bush" as they wandered a twisting path through the barren country. Finally, on June 20, they arrived, magically, at the town of Cheyenne, Wyoming Territory. All the men were travel-worn, dirty, grubby hungry and tattered. Even the knowledge of the value of the large saddle bag of gems Arnold clutched tightly to him did not allow the good spirits of previous days to endure. The men were glad to go their separate ways while they waited for the train to carry them to New York to arrive. Harpending and Dodge headed for the hotel and a bath. While Arnold took the stock to the local livery, Janin went into the telegraph office to compose a cryptic message to lawyer Barlow in New York and banker Ralston in San Francisco:

"Aunt Dorodo even better than expected STOP New baby is robust STOP Returning with sample of fabric. Complete arrangements with all possible speed."

Chapter Twelve

Tuesday, June 24, 1872
New York, New York

Asbury Harpending, Bill Lent, Henry Janin and General Dodge were amazed to learn that the news of their discovery of an American El Dorado had arrived in New York even before they did, despite their having traveled as rapidly as the trains would allow. They were soon to learn that the news had reached San Francisco with equal rapidity, and a telegram from Baron Rothschild in London verified that the information had "crossed the pond" as well.

"How in hell did so many people find out about this?" Lent wondered aloud in Barlow's office.

"Any secret with so many people in the know isn't gonna stay a secret very long," Harpending advised. "The word's even out that Tiffany's evaluation of the stones we brought back was only $8,000."[84]

"That's way too low," Janin asserted. "Considering the diamonds alone at $35 per carat – and some of them are worth more – they're worth $30,000. And that's not even counting the rubies and other gems."

"You seem pretty sure about that," Lent observed.

"I'll bet you money I can take twenty rough laborers out there and wash out a million dollars worth of diamonds a month," Janin retorted.[85]

"Hold on here," Barlow advised. "We are going to have to be very careful about returning to the site. The newspapers are full of speculation about where it is."

"Yes," Harpending said, "but nobody really has any idea. I heard that after one paper advertised the fact that our site was in Arizona, within the month the population of that territory increased by thirty percent."

"That's right," Lent added, "and then they all rushed to New Mexico the next week based on the speculation by another paper that that's where it is."

"The *Denver Times* has offered a reward to the first man who finds a diamond in Colorado," Dodge said.

"Enough of this foolish talk," Barlow advised. "Mr. Janin, are you ready to make your report to these gentlemen?"

"Yes. Gentlemen, I have a preliminary draft here that I turned over to Mr. Barlow yesterday," Janin said, accepting a paper from the lawyer. "As you'll see, I said that the sum total of work done in washing out diamonds while we were there would amount to about eight man-days."

"I'd agree with that," Harpending added.

"Well, my report indicates that we washed about one and a half tons of gravel and produced 814 carats of diamonds and 7,200 carats of rubies. So, on a conservative commercial and selling basis,I estimate that every ton of gravel washed will bring about $5,000 worth of gems."[86]

"I might point out, too," Dodge said, "that we dug no deeper than a foot or so. Who knows what deeper exploration would reveal?"

"For the record, gentlemen," Janin said, his eyes falling back to his report, "I'd like to read this for you. 'I particularly desire to impress upon the mind of any proposed purchaser that I am not in a position to say, owing to the limited time allowed me for prospecting the ground, how extensive the area of rich gravel is, or how much of the tract will be found available and profitable for washing. My report must necessarily be unsatisfactory and incomplete on these points. Nevertheless, the investigations made were satisfactory as far as they went, and no evidence was gathered which could authorize me to do other than recommend investment....'" Janin paused in his reading to glance at Lent and Harpending. Again his eyes returned to the report, "'at the price of $40 per share.'"[87]

"That's good enough for me," Barlow said, clapping his hands gleefully. "Anything else you want to say about it, Henry?"

"Well," Janin said, scratching his chin, "I suppose I should inform you all that I did say that I was sure that any money invested would speedily be repaid in dividends."

"There's little doubt about that," Dodge commented.

Janin ran his eye over the report. "'In conclusion,'" he read, "'I would say that I consider this a wonderfully rich discovery that will prove extremely profitable. While I did not have time enough to make the investigations which would have answered some very important questions, I do not doubt that further prospecting will result in finding diamonds over a greater area than is yet proved to be diamond-bearing; and finally, I consider any investment at $40 per share, or at the rate of $4,000,000 for the whole property, a safe and attractive one.'"[88] With a sigh of satisfaction, he handed the report back to Barlow. "Let me say again that this report is preliminary."

The men sat silently for a few moments, each considering the possible impact Janin's report would make on the investing public. "I wonder how long it will be before this report hits the newspapers," Harpending said, breaking the spell.

"I did telegraph a copy of it to Mr. Ralston this morning," Barlow said.

"Then," Lent grunted, "you may be sure that the news is all over San Francisco by now."

"Speaking of which, what's going on out there?" Barlow inquired of Harpending.

"Well," Harpending began, "Mr. Ralston and I have agreed that our proposed company be incorporated in California under the terms already agreed upon."

"Capital stock of 100,000 shares at $100 per share?" Dodge interrupted.

"That's right," Harpending said, "but we're not going to offer any of the shares for public sale until we prove the total richness of the discovery beyond any possible question."

"What?" Lent exploded. "Why, we can sell shares for any price you could name. There's at least 50 or 60 million dollars...."

"Mr. Ralston is most emphatic that no stock will be offered for general sale." The tone of Harpending's voice put a halt to further discussion on that topic.

"Why," Dodge asked, "make it a California corporation when everybody knows that New York in the financial center of the world? I wouldn't want to overlook all those potential investors located here."

"Mr. Ralston assures me," Harpending answered evenly, "that the Bank of California will make available whatever sums of money may be required." He paused for a moment, then added, "Hence we will not need investors' money and we can keep it all in the family, so to say."

"And," Barlow added, "we're also to have an office right here in New York. We'll be prepared – and quite willing – to take care of any New Yorkers who care to invest in our project."

"That's correct," Harpending said with a satisfied air. "I'm happy to say that Mr. Barlow and General George B. McClellan have agreed to be the East Coast resident directors of the San Francisco and New York Mining and Commercial Company. The principal office, however, will be in California."

"Is that just your bias for San Francisco?" Janin inquired.

"A simple question of dollars and cents," Harpending assured. "We intend to cause the lapidary industries of the world to move from Europe to California. After all, gentlemen, all these stones we mine will have to be cut someplace. Why should we let someone else have the fun – not to mention the money – involved with that?"

"How's Arnold feel about all this?" Dodge mused.

"He's agreed to sell me his interest," Harpending commented. "That will make Ralston and me the principal owners. So, how he feels does not matter much."

"The hell it doesn't," Janin roared. "We must keep Mr. Arnold happy because he's the only one who…."

"What?" Lent exploded, interrupting Janin. He looked as if he'd been punched in the stomach. "Arnold has refused to sell more times than I can remember. Now, all of a sudden, he's sold out?" Lent sputtered a moment before demanding, "How much?"

Harpending glared at his fellow California investor for a moment before answering. "Not that it's any of your affair, but he's to meet me at my place in Tarrytown next week where I'll purchase his remaining shares for $300,000."[89]

"Just a damn minute here, Harpending," Lent roared. "You know, don't you, that as per my meeting with him on the Denver train platform, we'd agreed to give him $150,000 if the visit to the site and Janin's report were satisfactory as to the richness of the claim? We are obligated to pay Arnold that sum, you know."

125

"Yes, I know that Bill." He hesitated momentarily to let Lent cool a bit. "When I buy out the remainder of his interest, we will have paid him a total of $550,000 and then he'll be out of the picture."

"And good riddance," Dodge interjected.

"Well, as I was trying to say earlier, let's not write Arnold off quite so fast," Janin said. "I need to go back there so I can finish my investigations and Arnold will have to go with me."

"We better not be in a hurry about that," Barlow advised. "With all this crazy speculation going on, we might be well advised to lay low for a while."

"Yes, the point here, gentlemen," Lent added, "is that we may be dead sure that we're being watched."

"However that may be," Harpending added, "we must remember that we left Rubery and Slack there to guard the property. I imagine that they are running pretty low on supplies by now."

☙

"What? We can't just up and leave here," the normally laid-back Alfred Rubery was livid. "Our friends are depending on us to guard this place."

"Well, you stay if you're so inclined," John Slack retorted, "but as for me, I'd have been gone yesterday if you hadn't been damn fool enough to let the horses get loose."

"Do you mean to tell me that you'd betray our partners' trust in less than one day?" Rubery's temper was rising with each word.

"They might be your partners," Slack said, "but me, I'm just a lowly hired hand and I ain't hanging around here no longer. Two days is long enough." Rising from the ground, he began gathering his gear. "As for guarding this dust hole, have you seen anything more threatening than a coyote around here?"

"I guess you're right about that." A note of resignation crept into Rubery's voice.

"You're damned right, I'm right," Slack roared, pausing in his packing. "And, I'll tell you something else I'm right about."

"What's that?"

"It doesn't seem to have occurred to you that you're sittin' out here in the middle of nowhere with not the slightest notion of how to get back to the railroad." Seeing in Rubery's eyes that the Englishman realized the truth of what he was saying, he rushed on. "Now, I'm agoin'. If you stay behind, how will you find your way out?"

"I shouldn't have to worry. The others will be back." A tiny note of uncertainty crept into his voice.

"Maybe they will," Slack admitted, gathering up the last of his gear. "Are you willin' to bet your life on it?"

"Well, I cannot imagine that you'd think they would abandon all these riches...."

Slack cut him off. "It could be that maybe this place ain't quite as valuable...." Then he cut himself off. "Well, anyway, I figure there's enough food here to last the two of us maybe a week. Even if your friends tried, I doubt they could resupply us in that short a time." Again Slack sensed that he had Rubery's attention. "Now I'm gonna take some of those supplies with me, so you could hold out for, oh, let's say ten days, by yourself. What are you gonna do when the food's gone?"

"Well...."

"I'll tell you what you're gonna do, you're gonna starve, that's what. I'm leavin' right now. If you want to go with me, get your gear together and I'll lead you to the railroad." He heaved a disgusted sigh. "I'm through talkin' to you about it: stay here and starve, or go with me. Suit yourself, it makes no difference to me either way."

Giving in, Rubery said, "Well, it offends my British sense of fair play." He began gathering his meager gear. "After all, we did give our word." His voice betrayed a hint of persecution.

"I'll tell you this," Slack intoned, lashing the saddle bags to his horse. "If you stay here, if and when your friends show up, your honorable British bones will be bleached just as white as any dead American jack rabbit's."

"How far is it to the railroad?" Rubery mounted his horse.

"Oh, 'bout 20 miles." Slack urged his mount into motion.

"What?" Rubery pulled alongside. "It took us four days to get here."

"Well, we took what you might call the 'scenic route' on the way here," Slack informed. "We're going to take the more direct course to Black Buttes Station."

"What? We got off the train at Rawlins, didn't we?"

"Don't matter, Arnold just did that to add to the confusion. We're gonna get on at Black Buttes," Slack stated matter-of-factly. "It's the closest. We can do it in a day if we hurry."

"You know, one evening on the way out, I told Harpending I thought I heard a train. We've been within 25 miles of the Union Pacific line the whole time, haven't we?"

As Slack made no reply, Rubery kept his thoughts to himself, but he had questions. Taking an indirect route to the diamond field was not, in itself, so suspicious – he could see that Arnold and Slack were not eager to have any-body find it again without them. But, considering the value of the diamond find, if Slack actually thought there was any chance that the other men might not return, then clearly everything was not as it appeared.

When the men reached the railroad station at Black Buttes, Wyoming, they sold the horses and checked the train schedule. Wordlessly, they sat side by side on a bench outside the station until the westbound train arrived. Ru-bery stood, his ticket in his hand. "Well, old chap," he said, offering his hand, "your eastbound train should be here…." John Slack simply turned his back and walked away.[90]

❧

As Philip Arnold walked up the wide, flower-lined walkway leading to Asbury Harpending's magnificent home overlooking the Hudson River at Tarrytown, New York, he marveled at his friend's behavior. He had spent many hours in Harpending's company in all kinds of locations and circum-stances. Never had he seen any evidence of the fortune he knew the man had amassed. But here, on display for the world to see, was a mansion in a setting that bespoke considerable wealth.

The train ride from New York City had taken less than an hour to cover the 25 miles, but the scene was as different from the crowded, dirty city as could be imagined. Across the river, on the west side, the trees were in full summer glory, showing off the silver side of their leaves in the riffling breeze. He paused a moment on the stoop, drinking in the beauty of the setting, be-fore he rang the bell. A nagging thought in the back of his head brought *The Legend of Sleepy Hollow* to mind as he remembered that this location was the setting for Washington Irving's classic tale.

Much to Arnold's surprise, Harpending himself answered the door. "Hel-lo, Phil," he greeted pleasantly, "come on in."

Arnold took Harpending's proffered hand as he moved into the ornate gray stone entryway. "This place reminds me of some of the pictures I've seen of medieval castles in Europe."

"Well," Harpending said dismissively, "be it ever so humble. It's my East Coast get away. My family and I enjoy spending our summers here." He led the way into his study adjacent to the entryway. Motioning Arnold to a stuffed chair upholstered in red leather, the host took a seat behind his massive mahogany desk. "Pleasant trip?"

"Train rides are never pleasant," Arnold replied.

"Just so. I'm sure you're parched. Can I offer you a brandy?"

"I wouldn't be insulted," Arnold replied with a smile.

"Before we get to the business at hand," Harpending said, handing his visitor a glass of amber liquid," I have a telegram here that might interest you." He extracted a slip of paper from a desk drawer.

"Yeah?"

"It's from Baron Rothschild in London."

"Word has spread plum over there, has it?" If the thought that the reason for his trips to London had been discovered even entered his mind, his easy manner gave no indication.

"For sure. The Baron says he's been in touch with William Ralston and understands that we've made a personal visit to the diamond fields and received a first-rate report from the mining expert and a satisfactory evaluation from Tiffany's. He wanted me to confirm the results of our observations."

"Have you answered?" Arnold took a sip of his brandy.

"I told him that half the truth hadn't been told and that the diamond fields are rich beyond calculation."[91]

"What do you suppose the Baron has in mind?" Arnold drained his glass. If he had any inkling that the Baron was suspicious of his European activities, his behavior was no give away.

"Another?" the host asked, indicating Arnold's empty glass. Seeing Arnold shake off the offer, he went on, "Oh, I'm sure that when he thinks the time is right, he'll be wanting to be the European representative of our company."[92]

"As long as the money's right, it's fine by me." He made a dismissive wave with his hand.

"Speaking of money," Harpending said, rising from his chair. He walked across the room and swung a hinged picture frame away from the wall, revealing a hidden safe. Spinning the dial, he opened the door and extracted a thick wad of bills. "Here's yours." He handed the stack to Arnold.

"Very good," Arnold said, trying to conceal his excitement. "$300,000?"

"Count it if you like."

"No. No. I'm sure it's OK." After he fondled the bills for a moment, he started to rise. "Well, I guess that about does it."

"Hold on. There is another issue we need to discuss." Harpending said, resuming his seat behind the desk. "Mr. Janin has been appointed superintendent of our company, you know. He wants to return to the diamond fields with survey equipment. It's imperative that we gain a government patent on the land." Harpending paused a moment before he came to the point. "You're still the only one who really knows where it is."

"I'll be happy to make sure he gets there whenever he wants to go," Arnold said agreeably.

"Very well, thank you, Phil. Now, we need to talk about guarding the property."

"Slack and Rubery are there," Arnold reminded. "As remote as the site is, I doubt they'll have any trouble."

"I don't anticipate they will, either." Harpending shifted in his chair. "But they need relief right away, and we ought to make the grounds more secure until we gain title to everything we want. And, we'll need a bunch of laborers – somebody has to do the work, you know."

"That shouldn't be a problem," Arnold advised. "We can surely hire as many men as we need."

"Ah, but there's the rub," Harpending sighed. "We want to make damned sure we get men we can trust."

"Agreed. What are you getting at?"

'Well," Harpending drew the word out, "to be frank, I don't think we can trust white men with our secret."

Arnold let that soak in before he spoke. "So, what are you saying? We should get Mexicans? Indians?" Uncertainty tinged his voice.

"No. All other things aside, we'll want 'em to speak English."

Arnold waited for him to go on. When it became apparent that Harpending was waiting, Arnold offered, "Negroes? You want to entrust the security of our place to a bunch of Negroes?"

"That's it," Harpending said matter-of-factly. "That's the way there're doing it in the South African diamond mines, and it's worked out fine. Do you know where we might find forty or fifty reliable colored men?"

"Well, I reckon we can find as many as we want in my home town in Kentucky. I've got friends there."

"Elizabethtown?"

"Yep," Arnold said, "there's a lot of ex-slaves laying around there waiting for work."[93]

"All right," Harpending said. "I'll get you some expense money from the company so you can go on to Kentucky and recruit a bunch of coloreds who are willing to go west. Tell 'em that they may have to go armed some of the time and that there may be some physical labor involved, but beyond that, tell 'em as little as possible."

"OK," Arnold agreed. "Now, what about Janin?"

"He's still in New York City," Harpending informed. "I'll arrange to have him meet you somewhere along the way after you leave Elizabethtown."

❧

"Gentlemen, gentlemen, please calm down," Bill Lent, President of the company shouted. "I know we're all excited, but I call the first share-holders meeting of the San Francisco and New York Mining and Commercial Company to order. Now that the company is officially incorporated in the State of California, the first item of business is to elect the other officers."

As the room quieted, nominations were made, and in short order, William Ralston, as he was a banker, was elected treasurer and William Willis was installed as secretary. David G. Colton, the railroad engineer who had, blindfolded, accompanied Arnold and Slack to the diamond fields agreed to resign his current job to assume the duties of general manager.[94]

With that out of the way, Lent decided to restate the intentions of the company for the record and to avoid misunderstandings. "We intend to carry on the business of exploring and mining for gold, silver and other precious metals and substances of every name and nature in any and all of the States and Territories of the United States and to do such commercial business connected therewith as the interests of said company may require."[95] That statement, although it did not specifically mention diamonds, met with wild applause. When the noise died off, he added, "We also intend to give the great lapidary establishments of Amsterdam a run for the business."

The discussion then turned to who should serve on the board of directors. The most influential men in California were in the room, and each hoped to be named to the board. In the end, a virtual "Who's Who" of the financial world was appointed: William Ralston, William Lent, Thomas Selby, Milton S. Latham, Louis Sloss and several others, including Alfred Gansl, the Pacific Coast representative of the House of Rothschild, were pleased to hear their names called. Additionally, General McClellan and Samuel Barlow, headquartered in New York, would serve as directors.

Immediately following his election, Alfred Gansl asked to be recognized. "I suggest we send a large representative sample of the diamonds to Europe for evaluation," he shouted.

"Why?" Lent asked. "We already have Tiffany's appraisal."

"An evaluation from the prestigious House of Rothschild will carry a much greater impact on the world's financial community, not to mention that we could allow them to sell a portion of the merchandise, thereby raising some additional capital."

The motion to send a representative sample of the goods most recently retrieved from the diamond fields was unanimously approved.

"Now then," Lent said, "there's the slight matter of how we will allocate the stock." The room erupted with everyone yelling at once.

"Here, here," Ralston shouted above the din. "I have the plan." As the noise subsided, the treasurer emphatically went on, "We will offer no sale to the general public until all the patents are gained and the surrounding territory is explored…." Again noise erupted. Ralston simply waited. When quiet again returned, he said, "I know that there are many millions of dollars that could be had by quick sale, but this point is simply not open for discussion." He paused to let that sink in on his listeners. "Now, I propose that we initially allow 25 influential men to subscribe. This will allow us to bring more powerful influences to bear, enabling us to better hold our claim than could possibly be done by three or four individuals."[96]

"What did you have in mind, Bill?" Lent asked.

"I think that $2,000,000 should be sufficient to cover all our initial expenses," Ralston said. "So, I suggest that we allow each of the 25 chosen investors to purchase up to 2,000 shares of stock at the $40 per share price we've agreed on all along. If they all each take the 2,000 shares, that will bring $80,000 from each of them and put the $2,000,000 in our bank account."

"OK, but why not sell as much as we can? We can get any price we ask," someone demanded.

"Aside from the fact that to do so would be unethical," Ralston answered patiently, "an American El Dorado is simply too good a thing to share with the general public. Also, the hectic atmosphere a public offering would create would completely disrupt the financial structure of this entire nation."

Despite some grumbles of discontent, Ralston's plan was adopted. Within a day, the 50,000 shares of stock were sold and the money was deposited in the Bank of California. In the lobby of the plush offices of the San Francisco and New York Mining and Commercial Company, located in San Francisco's Harpending Building on Market Street between First and Second, a huge map of the American El Dorado was posted. The map showed the general outlines and physical characteristics of the 3,000 acres claimed by the company and the relative positions of Discovery Claim, Ruby Gulch, Diamond Flat, Sapphire Hollow and other locations with names similarly suggestive of incredible wealth.[97] As would-be investors scurried hopefully in and disappointedly out of the building, many a longing eye was cast upon that map.

Chapter Thirteen

Tuesday, July 23, 1872
Elizabethtown, Kentucky

Philip Arnold had much to occupy his thoughts on the hot, dusty train ride from New York. At the top of that list was how he would immediately deal with the $300,000 Asbury Harpending had put in his hand a week before. Additionally, he had to find a way to bring his wife up to date on all that had transpired, locate Janin somewhere along the way and ensure that the necessary surveying and mining equipment would be available when all else was ready for another trip to the diamond field. Even with all that on his mind, he still had to stop off in Elizabethtown, having agreed to recruit a company of colored men to accompany him to El Dorado where they would act as guards and laborers.

He found a partial answer to the first problem when he discovered the home of attorney William Wilson, located at the end of Poplar Street on the outskirts of town, for sale. With little negotiation, Arnold purchased the house, most of its furnishings and some livestock for $17,875. The price, which he paid in cash, also included the 34 acre lush Buffalo Run/Valley Creek farm on which the house sat.[98] As an added benefit, Arnold and Wilson became friends. Arnold deposited the remainder of his newly gained riches in the Elizabethtown bank owned by his friends Thomas, Polk and Company and wired Mary in San Francisco to place their home there on the market and pack up her belongings as they'd be moving to Kentucky as soon as he returned.

He lingered in his home town long enough to renew some dormant business and personal relationships, investigate other Hardin County lands for sale and check in with his wife's relatives. With that groundwork laid for his return to Kentucky, he enrolled some twenty colored men and used the Company's expense money to purchase a Winchester rifle and a Colt pistol for each man.[99] With the men in tow, he boarded a train bound for Laramie in the Wyoming Territory where he was to meet Henry Janin.

∾

"MacIntyre," Arnold yelled, entering the low, dank building bordering the railroad track. Here, on the outskirts of Laramie, he'd found an ideal location to house his impromptu militia away from the ever-present prying eyes, yet near enough to the diamond fields to allow easy access when all was in readiness. "Where the hell are you?"

"Rat cheer, Boss," Lloyd MacIntyre answered peeking out of a musky room. MacIntyre, a grizzled ex-slave whom Arnold had known in Elizabethtown before he left there to go west back in '49, was the titular leader of the colored contingent Arnold had lured west with the promise of $2.50 per day in wages and an interest in the profits derived from the fabulous American diamonds fields.[100] "What's doin'?"

"It's time to shoot. Gather your boys and take them, with their weapons, over to the shootin' range." Arnold ordered. "You start the target practice and I'll meet you over there in a few minutes."

"Yas suh, Mista Phil, rat now," MacIntyre said agreeably. As Arnold turned to walk away, MacIntyre informed him, "but you know, we's runnin' low on whiskey and tobaccy over yere."

"I'll tell you what," Arnold grumbled, "you worry about learnin' to handle the firearms right now. I'll worry about your drinkin' and smokin' later."

As the colored men scrambled to gather their weapons, ammunition and walk across the tracks to their make-shift rifle range, Arnold walked purposely into town to the hotel where he knew he'd find Henry Janin, now the company superintendant. Janin was, as usual, at his post near the telegraph office. "What's goin' on, Henry?" Arnold inquired.

"Damn it all," Janin exploded, slamming the newspaper he'd been reading to the desk. "Your California friends, Barlow, Ralston and Roberts, have made my report public. They knew that my report was preliminary and private. They've made a laughing stock of me! Damn it all to hell!"

"Now, calm down, Henry," Arnold pleaded, "It ain't as bad as all that, is it?"

"Well, just look at this," Janin waved a newspaper beneath Arnold's nose. It says here that Roberts told this reporter that I'm at the diamond fields right now with an armed force guarding me! Roberts and Harpending know damned well where I am. Why, they're so worried about somebody learning where the diamonds are that they ordered me not to make a move – to stay right here in Laramie!"

"They're obviously just trying to throw the scent off," Arnold soothed.

"Listen to this," Janin shouted, reading from the paper, "'His reports have been such that all his friends in San Francisco have put their money in, and he himself has invested all he has. He expects to bring out, all the time he is down there, a million dollars a month.'[101] Preposterous!" He paused, seemingly out of steam for a moment, but then gathered himself and roared, "And everybody involved knows that I paid $10 a share for the 1,000 shares I bought! A far cry from 'all he has!'"

"Well, Henry, a million a month is pretty much what you said in New York," Arnold tried to placate.

"I know damned well what I said," Janin exploded, "But that was in private. Had I had any thought that they'd publish my report, I would have been more careful with my wording and more conservative in my predictions! On top of that, I cannot understand why they are trying to draw attention to what we're doing here. There are so many people watching us that I feel eyes on me every minute of the day as is, and now there's this." He slammed his fist on the newspaper. "If we make a move from here, we'll have such an army following us that it'd look like the contrabands following General Sherman through Georgia."

"Did your surveying equipment arrive?" Arnold asked, attempting to change the subject.

"Yes, everything is complete." Janin simmered down enough to ask, "And on your end?"

"I've secured the necessary horses, wagons and pack animals," Arnold informed. "Now we just need the 'go' from Ralston or Harpending or whoever it is that's got us on hold."

"I'm sure it's Ralston," Janin said. "I wired him yesterday saying that he cannot keep on reporting me as being at the diamond fields. That statement will, no doubt, soon be discovered as a lie. So, we'll be found here before we even set out, and then the whole expedition will have to be abandoned…." His voice tailed off in exasperation.

"It does seem that they are putting the reputation of the company at risk," Arnold agreed. "I've certainly done my share of misleading about the location of the field, but there is no need to outright lie about it."

Janin started to say something, but a loud report of rifles from across the way interrupted him. "And that! You and I just might be the famous characters in the territory, you know. And, on the off chance that there still might be a man in this country who doesn't recognize us by sight, why we'll set off fireworks to draw his attention to us. We're doomed, Arnold. There's no way in hell we will ever get back to the diamond fields without being found out and followed."

"Rubery would say we might as well hire a bloody brass band," Arnold said, hoping to lighten the mood.

Instead, Janin exploded anew. "Oh, did you hear? Rubery is back in San Francisco."

"What? He and Slack aren't still guarding the diamond fields?"

"Hardly. They lit out the day after we left 'em there," Janin informed. "According to Harpending, they took off practically as soon as we were out of sight."

"No kiddin'? You say Rubery's in California? And Slack? Where's he at?"

"Nobody knows. Rubery told Harpending that when he and Slack got to the railroad, he went west and Slack went east. So much for friendship and trust," Janin mused, shaking his head. "All the more reason we've got to get back there and survey our claim and complete the legal formalities." Another burst of gunfire interrupted the conversation. Janin jumped to his feet, "Go put a stop to that."

"Henry, they've got to learn…."

"If they never get there, they'll never have to guard anything," Janin pointed out. "Put an end to that infernal racket."

Arnold had reached the railroad tracks when he saw Lloyd MacIntyre running to meet him. "Mista Phil," MacIntyre gasped, "Hit's Mose."

"What?"

"Hit's Mose," MacIntyre repeated, "He's done took powerful poorly. He wants you to go fur the doctor."

"All right," Arnold said, "I'll go get one right now."

"Hold on," MacIntyre said, "He wants the hoss doctor?"

"What? He ain't a horse, and odds are he ain't got no horse ailment," Arnold protested. "Why does he want a horse doctor?"

"Well, you see, Mose don't rightly know what ails him. When a regulation doctor come to see you, he can talk wid you, ax you whar it hurts, what you been eatin' and so on like dat and you can tell him. But a hoss doctor, bein' unable to talk wid his patients, is jest natchelly 'bliged to know hisself what ails 'em. No suh, you get the hoss doc."

☙

The next day Janin received an encoded telegram from Harpending. Fearing that the entire operation had been compromised by too much publicity and speculation, Harpending's message ordered him to leave Laramie immediately and report to San Francisco. The message also instructed Arnold, for the same reasons, to wait three days, then dismiss the Negroes and send them home.

The day after Janin departed, an especially outfitted private rail car was pulled into the Laramie station siding. As Philip Arnold milled in the crowd, speculation of who and what its arrival meant was rampant. Looking toward the end of the car, he noticed someone pointing him out to a uniformed railroad man. The officer directly approached. "Are you Philip Arnold?" he asked.

"Yes. What's goin' on?"

"I'm an employee of the Atlantic and Great Western Railway," he advised, "General McClellan's aide." Indicating the rail car, he added, "This 'Palace Pullman' is our President, General George B. McClellan's, car. The General desires to meet with you as soon as possible."[102]

"All right, but I'd like to go clean up a bit before I meet with him," Arnold pleaded.

"The General is most insistent that he see you immediately." The man waited impatiently.

"All right," Arnold agreed, allowing himself to be led by the arm to the rear of the "Palace Pullman." As soon as the man opened the door and ushered Arnold inside, he saw that the car was aptly named; it was as elegantly appointed as anyplace the prospector had ever seen. The walls were covered with French wallpaper featuring velvet figures the color of which was an exact match for the plush green carpet. The gleaming walnut chairs were arranged around a matching table, which was set with sparking crystal glasses.

Just as his eyes adjusted to the dim interior lighting, a door at the opposite end of the car opened and General McClellan stepped into the room. "Mr. Arnold?"

"Yes." Arnold took in the trim little man with dark eyes and dark hair. This was the man who President Lincoln had appointed General of the Army of the Potomac at the beginning of the war. While McClellan was beloved by his soldiers, his army was never ready to fight, so Lincoln had had to relive him and then subsequently reappoint "Little Mac" when no satisfactory replacement could be found. "You and I met in New York at Mr. Barlow's home." Arnold extended his hand.

"Ah, yes. Please take a seat," McClellan said, ignoring his visitor's proffered hand. "May I offer you a brandy?" The General picked up a stylishly cut decanter. As Arnold shook his head negatively, the General poured for himself. "I must ask you to keep your voice down," he whispered. "My wife is ill." He inclined his head toward the rear of the car from which he had emerged. "We're traveling primarily for the benefit of her health."

"Very well," Arnold said softly. "What can I do for you, General?" McClellan was every bit the vain, strutting peacock that reputation had him.

"You know, do you not, that I am the New York resident director of the San Francisco and New York Mining and Commercial Company?"

"Yes, sir, I do know that."

"As such," McClellan took a sip of his brandy, "that makes me your boss."

Clearly, Arnold thought, the man was accustomed to command, not an admirable trait in a business partner, in his view. "So?"

The General carefully sat his glass on the table. "I demand to know the exact location of the diamond field."

Arnold took a moment to remember he'd been asked to be quiet. "Sir, I understand your position, but surely you understand that the location must remain secret until we obtain all the necessary rights." He congratulated himself on his restraint. Seeing McClellan's glare, he added, "I'm sorry, General, but there will be no compromise on this point." Arnold remembered that this was the man who had flatly refused to share his plans for invading the South with President Lincoln.

Apparently realizing that he was no longer in a position to command, the General changed directions. "Do you understand that I value my character too highly to allow my name to be associated with dubious enterprises?"

"Well, what you allow is your own affair."

"Something does not smell right about this whole business," the General opined. "I'm to meet with Mr. Harpending, Mr. Lent and Mr. Ralston when I arrive in California," McClellan confided. "If I don't get some answers about the location of the fields and some confirmation that the stones I've seen actually came from this site, wherever it is, I may have to withdraw my name from the enterprise."

Arnold thought about saying that if that was a threat, the General was wasting his time with him. Instead, he said, "Well, you can take that up with the men in San Francisco."

General McClellan stood. "You are dismissed," he announced as he exited back into the other room.

❧

As directed, three days after Janin's departure, Arnold assembled the Elizabethtown men outside the building which had served as their barracks.

"Men," he shouted, "the mine has been sold. Our work here is done." Then, addressing MacIntyre, he inquired, "How much do you figure I owe you?"

"Well, I reckon we've been yere'bout a month," MacIntyre reasoned. "So, that'd be...."

Before he could go on, Arnold pulled a wad of bills from his pocket. "How about $150 each?"

"Dat's fine."

"All right," Arnold said, counting out the money into MacIntyre's hand. "Pay 'em off, Lloyd. There are tickets for this afternoon's train waiting for you at the window. You boys just go on back to Kentucky."

"Yas suh," MacIntyre sighed, "but I shore is gonna miss all we had to eat and drink around yere. I shore is."[103]

As Arnold turned to walk away from the assembly, a young man with a pencil poised above a pad approached him. "I'm a reporter for the local paper, the *Sentinel*," he announced. "I'd like to ask you a couple of questions."

"OK," Arnold said, "but I'll tell you now that I will not reveal the location of our diamond fields."

"Oh, I suppose we've had speculation enough about that," the reporter said. "But would you mind telling me why you and your party are here?"

"Well, I guess you've got me down a hole," Arnold replied. "I came here for the purpose of fitting out an expedition, supposing that it might be done without our intentions or destination being discovered. The San Francisco papers have been working in the dark, publishing all sorts of nonsense regarding this important discovery, but you are the only one who has yet to hit us hard." As the reporter scribbled furiously on his pad, Arnold allowed himself a smug grin as he went on, "I go to Cañon City, Colorado, from which place I shall start with 100 picked men and experienced miners." He paused a minute to let the writer catch up. "From Cañon City, our route lies southwest through St. Louis Valley, 300 miles and south of the Moquis Villages near the Flax River."[104]

As the young reporter scurried away to file his "scoop" on the location of the diamond mine, obtained directly from the man who knew, he didn't stop to recognize that Arnold's "directions" were utter nonsense.

Chapter Fourteen

Friday, August 15, 1872
San Francisco, California

Following his orders to abandon the contemplated trip to the diamond mine, Henry Janin returned to California a thoroughly discouraged man. In San Francisco, he met with an equally discouraged banker, William Ralston.

"I'm very disappointed," Janin said, "that I have been unable to complete my work at the diamond field."

"As am I," Ralston agreed. "I've made every effort to ensure that all of our dealings have been straightforward and above board. The fact that we have yet to perfect our title to the land disturbs me greatly. This is simply not how I prefer to do business."

"It's all these damned rumors running rampant," Janin moaned. "The only people who aren't running off to Arizona or New Mexico or someplace to hunt for diamonds are those who are too busy watching me and Arnold to see what our next move will be. There's no way I can go back there until we gain title to the land and we can't do that until I finish my work. It's extremely frustrating!"

"Well," Ralston said thoughtfully, "it doesn't necessarily have to be you personally who completes the survey, you know."

Janin was taken aback. "Why, I never even considered that another engineer might finish the job."

"Well, it seems obvious to me that it's gonna have to be someone else. As you say, you are being watched too closely to do the job." For emphasis, he slammed his fist to the surface of his desk as he added, "and, the job **must** be done."

"Yes, you're right," Janin agreed. "As a matter of fact, I've been thinking that it might be better if I sold my stock in the company anyway."

Now it was Ralston's turn to be taken aback. "What? Why?"

"It just doesn't seem fittin' for me to remain a stockholder and speculate in the value of the stock in a property which I experted," he said. "Besides, if I sell out, maybe they'll quit watching all of us so close."

Ralston digested that thought. "This is not a snap decision on your part?"

"Certainly not. I had plenty of time to think about it while I was sittin' around doing nothing in Wyoming."

"I see," Ralston said thoughtfully. "You own 10,000 shares?"

"That's right."

"What do you want for them?"

"Well," Janin began, "I've given that matter some thought, too. With all the speculation going on, I suppose that if I advertised the fact that I have stock in the San Francisco and New York Mining and Commercial Company for sale, I could get any price I'd care to ask."

"I'm sure you could," Ralston said, "but I would consider...."

"Yes, you're right," Janin interrupted. "It would indeed be a breach of ethics, so I thought perhaps you and Mr. Harpending and Mr. Lent might be willin' to buy me out. I certainly wouldn't want to bring in any outsiders."

"Nor would I." The banker considered before he went on. "I'm sure that buying your shares can be arranged. What would you consider a fair offer?"

"Well, you gentlemen flattered me by asking me to be involved and then allowed me to buy the stock at a mere $10 per share, so I wouldn't dream of holding you up...."

"We all figure to profit in this enterprise and that should include you," Ralston interjected. "The price we've discussed every step of the way has been $40 per share."

"Why that's certainly more than fair," Janin exclaimed.

"Consider it done then," Ralston said, reaching across to shake on the deal. "I shall consult with my partners and have your $40,000 ready for you on Monday, if that's satisfactory."[105]

"Very well." Janin hesitated a beat, then asked, "What are we going to do about getting the patents on the property?"

"I'll tell you exactly what we're going to do," Ralston nearly shouted. "Plans are underway. Harpending, Roberts, Lent and I have already picked a party of men to go to the diamond fields to complete the work. The preparations are nearly complete; I think they will be ready to depart next week. Do you know Mr. John F. Boyd?"

"I know of him," Janin replied. "A mining engineer of no small reputation."

"But not of your stature," Ralston said with a smile. "Mr. Boyd was a member of the party that we organized to meet your group at the diamond site on the first expedition."

"The group Arnold had Harpending turn back?"

"That's right. Mr. Boyd has read your report, of course, and assures us that, from what he knows, you were quite conservative in your evaluations and estimates."

Janin allowed himself a satisfied smile. "Who else will be going?"

You probably don't know most of them, but I assure you they are all able to handle themselves in the wild and represent the best financial interests in this state. George Roberts' brother, Joseph, will be in charge."[106]

"How 'bout Arnold? Lent?"

"No," Ralston responded. "Mr. Lent wanted to go, but we thought it best that he stay away this time. You seem to be unaware that Phil Arnold has moved back to Kentucky."

"Really? He's gone?"

"Yes. His wife arranged the sale of their home here while you and Arnold were holed up in Laramie. After you left there, as we instructed, he sent the Negroes home and arrived in California a few days after you. She had everything ready, so he collected the money from the sale of his house and lit out for old Kentucky." The banker paused a moment, then went on, "Also, you probably don't know that Arnold met with General McClellan at Laramie shortly after you left there."

"No, I didn't know. What did the General have to say?"

"Not much then, but by the time he arrived here, he'd decided to withdraw his name and sever all his connections with the San Francisco and New York Mining and Commercial Company and promptly did so."

"Damn! Why?"

"He didn't actually say, but I gathered that he wanted out in part, at least, because nobody would tell him where the diamond field is. I think the fact that he couldn't order everybody around was a factor, too."

"I could see that. As far as I'm concerned, good riddance to the pompous little ass," Janin said. After a moment's thought, he asked, "so Philip Arnold's done with the diamond business?"

"Financially he is, but he did agree to provide any help we might require."

"That's good." As an afterthought, he asked, "What about his buddy Slack; where's he?"

"Who knows? Evidently he took the money and ran, as they say."

That comment struck a chord with Janin. "Well, this new expedition then. What with Arnold and Slack gone and me and Harpending and Lent ruled out, who's gonna lead the way?"

"Oh, Mr. Harpending's pal, Alfred Rubery is going. You'll recall that he was along when you went, so he knows the way in."

Recalling that Rubery and Slack had violated the trust placed in them when they abandoned guarding the site as soon as the rest of the party was out of sight, Janin's first impulse was to say that he suspected Rubery would know the way **out** better. But, having agreed to sell his interest, he decided to keep his thoughts to himself. "Ah, yes," he said.

❧

Under the leadership of Joseph Roberts, a few of the exploratory party of fifteen men departed San Francisco on August 20, 1872.[107] The remainder of the group boarded the trains individually or in pairs over the next several days. In addition to Roberts and Alfred Rubery, included were John F. Boyd, the mining engineer; Edward M. Fry, a relative of Ralston's wife; Dr. Charles Cleveland, a journalist who was acquainted with both Harpending and Arnold and would supply the publicity when the time arrived; and Malcolm King, a civil engineer and mining expert who had done considerable surveying work at the Comstock Lode. While all these men were well known and trusted by the stockholders, none, with the possible exception of Rubery, was as conspicuous as Arnold, Lent and Harpending. As a hedge against trackers, Rubery traveled under the unimaginative alias William Brown.[108]

In addition to the various rumors as to the location of the American El Dorado and in spite of steadily increasing loud and numerous rumblings that the whole affair was a hoax, other diamond speculating companies where springing up like weeds, on the off chance that someone might stumble upon the genuine location, find a similar tract somewhere else, or, most importantly, follow this party to the actual site. At the station, Harpending expressed his concern to Dr. Cleveland: "I hope you will get there, but I am afraid you won't. If you get there, Doctor, you will find one of the biggest things in the world; but you won't get there. You will be followed."[109]

Taking every precaution against trackers, Roberts had the majority of the men leave the train at Green River, Wyoming, about 50 miles northwest of the site, while he and Cleveland and Fry went on to Rock Springs, where they would pick up the supplies and then backtrack to rendezvous with the others at Green River.

After a few days on the trail, two things became obvious: a tracking party was dogging their every step; and Rubery did not know where he was going. However inadvisable it may have been, given the uncertainty of the guide and the total ignorance of the others, a decision was made to split the party. A group of five, with Cleveland in charge, went in one direction, while the remainder moved in an opposite direction. The splitting and wandering had one happy effect: after a few days, the tracking party ran out of supplies and turned back.

"For one month, through the most difficult mountain country south of the Union Pacific Railroad, east of Rock Springs in the State of Wyoming, under two respected guides, we did anxiously, solicitously search for the diamond fields," Dr. Cleveland recorded.[110] "It was an ordeal of the most wearing, arduous, uncertain, violent, exasperating, perilous nature it is possible to conceive."

The fact that when Rubery was there previously the mountains were snow covered, while they were now bare, added to his confusion. Additionally, the stream in which they had washed the gravel was now dry, causing Rubery to ride right over the original camp site several times without recognizing it. By the last week of September, when Rubery finally identified the site where they had mined before, he was leading a most thirsty, exasperated, exhausted and quarrelsome group.

As before, arrival at the site (along with some whiskey) raised the prospectors' spirits. With only an hour remaining before sunset, everyone set out looking for precious stones. One member reported, "We scratched and dug with our knives among the sand and gravel down to the bedrock, which varies in depth from six inches to ten feet. The diamonds, varying in size from a drop of water to a white bean are found close to bedrock."[111] By sunset, the entire party had found 384 diamonds along with some sapphires, garnets and rubies. When one member of the party chopped down a cedar tree for firewood and found a diamond under the roots, he exclaimed, "I'll be damned if anybody could salt them there unless they did it long enough ago for the tree to grow."[112]

The next morning, the men settled down to the business that had brought them there: surveying the site to obtain the government grant. With Malcolm King in charge and everyone taking a hand in the work, the 3,000 acre tract was surveyed within a week. The work included laying out a town site, which they awarded the majestic title of "Brilliant City."

When the purpose of the expedition was accomplished, any thought of remaining to prospect was defeated by the bad weather. "It was too late in the season for mining," reported Joseph Roberts. "Besides, we had no water, and the weather had become severely cold. The place is simply too cold for winter operations."[113]

With no trackers to evade and the benefit of the experience gained going in, the return trip to Green River was accomplished without incident and required only two and one-half days. "Roberts rode a mule that wasn't bigger'n a rabbit, but he was the pluckiest little devil you ever saw. We rode sixty miles to reach the railroad, and he flirted his tail as spry as any chipmunk you ever saw."[114]

☙

"I tell you, they must be lost," George Roberts cried. He, along with Asbury Harpending and William Lent were assembled in Ralston's Bank of California office. "They've been gone for more than a month now and not a single word. With winter coming on and as bad as the weather can get in that country, they may be in serious trouble."

"Let's not panic here," Ralston reasoned. "We picked these men because they know what they're doing."

"As far as mining and surveying go, they do," Roberts said, "but I need not point out that my brother does not know the way to the site."

"Rubery does," Harpending reminded.

"Let's see," Lent said, attempting to add a voice of reason. "They left here around August 20; today is September 22. That's 33 days they've been gone. Let's give 'em seven days to get to Green River and another three days to form up and gather their provisions. That's ten days. The distance to the diamond fields is about 50 miles – three easy days. Then the survey work should be done in a week – that's another ten days. Even allowing a little time to dig for diamonds – it would be too much to expect 'em to resist – they should have been back at the railroad in a total of 25 days. They would have telegraphed us when they got back, and they haven't. By my calculation, they're at least a week overdue. So, I think we can safely assume that they are lost."

"You're right, Bill," Ralston said. "And I know George is worried about his brother. As far as that goes, I have kin folks out there, too."

"I say we organize a rescue party to go find 'em and bring 'em back," Roberts suggested.

"All right," Harpending agreed. "That's a good idea. Who'll lead it?"

"I recommend Janin and General Dodge," Ralston said.

"Are they not being watched?" Harpending asked.

"We cannot worry about it," Roberts said. "Even if they are, the rescue party will need their expertise."

"Let's not take any chances this time," Roberts interjected. "Let's see if we can get Arnold to go. They damn well won't get lost with him along."

"Good idea," Harpending said. "He did say that he would offer any help we needed. I'll go telegraph him right now."

Philip Arnold received Asbury Harpending's telegram in Elizabethtown the next day. Immediately, he replied, "I leave tomorrow."[115]

Notwithstanding the satisfaction Arnold's good faith generated, his help was not needed. The very afternoon Arnold's reply was received, the Roberts party announced their return to Green River by telegraph. Lent and Janin immediately left to meet them and get their report first hand. On the return trip to San Francisco, a reporter for the San Francisco *Chronicle*, aware of the surveyor party's mission, picked Joseph Roberts' brain. "We surveyed 3,000 acres of land and fully confirmed the truth and accuracy of Janin's report," Roberts said.[116]

Henry Janin was absorbed in deep conversation with engineer John Boyd, their heads close together so they could whisper over the clackity-clack of the wheels on the rails, when a man stopped in the aisle beside them and cleared his throat. "Excuse me, Mr. Janin?"

"Yes?" Janin looked up, a bit irritated at the interruption.

"Hope I'm not disturbing you, sir. I'm Sam Emmons."

Oh, yes, everybody in the profession knows a noted geologist like you, Sam. Sorry I didn't recognize you at first. This is John Boyd." The three men shook hands as Emmons took the seat offered him opposite the other two men.

"What brings you to these parts?" Janin inquired.

"The Fortieth Parallel Survey," Emmons replied. "You know my boss, Clarence King, don't you?"

"Of course," Janin said. "King is the most famous explorer, mountain climber, scientists and blizzard survivor in the country. Would it be fair to add 'politician' to that list?"

Emmons laughed. "If you're referring to his having convinced Congress to fund his grand survey along the route of the transcontinental railroad, I'd say that 'diplomat' would be a better term."

"Your work is over for the season?"

"Yes, praise be," Emmons sighed. "We just beat the bad weather. This is the end of the sixth year of the survey. I'll be happy to spend the winter at headquarters in the Montgomery Block building in San Francisco."[117]

Another man approached the trio. "Hi, Jim," Emmons said, "Join us. This is Jim Gardiner."

"Another Fortieth Parallel man?" Janin inquired, shaking hands.

"Yep," Gardiner said taking a seat. "I'm King's chief topographer." After a few minutes of "shop talk" among these professional men, Gardiner said, "Say Henry, I read in the papers that you're all wrapped up in the diamond mining business."

"Am I that famous?" Janin shot back.

"Oh, yes," Emmons said. "Even out in the wilds where we've been, word about your report on the American El Dorado seeps in. Does your being here got something to do with that?"

"Well, yes, in a way."

"I understood the diamond mine was somewhere in Arizona or New Mexico, 'way south of here," Gardiner said.

"If you wanna go on the rumors in the newspapers, you might as well go looking for it on the back side of the moon," Janin said with a laugh.

"Well, I don't much believe what's in the papers, but, as a matter of fact, I agreed with 'em that this whole business is a lot of hooey until I learned that you were involved. We saw you at breakfast," Emmons added, "and couldn't help but noticing your rough looking companions. We thought they might be a diamond prospecting party."

"Well, you're right," Boyd said. "We've had a rough month or so out in this country."

"I understand that," Emmons said, affecting a shiver. "Say, do you have any of those precious stones?"

Boyd looked to Janin who nodded. Boyd then extracted a buckskin sheet from his pocket. Unwrapping it, he displayed 50 or so of the new-found sparklers, diamonds and a few rubies, for the government survey men. "We went there to survey the land, not look for diamonds," Boyd explained, "but we did manage to pick up a few while we were there."

"Pretty crystals," Emmons commented, fingering the stones. "Would you mind telling us where these came from?"

"Hell, Sam," Janin exploded, "you know we couldn't do that."

"Oh," Emmons said apologetically. "I'm just interested in the geology of the area." Seeing Janin's dissatisfaction with that explanation, he added, "Of course, I wouldn't dream of staking out a claim of my own."

"Well," Janin said, softening, "I tell you what, as soon as we gain title to the land – and with our survey results, that shouldn't be long – you'll be the first to know."

"Fair enough," Emmons said. "Come on Jim, let's let these men alone."

As Emmons and Gardiner returned to their seats farther back in the car, Gardiner whispered, "The fact that they're on this train indicates the diamond field must be somewhere in the northwest corner of Colorado or maybe southern Wyoming."

"Sure does," Emmons agreed. "We've been all over that country and I didn't see any signs to indicate that diamonds might be found there."

"That's exactly what I was thinkin'," Gardiner agreed. "Also, it strikes me as mighty strange that diamonds and rubies occur in the same location."

"A geological oddity, for sure," Emmons agreed.

After the two men sat in silence for a few moments, Gardiner suggested, "Let's see if we can subtly poke around with some of these other boys and perhaps pick up some clues."

"Be careful," Emmons cautioned, "we don't want to make 'em suspicious of our motives."

"I saw Malcolm King back there. He's got to be their surveyor. I'll pretend that we've been confused about the exact boundaries of Utah and Wyoming and Colorado and see if I can get some information from him on that. He'll think that's a legitimate enough thing for us to be askin' about."

As the train slid down the west side of the mountains toward California, Emmons and Gardiner casually interrogated the Roberts party for information concerning landmarks, water ways, distances and directions. While the Roberts men had been advised to guard their information, they did not allow for the fact that these Fortieth Parallel surveyors had been meticulously over every inch of the ground they vaguely described.

When the train arrived in San Francisco on October 6, everyone was happy to be home. Most of the Roberts party men were enthusiastic in their descriptions of what they'd seen and assured everyone that the diamond fields were, indeed, as rich and extensive as Janin had initially reported. In response to a question about the diamonds having been "salted", the man who'd chopped the cedar tree replied, "Salting? Hell no! How could they? All damned nonsense. I picked diamonds away under tree roots and over an area of half a mile. They couldn't salt so much, could they, and in anticipation of our visit, which they couldn't expect."[118]

Roberts told the reporter that while the survey and mining work would be suspended for the season, they'd all, no doubt, be rich by spring. In response to the "salting" question, which was occurring more and more frequently, he said, "If we are deceived, we are the worst deceived and cheated men who ever lived."[119]

Chapter Fifteen

The slowly moving water of Valley Creek sparkled in the warm early fall sunlight as the it trickled over the limestone rocks on its way past the newly occupied residence of Philip and Mary Arnold on the outskirts of town. The Tudor style house, sitting on the edge of a prime 34-acre farm, was the most elegant residence in town when it was built by local attorney William Wilson back in 1869, and the recent refurbishment brought it well past that passé standard. Since his return from California, Arnold had purchased, in addition to the residence, seven other properties amounting to some 400 acres of prime farmland.[120]

If anyone noticed that he had taken care to ensure that each parcel was deeded in his wife's name, the fact caused no more than a raised eyebrow. The acquisition of all that property made him – or her – one of the largest land owners in the county.

"Oh, Phil, I'm so happy to be back home," Mary enthused. "California was all right, I guess, and the Lord knows San Francisco was good to us, but I'm glad we're back here to stay."

"Me too," her husband agreed, even if he lacked her certainty that the move was permanent. "Being a New Englander is a chore and being a Californian is a profession, but being a Kentuckian is an incurable disease. You can never get it out of your blood."

"That's right," she laughed. "And I love this house. I didn't like staying in town at the Showers' House with everybody prying into our business." She spread her arms wide and twirled, coming to a stop facing the stylish dining room. "Just think of the parties we'll have with all our friends and family laughing and singing in here. I'm as giddy as a school girl!"

"You throw the parties," he muttered, "I'll be on the back forty tendin' to the stock."

"Oh, you'll enjoy it too," she said, undeterred. "Why we'll be the very toast of Elizabethtown society."

"Yep, I reckon so," he sighed. "Why, with as many relatives as you've got around here, even if we don't invite anybody else, they alone wanderin' in and out of here will cause the nosy folks to pay attention."

"And the children will be so much better off here." If she took any offence at the mention of her family, she did not let it show. "With this big yard, they can run and jump and play outside and I'll not have to worry about all the pollution and crime of San Francisco. They'll be able to grow up like normal kids."

"I'm not sure how normal the girls are gonna appear," he said. "You've bought enough new clothes to keep 'em dressed to the nines for years, and all the furs and jewelry you've got for 'em make 'em look like European royalty.[121] Did it ever occur to you that the other kids will not have all that fancy stuff?"

Whatever remark she was about to counter with was interrupted by the crunch of heavy wheels on the driveway. "Oh, it's our new furniture," she shouted, running for the door. A look of disappointment replaced the excitement when she observed that the bed of the wagon slowly pulling up the drive contained only a large black box. "What's this?"

"I bought us a safe," Phil said, moving past her in the doorway.[122]

"Why?"

"To keep our bonds and cash in, for one thing." He walked to the edge of the porch. "Hello, Sid," he called to the driver.

The six work horses were more than happy to relax in their traces as the driver pulled them to a halt in the shade of the maple trees in front of the porch. Leaping from the seat, the driver wiped his brow with a red bandanna. "Arnold, what the hell are you gonna do with this thing?" he inquired.

"Just safeguarding my valuables," he said, shaking hands.

"Ain't the vault down at the bank good enough for you? This thing weighs a ton."

"Well, no, as a matter of fact, the bank vault ain't good enough, and actually, this one weighs a little more than that," Arnold said. "Where's the help to unload the safe?"

"Oh, they'll be along in a minute. Just gettin' this iron box up here was load enough for the horses, so I made the men walk."

"Well, sit a spell, then. Want a glass of lemonade?"

"That'd be mighty welcome," the driver said, taking a seat on the porch step.

"Mary," Arnold yelled, "bring me and Swanson a pitcher of lemonade." He took a seat alongside his friend. As an afterthought, he added, "please."

"What brought you back here, Phil?" Swanson asked, just making conversation. "The way I heard it, you was doing all right in California."

"You heard right enough, I guess," Arnold answered. He paused as Mary came onto the porch carrying a tray with a frosty pitcher and glasses.

"Why don't you boys sit up here in the chairs?" she asked, pouring.

"Thank you kindly, ma'am," Swanson said, standing to accept a glass. "This will hit the spot." He moved to one of the green-painted wicker chairs lined against the white weatherboard siding covering the exterior wall of the house.

Mary went back inside as Arnold took a chair beside Swanson. "Well, as to why I'm back here, in addition to being back home, and Mary's wanting to raise the kids here, I just figured I'd be safer in Kentucky."

"How's that?" Swanson asked, sipping his lemonade. "Are you in some kinda trouble with the law?"

"Nah," Arnold scoffed. "But it's just that some of the men I've had dealin's with out there might be a tad on the shady side. Bill Lent, for example, is one…." His voice trailed off as he decided he'd said enough. "Well, it could be that they'd come after me."

"Ha!" Swanson said. "Some of them California 'mine sharps?'"

"That's right. What they consider perfectly legitimate behavior among themselves don't go over too well some other places."

"Well, the talk around town is that you might have been involved in some fraudulent activity, all this diamond business, you know. But then there's also talk that maybe you simply out-Yankeed the Yankees, and if so, no court around here is likely to extradite you back to their playgrounds."[123]

"I hope it don't come to that," Arnold said with a satisfied air, "but I'm glad that's your opinion anyway."

The approach of a dozen men walking up the drive interrupted the conversation. "Well, to work," Swanson said, replacing his glass on the tray. "Thank your wife for me. Gettin' this thing in the house is gonna be a chore."

❧

"How you doin', John?" Philip Arnold greeted his old friend John Polk in front of Polk's bank on the town square.

"Evidently not as good as you," Polk answered, shaking hands. "You've cut quite a swath since you come back here."

"Aw, come on now…." Arnold protested.

"Well, let's see, you've established yourself as a gentleman farmer, what with purebred cattle and thoroughbred horses on your place out there, and become one of the political muckedy-mucks in the county, and that's quite a trick in this land of blue-bloods. Now I hear tell that you're thinking of putting up a new building over there." Polk pointed to a vacant lot on the corner of the square.

"I have no idea who might have told you that," Arnold said, "but as a matter of fact, that is one of the ventures I have under consideration."

"Oh? Really? I thought it was a joke."

"Yeah. I'm thinkin' of constructing a new business concern over there. A first class two or three story brick building would look pretty good sittin' there on that corner, don't you think?"[124]

"It might at that," Polk agreed. "What kind of business did you have in mind?"

"Nothin's definite yet, but I've been talking to Berry and Hargan. They've been thinkin' about settin' up a dry goods business, but they need a store. They say they'll do so if I'll construct a building and lease it to 'em."[125]

"Sounds a mite risky to me."

Arnold allowed himself a short laugh. "You bankers are too damned conservative, John. After all, this is the Gilded Age we're livin' in, you know."

"So I read in the papers," Polk agreed.

"Come to think of it, 'The Gilded Age' would make a good name for a new building. Let's walk over there and have a look." The two men walked to the corner of the public square. "Maybe I'll dig a basement there," Arnold mused, "or maybe…." He stopped in mid-sentence as he looked across the square. "What the hell is that?"

"What?" Polk looked where Arnold was pointing.

"That ball stuck in the wall up there."

Polk stared for a moment as if he did not comprehend what his friend was asking. "Oh, I forget that you weren't here during the war. That's a little souvenir of John Hunt Morgan's Confederate cavalry raid."

"Morgan raided here? I thought this was a thoroughly rebel town."

"Well, actually, his goal was to destroy the railroad trestle up at Muldraugh Hill, but the fact is that the 600 or so Yankee troops stationed here got in his way."

"I see," Arnold said. "When was this?"

"Just two days after Christmas, back in, oh, '62 it was. Morgan posted his artillery up there on the cemetery hill," Polk informed, pointing, "and shelled the town for a while just to get the Federal troops' attention. That ball stuck in the brick up there and we just left it lest we forget what an exciting time that was."[126]

"Well, anyway," Arnold returned to the building he planned to construct, "what would you think of calling a building 'The Gilded Age?'"

"Not bad," Polk said. "it does has a certain ring to it." Then, remembering what he wanted to mention to Arnold, he hesitated a moment before he changed the subject. "I also heard you put a safe in your house. Don't you have any faith in our vault? We do have one of them fancy new time-lock gadgets, you know. Nobody is gonna get into our safe."

"Oh, it isn't a matter of faith," Arnold said with a shrug.

"What then?" Polk prodded.

"Well," Arnold said reluctantly, "A court order will get into your vault, but a man's home is his castle."

Polk let that remark soak in for a moment, then changed the subject. "Have you given any additional thought to what we talked about the other day?"

"You mean my buying into the bank?"

"Yes. I see hard economic times on the horizon; some extra financial resources might come in handy. We'd welcome you as a partner, even if you do have to maintain your own lock box at home." He hoped his smile would lessen the tension.

"Well, I've got some other irons in the fire right now. I have a feeling that something is about to pop for me. Let's just let my involvement in your bank ride for a while until we see what's gonna happen."

Chapter Sixteen

When Clarence King finished his work on a chemistry degree at Yale – he was a member of the first class to graduate from the Sheffield Scientific School – in 1862, he took the famous advice to "go west" and headed for California, where he soon became engaged in the California Geological Survey. Over the next five years, he was to prove himself such an intrepid explorer and careful scientist that, by 1867, he was in a position to lobby the United States Government (in the person of the redoubtable Secretary of War, Edwin M. Stanton) to commission the Fortieth Parallel Survey with himself in charge. King's position was that because the area to be traversed by the transcontinental railroad should not be unexplored and uncharted territory, the United States needed a survey to map the land. Additionally, he would learn the geological make-up and natural resources contained in a swath forty miles either side of the tracks from western Nevada to eastern Wyoming. The survey work consumed six years, so when King published his quintessential work, *Mountaineering in the Sierra Nevada* early in 1872, he established himself as the leading geologist in the country.[127]

Thus it was that when King got wind of diamonds having been found in the territory he'd explored, he became concerned. If there were indeed diamonds just lying on the ground and he had not discovered them, he and his survey would look foolish, a possibility he could not even bring himself to contemplate. So, as soon as his men Sam Emmons and Jim Gardiner returned to San Francisco following their chance encounter with Henry Janin, King summoned them, along with Emmons' topological assistant, Allen Wilson, to his office.

"All right, boys," he began, "let's compare notes and see if we can't figure out where this so-called diamond field is."

"Well," Emmons began, "we happened to find Janin on a train in southern Wyoming. That tells me that the diamond site is not in Arizona or New Mexico, as they've claimed."

"Oh, I'm sure about that. We can totally dismiss the idea that it's that far south, and if it is, it's out of our area of interest, so we don't care. But, from all appearances, it seems obvious that the place we're looking for is somewhere in northern Colorado or south-central Wyoming," King agreed. "Before we go on, let's set down a ground rule here, lest we all end up looking foolish. Even among ourselves, let's never refer to diamonds; rather, let's say 'carboniferous fossils.'[128] Now then, Jim, what do you have to say?"

"The only place we've studied which has the geological qualifications to actually produce diam – uh – carboniferous fossils is the northwest corner of Colorado."

"I'd reached the same conclusion," King commented. "There's a narrow band there where the geology is right."

"That's near where we encountered Janin," Emmons said, "and it coincides with what I got out of Malcolm King about his survey work for Janin's outfit."

"In the corner of Colorado just south of Wyoming and just east of Utah?" King asked consulting the map.

"Yep," Emmons agreed. "Malcolm was mighty interested in learning what we knew about the territorial boundaries in that area. It makes one wonder why he was so interested in what we knew."

"Janin's report said the spot was on a mesa near pine timber," Gardiner informed. "We've tramped all over that area, and there's only one place in the whole region that would qualify."

"Right. I've got it figured this way," Wilson said, spreading the map on the table before them. "The place has to be east of the Green and north of the Yampa River. As these two streams are almost impassable at the time of year the Janin party visited the country, it seems that they must have gone to some point in the region where we've been working this season. Yet, I didn't believe any, uh, fossils had been found until I got back here and saw the gems they said had been picked up in the field."[129]

"Seems to me like the information we're basing this on is pretty meager," Gardiner commented.

"It might be to somebody else," Emmons said, "but, Jim, with our intimate knowledge of the geology and topology of the region, we have a leg up on most folks, and we're probably right about it."

"I would say it has to be within a radius of fifteen miles of this spot," King said, placing his finger on the map in the corner of Colorado. "Now, we must go there and have a look for ourselves."

"Gettin' pretty late in the year to be goin' back out there," Gardiner observed.

"We cannot let that bother us, Jim. Our professional reputations are at stake here." King hesitated a moment, then went on, "Not to mention that if this thing is a hoax – as we all know damned well that it is – and we're in possession of that knowledge, we have a moral obligation to expose it."

"The weather wasn't too bad when we were out there two weeks ago," Emmons said. "If we go right now, we might get in and out before the hard winter sets in. Clarence, do you want me and Jim and Wilson to go?"

"Yes, certainly." He hesitated a beat then added, "and I'll go along myself."

That revelation surprised Emmons. He considered King a single-minded, dedicated scientist, and hence uninterested in the diamond fields as a source of wealth. "Are you sure you want to go, Clarence? It's liable to be mighty cold."

"Yes," King said without hesitation. "We're going to have to be very careful to keep our activities a secret. In the first place, the reason for our going is to try to prove this whole affair is a hoax. But, we do not want to make our friend Henry Janin look bad either to the men who employed him or to the public. Additionally, it just could be that we're wrong. Should that prove to be the case, we sure as hell don't want anybody knowing what we tried to do." He paused to look at each man. "How soon can you be ready?"

"How 'bout Monday?" Gardiner suggested. After all agreed that October 21 was all right, Gardiner asked, "Where shall we depart from?"

"Our mules are wintering at Fort Bridger and we left some camping supplies there," Emmons reminded.[130]

"Fort Bridger?" Gardiner erupted. "Hell, man, that's in the southwest corner of Wyoming. It'd be, oh, 150 miles west of where we want to go. Black Buttes Station or Rawlins would be a hell of a lot closer."

"Yes, but having the supplies ready would save us some time," Wilson pointed out.

"Hold on," King interrupted. "You're both right, but keep in mind that above all else we do not want to be found out. In conjunction with our survey work, we have a perfectly legitimate reason for going to Fort Bridger, so departing from there would certainly provide no hint as to our true purpose to anyone who might be watching."

♋

Traveling separately to avoid suspicion, Wilson, Emmons, Gardiner and King assembled at sunset on October 24 at Fort Bridger, Wyoming. The hoped for break in the weather did not eventuate; conditions were brutally cold. Emmons set about having some necessary testing equipment made while Wilson purchased food and other supplies and Gardiner contracted two trusted camp men, Hunter and Hill. Some trouble was had assembling the necessary gear, so they were not ready to travel until late afternoon on October 28. Emmons reported the temperature at eight p.m. that evening as eleven degrees.[131]

It was noon the next day before the party got on the road in extreme cold and a howling wind. Emmons recorded, "It was a bitterly cold journey, on tired and worn out animals, whose legs, from crossing the frequent, thinly frozen mountain streams, became encased in balls of ice, which rattled as they went like rude castanets. The wind that sweeps over these elevated, barren plains is even fiercer and more constant that that which prevails at this season on the Great Plains."[132]

The next few days were passed in conditions as favorable as could be expected given the season. About noon on November 2, the party arrived at a "clear spring in a deep narrow gulch, sunk some 600 feet below the uniform level of the surroundings mesas, and where both we and our animals were effectually concealed." A decision was made to spend the night in this protected and obscure location.[133]

While the camp men set up, King, Emmons and Wilson went out to look for an opening allowing passage up the walls of the ravine to the mesa above. They had ridden only about 500 yards when Wilson cried out, "Look, there's a small fresh blaze on that cottonwood tree over there."

Rushing to the tree, they began to search around the area. In a moment,

King shouted, "I've found something!" as he held a slip of paper aloft fluttering in the wind.

"What does it say?" Emmons demanded.

Unfolding the slip, King said, "it says that the water privileges in this gulch belong to the San Francisco and New York Mining and Commercial Company. It's signed, 'Henry Janin, June 15, 1872.'"

"Hot damn! We've found it." Emmons enthused.

"We sure have," Wilson, a hundred yards away, shouted. "I've found some tracks over here."

By following the tracks just discovered, the three men were soon atop the level mesa above their camp. The tracks converged on an outcropping of rust-colored sandstone about thirty yards long. "This is exactly what Janin described in his report," King shouted.

Certain that they had found the source of the "carboniferous fossils," all three men jumped to the ground and, on hands and knees, began examining the sandstone. In only a moment, Emmons shouted, "Hey! I found a ruby!"

Before King could go to Emmons' side, Wilson yelled. "I found a diamond." No one objected to his not calling it a carboniferous fossil. The three geologists needed only a moment to determine that the tiny sparkler, having a steely tinge, was, indeed, a genuine diamond.[134]

Despite the scientific training of these men and the object of their mission, an epidemic of "El Dorado fever" struck with the same ferocity as it had the other parties who had visited the site. While daylight lasted, they continued scurrying around the mesa, picking up precious stones. Despite the numbing cold, howling wind and lack of diamond hunting training, by dusk the men managed to find about 100 rubies and four small diamonds.

By the campfire after dark that night, Emmons opined, "Well, it looks to me like Henry Janin knew what he was talkin' about after all." The flickering fire light revealed the seriousness on his face.

Wilson agreed. "If a man was to come here in daylight when it wasn't so damned cold, it's untellin' what fabulous wealth he'd be able pick up."

"Well," King admitted, rubbing his hands before the fire, "the geological make up this country is similar to other spots in the world where diamonds have been found. There is no reason why the gems should not occur in this sandstone. We're in a remote and basically unexplored spot – as secluded and out of the way as anywhere I ever wandered – so, despite what I thought, I have to allow that it is possible that this whole affair is as advertised." A certain wistfulness tinged his comment.

"One thing, though," Gardiner said, "does it strike anyone besides me as odd that they'd leave this place unguarded?"

"That's not so strange," Emmons commented. "As Clarence said, this spot is about as remote as anywhere on the face of the earth could be, and everybody believes that the diamonds were found in Arizona or somewhere well south of here. So, it's unlikely that anyone would come here, especially at this time of year."

"Any reasonably sane human being wouldn't come here in this weather, that's for sure," Gardiner said sarcastically, rotating his back to the fire.

"That might be a part of their thinking," King added. "Perhaps they didn't bother with a guard because they were sure nobody would come here, even if they could find the place, until spring. By then, the winter snow and rain would wash away the tracks. Don't forget that we wouldn't have found the spot so easily without those tracks."

"Well, let's get some sleep," Emmons suggested. "We'll see what it looks like and how we feel in the cold, hard light of day." The men turned in, each secretly wondering if he was the only one who had thoughts of abandoning their mission in favor of gathering the wealth that apparently was theirs for the taking.

Chapter Seventeen

Sunday, November 3, 1872
American El Dorado
Northwest Corner, Colorado Territory

The winter morning brought a feeble – but sobering – light to the men camped atop the mesa. By the time the scientists were up and about, the camp men had a roaring fire going with the aroma of bacon and coffee wafting through the frigid air. Clarence King, Sam Emmons, Jim Gardiner and Allen Wilson gathered near the fire over breakfast.

"Well," Wilson opened, "more mature thought leads me to the conclusion that the gems we found have to have been planted here." The notion of gaining wealth for themselves was totally gone now.

"Oh, I agree," Emmons chirped in. "It is not natural for us to find a dozen rubies for every diamond we pick up." As he stuffed a biscuit in his mouth, he added, "as a matter of fact, diamonds and rubies occurring in the same place – in any proportion – seems a mite strange. I'm now positive that it's a hoax."

"Now, hold on," King cautioned, setting his tin coffee cup aside. "Let's not forget that our friend Janin certified this site as genuine. Even if it is a hoax, and I'm not saying that it isn't, given how excited we got yesterday, you would all agree that it's easy to see how he was fooled."

"You're right, Clarence," Emmons said. "We need to determine a well thought out, scientific plan of investigation."

"I have a couple of ideas," Wilson offered.

"OK," King, the man in charge, said, warming his hands at the fire. "Let's go back over there and poke around separately this morning as we each formulate our opinions and ideas. We'll come back here at noon, compare notes and come up with a plan."

When breakfast was finished, the four scientists walked to the sandstone jutting above the surface of the mesa. King, recognizing Henry Janin's narrow boot width, followed the tracks. The first thing he noted was that another set of boot prints accompanied Janin's tracks. King concluded that these footprints must have been made by Philip Arnold.[135] Following these tracks through their wanderings all around the mesa, King observed that as long as he traced the footsteps, even though he did not try, he would find an occasional gem, but not a single stone was to be found when he wandered as much as ten feet from the trail.

At the same time, Sam Emmons was examining the many anthills to be found around the area that the prospectors had dubbed "Brilliant City." Emmons observed that while nearly every hill near the sandstone yielded a ruby, those at any distance from the central axis contained no gem. While every anthill had one hole in the top which the ants had fashioned as an entry/exit portal, some of the hills had another hole in the side of the crust. He also noted that the two-hole anthills always had footprints near them and invariably contained a ruby. Emmons concluded that the second hole must have been created when a ruby was pushed into the anthill with a stick.[136]

Allen Wilson wandered about in a random pattern using one of the sieves they had had constructed for the purpose of sifting the soil. In areas where the ground had been disturbed, a sievefull of dirt sometimes yielded as many as twenty to thirty rubies as well as an occasional sapphire, emerald or diamond. No matter how much sifting he did in areas where the soil appeared undisturbed, no gem was produced. [137]

After the men had discussed their observations around the fire at noon, Gardiner added that he had found a diamond perched on a small point of rock about two inches above the surface of the surrounding area.

"Why wouldn't the wind have blown that off?" Emmons asked.

"Exactly," King answered without further comment.

After Wilson informed that he had found fifteen to twenty rubies for each diamond, King voiced the question on everyone's mind: "Do we all now agree that this diamond business is, beyond doubt, a hoax?"

Neither Emmons nor Wilson nor Gardiner felt the need to speak; their silence acknowledging their complete agreement.

"Well, then," King said, "let's rest up today. In the morning, we'll dig a bushel or two of soil samples from various sites all over this mesa. We'll sift each to see what we find and then we'll wash out both the saved gravel and the dirt that we sifted out. In addition, we'll trace the existing tracks, examining everywhere the Janin/Arnold party stopped, and we'll dig up every damned one of these anthills."

"When we finish that," Emmons opined, "we'll know for sure."

King grunted. "We already know for sure, Sam. What we're gonna do now is remove any shadow of doubt. You do realize we're going to have to confront the men who claimed this property, don't you?"

"I do," Emmons said, "and you're right, we want to be damned sure of what we're saying."

"I like Clarence's plan," Wilson added. "If we follow it carefully, we can leave here knowing that we overlooked nothing."

"And, therefore, whatever we conclude is absolutely correct," Gardiner added.

King's plan was implemented through the entire day on November 5 despite the numbing cold. At the end of the day, not a single diamond or ruby had been found away from the central sandstone rock or off the Janin/Arnold track. Additionally, the gems were mixed – as nature would dictate – with quartz pebbles of various sizes and concretions of iron oxide. The gems' specific gravity being intermediate, they should have settled through to bedrock. In more than thirty tests panning and washing the soil all the way to bedrock – in some cases as much as ten feet – not one gem was located more than two inches below the surface.[138]

The next day, the men examined the cracks in the sandstone. The cracks varied from a few inches to nearly two feet in depth and some showed signs of tampering. Every one of the disturbed cracks yielded a diamond or rubies in the previously observed proportion. Not a single gem of any kind was found in the crevices filled with untouched earth and overgrown with grass. Around the fire that evening, King spoke for the group: "Well, boys, this sandstone rock has produced four distinct types of diamonds, a few oriental rubies, garnets, spinets, sapphires and amethysts…." He paused a moment to let the significance of what he was saying soak in, then concluded, "An impossible association of minerals to occur naturally." The others' silence again signaled their agreement.

While involved in additional test on the morning of November 7, the men were startled when "a stout party, city dressed and looking very much out of keeping with the surroundings[139]" appeared riding a fine looking horse. "We've been followed!" Emmons whispered to King as the interloper approached.

"By a clown, evidently," Wilson observed.

"I say, gentlemen," the visitor inquired, "have you found any carats around here?"[140] That comment erased any thought that the man had stumbled upon them by accident. The round man was wearing a lime green three-piece suit divided into a grid by narrow horizontal and vertical black stripes. Patent leather shoes with white spats covered his feet. His overcoat and hat of buffalo hide gave the appearance of a ball of fur mounted on a horse.

Taken aback by the sudden, unexpected and comic emergence, King stammered, "Who might you be, may I ask?"

"Certainly you may," the gentleman said, dismounting. "My name is J.F. Berry. I'm a New York diamond dealer." He removed his kid glove and extended his hand. "Happy to make your acquaintance."

"Clarence King," King muttered, still in shock. "Where the hell did you come from?"

"Well, it's a long story," Berry said with a short laugh. "What do you say we go sit by the fire and I'll tell you all about it? Beastly cold out, you know." He hugged himself to indicate his discomfort.

Around the fire, Berry made himself comfortable, settling his considerable bulk on Emmons' pack. "I had interest in some mining ventures in Utah for some time when I heard about the diamond fields some six months ago," he began. "Being in the diamond business, I was naturally interested in learning the exact site of the discovery. So, I've had men watching the railroads hereabouts with great intensity all summer. We were particularly fascinated with the comings and goings of one Mr. Henry Janin. As a matter of fact, we hit upon the ruse of hiring Mr. Janin ourselves to give us his opinion of one of our mines. Despite all our efforts to wine, dine and charm the ever-professional Mr. Janin, he would disclose no hint as to the location of his source of diamonds, so we were reduced to paying attention to the railroad stations." Berry paused in his narrative to fish a full-bent meerschaum pipe out of his coat pocket, meticulously pack it with tobacco and carefully light it with an ember from the fire before he went on speaking. Contently exhaling a cloud of smoke, he continued, "You can imagine my delight and piqued curiosity when men of the stature of you gentlemen appeared at Fort Bridger and started equipping for an adventure at this odd time of year."[141]

King looked at Emmons and Wilson as if to say that the man obviously knew who they were and why they were there. "You followed us all this time? How did you get onto me?"

"Mr. Janin did let it slip that Mr. King was doing the surveying of the diamond field. When I learned that you had left San Francisco, I located you at Fort Bridger, and here we are." As Berry sucked on his pipe, King started to point out that the man Janin had referenced was not he but rather Malcolm King, but decided that there was no point in correcting Berry's confusion. "And, yes, my eight men and I have been observing your activities through a spyglass from atop yon mountain." He pointed to a peak a mile distant to the north. "I might add that it was bitter cold work for us, too." Drawing on his pipe, Berry smiled as he rubbed his hands before the fire.

"What do you want from us?" Emmons asked.

"Well," Berry said, "other than learning the actual location of the diamond fields, I'd be interested in what, if any, conclusions you gentlemen have reached. I've observed all the testing you have been doing and, given your reputations, I'm sure your results will be valid."

King glanced at Emmons who simply shrugged. Gardiner volunteered, "It doesn't matter now, Clarence."

After a moment's thought, nodding in agreement, King said, "That's right. As the entire thing is a swindle, it makes no difference if the whole world knows this location. Any gems to be found here have been salted and are of virtually no value, so the claim is worthless."

Berry drew slowly on his pipe. "I see. That's just as I suspected and I am satisfied that you gentlemen know what you're talking about." Exhaling a dense puff of smoke, he thought aloud, "What a chance to sell short on the stock!"[142]

❧

By the camp fire that night, King and his men could see Berry's fire in the distance; he evidently having decided that there was no longer any need to attempt to conceal his presence. King turned to Emmons, "We've made a mistake here, Sam."

"How's that? We couldn't have kept him from following us. Besides, like Allen said, it doesn't matter now who knows where this place is."

"Oh yes it does!" King snapped. "Berry's comment about selling short bothers me. I don't know if he owns any stock in this fraud, but if he does, he'll make a beeline for San Francisco and sell it as fast as he can so he can cash out before we burst the bubble. Maybe he's in cahoots with some of the other men who laid claim to this property. With all the excitement this deal has caused, we're going to have enough difficulty getting anyone to believe us. I can see that there will be thousands of people rushing here to get in on it if he discloses the location before we can expose the swindle."

"Hold on, Clarence," Emmons said. "We don't know what Berry is gonna do."

"That's just my point. I wouldn't trust that fat clown any farther than I could throw him," King exclaimed.

"I'd say we'd better beat him back to California," Wilson commented.

"Right you are, Allen. We've got to get to San Francisco and expose this business as a hoax before Berry has any chance to make mischief." If Clarence King feared that Berry might steal his thunder by announcing the fraud first, he did not mention that possibility to his colleagues.

"Other than Janin, do you know any of the people involved in the diamond company?" Emmons asked.

"I know that Asbury Harpending and William Ralston have a hand in it," King answered, "but I don't really know either of them. Do you?"

"No," Emmons said. After a moment, he added, "I do know Henry Janin, though, and I know he's a stock holder in the company they've formed."

"That's it!" King cried. "Sam, you and Jim stay here, try to make it look like we're still working and get everything finished up. Me and Allen will head out the first thing in the morning. We'll make a straight line for Black Buttes Station – no need for deception now – and get home. As soon as we get there, I'll make an appointment with Henry and expose this colossal fraud."

"All right," Emmons agreed. "Do you think you can you beat Berry to San Francisco?"

"I'll bet he doesn't know any way out of here except the way he followed us in," King said. "Black Buttes Station is a whole lot closer, so beating him back to California shouldn't be a problem."

"Unless he follows us again," Wilson offered.

"Damn!" King exploded. "Allen, pack up your gear. We'll leave right now while it's still dark. Sam, you keep the fire going so he'll never suspect we're gone."

❧

The route to Black Buttes Station was, indeed, more direct, but the terrain was also more difficult. "We had a long ride," Wilson reported, "without track or trail, over sage-covered hills and plateaus. We crossed ridges, gullies, washouts, and, late at night, with only stars as guides during the latter part of the trip, we arrived at the station."[143]

After they awoke the station agent, they procured passage for their mules on a west-bound freight and settled in to wait for the next passenger train. "Don't you think we ought to report to somebody?" Wilson asked.

King considered that idea for a moment. "No. I'm afraid to," he answered. "We must ensure the secrecy of our knowledge until we can release it in an honorable fashion. If we send a telegram, word of the hoax will instantly be all over the country. No, the announcement will have to wait until we arrive in San Francisco and have a chance to speak with Janin."

Wilson started to object, but as he now realized that his boss was determined that he, Clarence King – and Clarence King alone – would be the one to expose the swindle; he kept his opinions to himself.

Chapter Eighteen

Sunday, November 10, 1872
San Francisco, California

The fog was just beginning its evening crawl up from the bay when Clarence King arrived at the ferry wharf. Although he was glad to be home and back in the warmer climes of California, he walked ashore through the swirling mist with a heavy heart. Having telegraphed the time of his arrival ahead, he knew that Henry Janin would be expecting him straightaway. Picking up his baggage, he hailed a waiting hack and gave the address of his office to the driver. Telling the driver to wait, he lingered there only long enough to drop off his bags before returning to the hack and directing it to Janin's residence.[144]

"Hello, Clarence," Janin said, his voice laced with anxiety. "Welcome to my home."

"Thank you, Henry," King said, shaking hands and trying to sound cheerful.

"Come in. Let me take your coat. Let's talk in here." Janin ushered his visitor into his library on the right of the entryway where he waved King to a green leather upholstered chair. As he moved around his desk, he asked, "May I offer you a brandy?" At King's nodded refusal, he sat and heaved a great sigh. "Well, then. What can I do for you, Clarence?"

King looked intently into his host's eyes a long moment before he spoke with a sigh. "Henry, do you know that I've only today returned from your diamond field?"

"No, I didn't know that. Are you sure you found the right place? They went to no small trouble to disguise the location, you know."

"Yes, I do know, and yes, I'm quite sure. We found some of your marker stakes with notes signed by you and the outcropping of sandstone you described in your report. Despite the efforts your employers made to misdirect all attention, there is absolutely no doubt I located their diamond field."

"I see," Janin said, standing. "I think I'd better have a brandy myself. Sure you won't join me?"

"On second thought, perhaps I'd better have one."

Janin brought a crystal decanter and two glasses from the sideboard across the room to the desk. As he poured, he urged, "Go on, Clarence."

"Well," King sighed, sipping from his glass, "Henry, the long and the short of it is that you've been duped. The entire proposition is a hoax – a swindle – and every last gem that has been found there was salted into the ground." He leaned against the back of his chair.

All the color drained from Janin's face and his hand shook so violently that he spilled most of his brandy. Deliberately placing his glass on the desk, he tried to speak, but the words log-jammed in his mouth. Clearing his throat, he tried again. "I know you're competent, Mr. King, but that simply cannot be true." The words were hardly above a whisper and sounded more hopeful than factual.

King leaned forward as if to add sincerity to his words. "I'm sorry, Henry, I really am. Please believe me, I'm not questioning your competence. I assure you that the evening we first arrived at the site, Emmons and Wilson and Gardiner – you know them – and I were all quite convinced of the wealth to be had there. I can readily see how you were fooled...."

"Hold on here," Janin interrupted, "did you in fact find diamonds there?"

"Yes, of course we did, and we also found rubies and emeralds, but in places and proportions...."

"All right, then," Janin broke in.

"Philip Arnold, I don't know the man, but isn't he the brains behind this whole deal? Isn't he the man that led you there?"

"Yes, that's so."

"Well, then, from the tracks I followed, didn't he accompany you in every step you made?"

"No!" Janin bellowed. "Certainly not. I did the surveying and staking all alone. Arnold didn't even offer to go along."

"I'm sure that's right, Henry. What I'm asking is, didn't he go everywhere you went *looking for gems?*" King punctured the air with a finger to add emphasis to the last phrase.

"Well," Janin said slowly, "now that you mention it, I suppose he did, but I didn't go there looking for diamonds. I went to appraise the property."

"I know, and you did an excellent job of that. But, as far as the value of the property for finding gems, they managed to pull the wool completely over your eyes." Seeing Janin's confidence crack a bit, he pressed on, "Did you see any traces that anyone had been there before?"

"No! There was not a boot print anywhere around." Seeing King's mouth open, Janin beat him to the punch. "Come to think of it, Arnold wouldn't lead us there until spring broke. By then the winter snow, wind and rain would have erased all traces." He thought for a moment, then added, "I'm sure that you would agree that in view of the weather in that country, the delay was reasonable."

"Yes, but consider the fact that waiting until the weather had erased all traces of anyone having been there was not a unwelcome side effect. You yourself said that your report was necessarily incomplete," King pointed out. "I am sure that you were not allowed enough time to examine the properties carefully. Did you find any gems more than, say, two inches below the surface of the ground?"

"I told you," Janin exploded, "I didn't go there to hunt for diamonds."

"In what time you did spend looking for stones, did you find any lying on the surface of a rock?"

"A few," Janin admitted.

"Didn't that seem strange to you?"

"Why," Janin sputtered, "I only looked for gems that first evening. Besides, I'd been assured by Harpending and Arnold and Slack that the field was unbelievably rich. Anyway, there was so much excitement, what with everybody finding diamonds and about as fast as…." His voice tailed off as his gaze fell to the desk. "I did say in my report that I did not have time enough to answer some very important questions."[145]

And so it went for the next several hours. In view of King's careful tests and observations, Janin slowly and reluctantly came to understand that the diamond field had been salted, that he had indeed been duped, and then, in turn, his glowing report had unwittingly drug others into the swindle.

Early morning light was streaming through the windows when King finally said, "Henry, we have to advise the principals of your company that they've been hoaxed, and the sooner, the better."

"I suppose so, but I dread that," Janin sighed. "I'll be made an utter fool. My career is over."

"Don't sell yourself short, Henry. I'm sure no one will question your integrity." King hesitated a moment then asked, "May I ask you something?"

"What's that?" His voice was tinged with resignation.

"Has any stock in this enterprise been sold to the public?"

"Not to my knowledge. Investment has been limited to a select group of businessmen, I believe."

"Well, then," King said cheerfully, "it could be much worse, couldn't it?"

"That's small consolation," Janin commented with a sigh. "Well, they must be told. Do you want to go with me to break the news?"

"I suppose I'd better. Your employers will, no doubt, be as shocked as you, and I'm sure they will want to question me."

"Very well," Janin sighed. "I'll make arrangements to have the principals gather at their offices. Where can I reach you?"

"At the survey office."

"Do you want to get some sleep first?"

"No!" King snapped, then softened a bit. "This is too important to be held. With so much at stake, we must make this information public as soon as possible." He did not mention the fact that he was determined that the one to burst the bubble would be Clarence King, not Mr. J.F. Berry.

"All right," Janin said. "I'll get the men together this morning as soon as I can. I'll call at your office to let you know what time."

❧

Back at the diamond field, Sam Emmons and Jim Gardiner, not knowing if Berry was watching or not, made a show of digging around near the sandstone rock for a full day after King and Wilson departed. The next morning, they packed up the camp and headed back to Fort Bridger. Upon arrival, Emmons was startled to learn that Berry had been there two days before, exhibiting the diamonds he had carried from the diamond fields and passing out a few of them as souvenirs. Despite Emmons' assurance that the diamond find was a hoax, the population of Fort Bridger was in a state of excitement.

Even in the frigid weather, several parties began outfitting for prospecting, Berry having disclosed the location.[146]

Berry had not lingered at Fort Bridger. Letting no moss gather on the knowledge he possessed, he moved on rapidly, arriving at Salt Lake City at about the same time King was briefing Henry Janin in San Francisco. Berry announced to all who would listen that he had located the diamond field and, taking a lesson, perhaps, from Philip Arnold, displayed two dozen small diamonds and some rubies to prove it.[147] When he put the stones on exhibit in a local bank, an epidemic of "El Dorado fever" broke out in Utah. Clarence King had judged Berry correctly. The problem now was to ensure that whenever Berry did decide to divulge all he knew, it would be too late.

℣

In the offices of the San Francisco and New York Mining and Commercial Company in the Harpending building, the company's principals, Asbury Harpending, William Lent, William Ralston, George Roberts and General George Dodge, had assembled at Janin's behest. As soon as the door opened to reveal the august gathering within, Henry Janin almost physically recoiled from the glares directed at him. Only the presence of Clarence King behind him prevented his being pushed away. Although Janin had conveyed no hint as to the purpose of the meeting, everyone was on edge.[148]

"Come in, gentlemen," Harpending greeted, as he extended his hand. "Mr. King, I presume?"

"You have the advantage of me, sir," King said, taking his hand.

"I'm Asbury Harpending. Please come in. Everybody in California knows you, at least by reputation." Each of the other gentlemen nodded politely, but coolly, to King as Harpending made the introductions.

"May we offer you some coffee?" Ralston said. He was really asking why they had been called there.

"No. Thank you," King said, clearly uncomfortable.

"Well, then," Lent demanded, "why have you dragged us out here so early in the morning?" His ominous glare added to the anxious atmosphere.

"Henry?" King said, deferring to Janin.

"Gentlemen," Janin began with a deep sigh, "I regret to tell you that Mr. King has brought me information proving that we are victims of a hoax and appallingly mistaken as the value of our recent diamond discovery. Mr. King's conclusion, reached after laborious investigation, is that the whole thing is a well-planned fraud and 'salt.'" He paused a beat, then added, "apparently I'm the biggest fool of all." He sank deeper into his chair.

"What?" Lent shouted. "What are you saying? You cannot be serious!"

"Quite serious, I assure you," Janin said. "Trust me, I did not want to believe it either, but Mr. King has proved beyond doubt that the diamond fields are fraudulent and every stone to be found there was salted."

"But diamonds are so precious, how could anybody afford to buy enough to salt them?"

"High quality cut diamonds are expensive," King said. "The low grade raw ones you men found, especially if purchased abroad, are cheap enough that the cost of planting them wouldn't be prohibitive."

Anger, consternation, disbelief and anxiety filled the room as the principals questioned King on every point. The geologist patiently went over all the issues he'd covered with Janin the night before until each man in the room was satisfied that they had been taken in.

"This clearly means that we cannot go through with the public offering of stock we've been planning," Harpending commented.

"Hold on, here," Lent shouted. "I see no reason why we need be in any hurry to make this information public – even if it is true."

"Oh, it's true, right enough," King assured.

"Would you be willing to lead an expedition back to the diamond fields so we can confirm what you're saying for ourselves?" Roberts asked.

"Certainly," King said, "anytime you say. But, if you gentlemen do not make a public announcement right away, I'll do it myself. There are millions of dollars and many peoples' fortunes at stake here."

"My own fortune among them," Lent shouted. "What if we made it worth your while to sit on this information for a while, Mr. King?"

Clarence King recoiled as if he'd been shot. Taking a moment to compose himself before he spoke, he said evenly, "There is not enough money in the Bank of California to make me delay the publication a single hour! If you do not, I will, but it will come with much better grace from you. Stop all transfers of stock; appoint competent men to represent you, and I will give you my camp outfit and take them to the spot, where they may convince themselves."[149]

"Henry, will you be willing to go?" Harpending asked, demonstrating his retention of faith in Janin.

"Certainly," Janin said, trying to express his gratitude for the vote of confidence.

"I want to go – I demand to go," Lent shouted.

"No," Ralston, ever the voice of reason, said. "This will be a purely scientific expedition. I suggest we send our new general manager, General David Colton. He's a good, knowledgeable, competent and trustworthy man."

"Isn't that the man who went there blindfolded before I became involved?" Janin asked.

"Yes he is," Roberts said. "He was a good man then and is still. We should also send Edward Fry and John Bost."[150]

"All right," Harpending said. "Mr. King, are you willing to defer a public announcement until this party returns with definitive information?"

"As far as I'm concerned, the information is already definitive," King asserted. "But, I can certainly see that you gentlemen would desire your own evaluation. If we go right away, and if you will agree not to sell any stock in the interim, I will hold my tongue until we return."

"Very well, thank you," Harpending said. "With the generous offer of your camp outfit, Mr. King, I think the mission can depart the day after tomorrow."

A profound silence settled over the men around the polished table. Finally, Ralston offered sadly, "I suppose we will have to make good on all the investment money we've collected so far."

"It's that damned Philip Arnold that will have to be made to make good!" Lent thundered, pounding his fist on the table. "Where the hell is he?"

"Gone to Kentucky, so I understand," General Dodge informed.

"Well, I suppose they have laws even there!" Lent roared angrily. "I say we go after him!"

"Let's not forget about Slack." Roberts asked. "Where's he?"

No one spoke for a long moment, each man searching the others' faces. Finally, Harpending said, "Well, Rubery says that he and Slack parted ways when Slack took an east-bound train from Black Buttes Station after they left the diamond site. Nobody knows where he went from there."

"Gentlemen," Henry Janin, having recovered to a degree, spoke up. "I

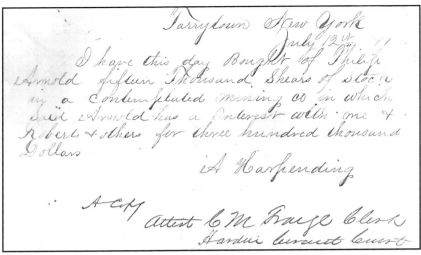

Arnold's receipt for selling 15,000 "shears" of stock to Asbury Harpending. This $300,000 represents the bulk of the money Arnold received. Courtesy of Kentucky State Archives.

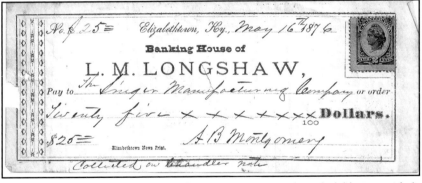

Despite the bad blood, some customers, such as A.B. Montgomery, obviously did business with the rival banks. Courtesy of Hardin County Historical Society.

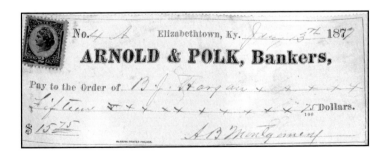

Philip Arnold's last will and testament gives no hint as to the value of his property. Courtesy of Hardin County Clerk.

(Page 1 of 1)

ed witnesses thereto and as such the same was established & ordered recorded.

Whereupon I have truly recorded the same together with this certificate in my office.

This May, 17, 1904.   F. C. Corley Clerk.

I Mary E. Arnold of the County of Hardin State of Kentucky do make this my last will and testament hereby revoking any and all former wills I may have made. First I gave and devise to my daughter Nora Arnold absolutely and in fee the whole of my property of every kind real, personal and mixed. Second I do hereby constitute and appoint D. C. Haycraft Executor of this my last will and testament. I do not will or devise any of my property to my other three children, or to either of them, because I have heretofore advanced to them towit: to my daughter Kate May, to my son Thomas Arnold and to my son Richard Arnold the sum of Ten Thousand dollars each. I therefore will and direct that the said Kate May, Thomas Arnold & Richard Arnold shall take none of my estate but that the whole of my property of every kind is hereby willed and devised as aforesaid to my Daughter Nora Arnold. In witness whereof I have hereunto set my hand this the eleventh day of August, 1894.   Mary E. Arnold.

Witnesses. D. C. Haycraft.

Virginie E. Cresap.

Katie A. May.

At a County Court begun and held for Hardin County at the Court House in Elizabethtown, Ky Monday May, 16th. 1904 the foregoing instrument of writing purporting to be the true last will and testament of Mary E. Arnold was produced to Court and proven in due form of law by the oaths of D. C. Haycraft & Virginia Cresap two subscribing witnesses thereto who also proved the attestation of Katie A. May the other subscribing witness thereto and also by the affidavit of said Katie A. May and as such the same was established and ordered recorded.

Whereupon I have truly recorded the same together with this certificate in my office

This May, 17th. 1904.

F. C. Corley Clk.

Mary Arnold's will, using the same exact wording as her husband's, leaves us wondering how much the estate was worth. Courtesy of Hardin County Clerk.

There was not much of the hoax money left by the time Katie Arnold's property was appraised in 1904. Courtesy of Hardin County Clerk.

Ralston's Bank of California about 1870. In 1996 the bank merged with Union Bank to form Union Bank of California and then, eventually, just Union Bank. Courtesy of Union Bank.

A run of the Bank of California in the wake of the Panic of 1873 spelled the end of William Ralston. Courtesy of Union Bank.

The Bank of California draped in black crepe following William Ralston's drowning. Courtesy of Union Bank.

This house on the "old May Place" is where the Arnolds lived before they went west. Courtesy of Hardin County Historical Society.

Gilded Age Building and Showers House, Public Square, Elizabethtown, Ky.

Arnold's Gilded Age building in downtown Elizabethtown about 1900. Courtesy of Hardin County Historical Society.

Arnold's Gilded Age building in its heyday. Courtesy of Hardin County Historical Society.

Built with hoax money, Arnold's Gilded Age building is still one of the most impressive on Elizabethtown's town square. The building at right with the printing on the awning was the location of Arnold and Polk's Bank. Courtesy of John Snell.

The building that housed Arnold and Polk's bank is now the Old Vault Deli. Courtesy of John Snell.

The lock dial still works, but no one knows the combination.

The actual vault now safeguards only paper napkins, drinking straws and bottles of ketchup. Courtesy of John Snell.

Built in 1825, the Hill House when Custer lived there, is now the Brown-Pusey house, a vibrant part of Elizabethtown's historic district. Courtesy of John Snell.

After the hoax was exposed, Harpending built this magnificent home near Princeton, Kentucky. Courtesy of Ron Pavellas.

John Slack's New Mexico grave marker. There is no known photograph of Slack, Philip Arnold's cousin and co-conspirator. Courtesy of Hardin County Historical Society.

John Hunt Morgan's cannonball lodged in the side of this building in Elizabethtown is a reminder of Civil War days. Courtesy of John Snell.

Still elegant, Arnold's home at the end of Poplar Avenue is now the Lincoln Trail Domestic Abused Spouse Center. Courtesy of John Snell.

The fireplace in the front room of the Arnold home speaks to the homes' former elegance. Courtesy of John Snell.

Towering over all others in the town cemetery, the Arnold family monument marks the final resting place of Phil and Mary and their children. The stones at right in the stair-step arrangement name the children. Courtesy of John Snell.

These stones, arranged in a stair-step pattern, commemorate the Arnold children. Courtesy of John Snell.

This view of Elizabethtown from the cemetery is much the same as Morgan's artillerist's saw in 1862. The Gilded Age building is the lighter colored structure in the center. Courtesy of John Snell.

This montage on display in the Hardin County Museum depicts some rather famous men who compose the cast of characters involved in the Great Diamond Hoax. Courtesy of John Snell.

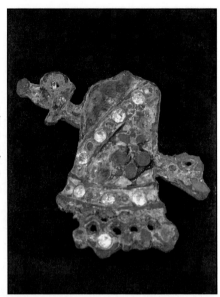

The grounds around the Arnold house have been well searched over the years. This diamond-studded brooch was found in the back yard of the Arnold home about 1995. Courtesy of John Snell.

A few small diamonds are all that remain of the vast horde of stones Arnold claimed to have located. Courtesy of John Snell.

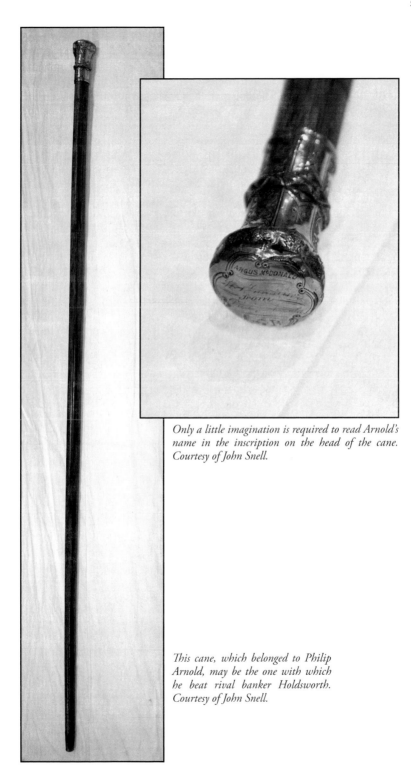

Only a little imagination is required to read Arnold's name in the inscription on the head of the cane. Courtesy of John Snell.

This cane, which belonged to Philip Arnold, may be the one with which he beat rival banker Holdsworth. Courtesy of John Snell.

This replica of Sutter's Mill, on higher ground than the original, marks the location where the discovery of gold in 1848 percipitated the rush to California the next year. Author's photos.

This map of the Union Pacific's route shows the relative positions of the various points of departure from the railroad for the diamond field as well as the distances to Fort Bridger, Laramie and Denver. Courtesy of Union Pacific Railroad.

now wish to put myself on record and say that I desire and intend to devote my own profits to the protection of innocent purchasers as far as the limited amount of my resources will permit. I wish to declare this intention before our suspicions are known and before any reclamations can be made."[151]

Everyone paused to consider the professionalism and courage Janin was displaying. At length, Ralston interrupted the troubled silence with, "Rather than sit here crying in our beer, let's get busy and get the expedition organized."

❧

The leader of the men who assembled at Oakland's Central Pacific station on the morning of November 13 was General David Colton, a man of "rare force and ability." He had been appointed as a brigadier general of the California militia back in 1856 following a skirmish with the Modoc Indians. Quite wealthy, Colton owned one of the more elegant homes on Nob Hill, a mansion located on the northwest corner of California and Taylor Streets. Perhaps his recent appointment as general manager of the San Francisco and New York Mining and Commercial Company and leader of this confirmation expedition was due to his previous experience with the company and the fact that he was a considerable force in local politics and business. Seeing no need at this point for subterfuge, the party headed directly for Black Buttes Station, where they speedily assembled their equipment. Ready to travel, the confirmation party departed from the railway on November 17. Even though the temperature was bitter, the winter snows had not set in yet, so they arrived at the diamond field about noon the next day. This time, not even a hint of "El Dorado fever" impacted anyone.

"Let's get to work," Colton directed as soon as the camp was set up. "Mr. Janin, please show me where you were instructed to look for gems."

Although he did not care for the implication of that request, Janin made no protest. He walked west of the central sandstone to an area that he remembered Philip Arnold had pointed out saying that it had "good prospects."

"Did you dig here?" Colton asked.

"No," Janin replied as calmly as he could manage. "I didn't spend much time searching for gems and what little time I did put in, I did not intend to be told where to look."

"I see," Colton said, dropping to his hands and knees. In only a moment, he had found a small ruby. "This must have been overlooked by the others who have been here," he announced, placing the gem in his pocket. Scratching around in the dirt for a few moments, he turned up a small diamond. "Worthless!" he declared. After looking around for a few more minutes, he stood and announced, "We'll dig clean down to bedrock right here."

Throughout the remainder of the day and the next morning, Colton directed the men to dig from surface to bedrock at more than 50 locations. Not one stone was found more than an inch below the surface. That afternoon, they examined "two crevices which showed unmistakable evidence of not having been tampered with," finding no diamonds or rubies there or elsewhere during the whole day." Unknown to his companions, on several occasions, Colton slipped a previously found gem into the area where someone was inspecting.

"Hey, I found a diamond more than a foot below the surface," Fry cried. Everyone rushed to see the discovery. Janin was especially interested.

As Janin examined the stone, he observed, "that's the first one at any depth."

"We haven't found one yet," Colton informed. "I salted that one while no one was watching."

"Why?" Janin queried.

"To demonstrate how easy it is for one person, who has the entire confidence of his associates, to commit numerous frauds without anyone suspecting it."[152]

Late in the afternoon, Colton gathered everyone around the fire. "Does anybody still have any doubts that this whole deal has been a colossal hoax?" When no one spoke, he summed up the findings. "All our investigations have forced on my mind the irresistible conclusion that the general assortment of precious stones found on this ground were strewn by the designing hand of one whose supply was only sufficient to place a limited number in the most conspicuous places."[153] Glancing at each man and seeing no disagreement, he added, "Mr. Ralston and Mr. Harpending dubbed our mission as a 'expedition of confirmation,' and we've done exactly that. Mr. King, I shall tell them that everything is exactly as you reported."

☙

The Colton party arrived back in San Francisco on November 25. At noon on that date, the board of directors of the San Francisco and New

York Mining and Commercial Company met in Ralston's office at the Bank of California. General David Colton stood to face the assembled business-men, his face a study in angst. "Believe me, gentlemen," he began, "I was not unmindful of the great responsibility of carrying out the expedition and of making this report, which today pronounces absolutely valueless a property having, when I left home, a cash value of millions of dollars."[154] Colton then explained the various tests he had conducted and how they were carried out. When he finished, a pin falling to the floor would have made a crashing sound.

At length, Ralston turned to Edward Fry. "Do you and Mr. Bost concur in that assessment?"

Fry slowly cleared his throat as he glanced at Bost. "We fully endorse Mr. Colton's conclusions as our own, as the result of our personal investigations on the ground with him. We believe his report to be a correct statement of our expedition."[155]

In the ensuing intense silence, Henry Janin got to his feet. "Gentlemen," he said, "I'm compelled to attempt to explain how I was hoaxed so deeply, and you may rest assured that I have given the matter abundant thought. While I discounted in my own mind the statements of Arnold and Slack, they still left me firmly impressed with the belief that such large sums had been ob-tained from this ground as to preclude any suspicion of salting. The diamonds and rubies were ranked as high average quality by New York lapidaries.

"I looked upon my investigation as undertaken not to determine the fact of discovery, but to ascertain approximately the extent and value of same. In view of all this, I now see that I was predisposed to being duped.

"Had I been allowed more time, it is possible, I dare say probable, that I would have detected the fraud. I can only say that a further explanation of the mistaken opinions of myself and others is found in the patient, ingenious and audacious nature of the fraud."[156] Thoroughly spent, Janin collapsed into a chair.

With a deep sigh, Ralston addressed Colton, "Well, sir what do we owe you for your commendable work?"

A look of surprise covered Colton's face. "Why," he sputtered, "I never even considered payment." Sparring for time while he gathered his thoughts, he said, "I only ask that you gentlemen spare neither time, money nor skill in finding the guilty parties of this unparalleled fraud and bring them speedy justice. The good name of our state and our mining interests demand it."[157]

"I heartily concur with that," Bill Lent roared, his face black with rage.

"Who can we trust to carry out such an investigation?" Roberts asked.

"Our stockholders will do," Ralston said.

✧✧

Thus it was that an "Executive Committee of Investigation" consisting of three of the men who had invested $25,000 and two of the company's lawyers was created and charged to "make a full, complete and thorough investigation" with the object of determining who was responsible for the hoax which utterly embarrassed so many prominent men.

After the committee heard testimony from all the directors and several other men, including Rubery and Colton, Asbury Harpending, Rubery and George Roberts where hanging around in an anteroom adjacent to the committee's meeting room at one of the lawyer's offices. "I suspect the committee will finish up its business soon," Harpending commented.

"Yes," Rubery agreed, "and I intend to be here when it does."

"Well, they have a chore," Roberts noted, "but it does seem as if they've interviewed everybody concerned."

At that moment, the outer door flew open to admit James B. Cooper, the man who had served as assayer in Harpending and Arnold's Pyramid Mountains venture back in 1870. "Cooper!" Harpending exclaimed, "what the hell are you doing here?"

"Oh, I have some information that this committee will possibly find interesting," he said evenly. Shabbily dressed, it was obvious that the years had not been good to Cooper.

"What might that be?" Harpending asked, deeply interested.

"You're welcome to come in and hear it," Cooper replied, knocking on the meeting room door.

Inside the committee room, Harpending, Rubery and Roberts lined the wall while Cooper took center stage. "You have information for us?" the chairman asked.

"I do indeed," Cooper said. "I understand that you gentlemen want to know who's responsible for the diamond hoax."

"We do. What do you have to tell us?"

"Well," Cooper said, relishing the moment, "I can tell you that it was all my idea."

In the shock registered around the room, Cooper proceeded to tell of how Philip Arnold had been his assistant at the Diamond Drilling Company and how he'd suggested the idea of "diamond framing" to Arnold. Although no one previously knew of Cooper having any connection with the swindle, his testimony rang true with what was known in every aspect of his testimony.

"I have a question," Harpending said when Cooper had finished.

"Yes?" Cooper said, turning to face the questioner.

"Why are you so willing to come here and so freely implicate yourself in this filthy business?"

"Because of the way Philip Arnold and John Slack dumped me," Cooper shouted. "It was my idea; they got rich and I didn't get a damned red cent."[158]

Harpending turned to Rubery standing beside him. "You've got to admire the way Philip Arnold pulled this off," he said. "He led us along the garden path, taking us through each carefully planned step with the skill of a master craftsman."

"Indeed," Rubery agreed. "You know, Harp, old chap, if Arnold had chosen to go on the stage, he surely would have been one of the greatest actors of our time."

"No question about that," Harpending mused. With a wry laugh, he added, "He salted the place with diamonds, rubies, emeralds and garnets. It must have been an oversight that he didn't sprinkle in a few pearls for good measure."[159]

◈

On November 27, the Board of directors of the San Francisco and New York Mining and Commercial Company met for the last time. The final report released to the public declared that the property claimed by the Company was "salted," and cited the confidence they had placed in Janin and Tiffany as factors in the success of the hoax. The board also ordered that all business be suspended and directed the attorneys to finalize all transactions. With that, the company ceased to exist.

As if to add insult to injury, the next day, a report arrived from London concerning the worth of the sample gems sent there for evaluation. The "gems" were almost worthless stones from the South African fields, the report said, and identified them as having been purchased by an American from Keller Jewelers nearly a year before. The report indicated that the entire lot could not have cost more than $37,000.[160]

Chapter Nineteen

As his handsome, new silver-appointed carriage rolled over the bridge below his home, Philip Arnold noticed that the unusually heavy winter rains had swollen the icy waters of Valley Creek over the limits of its banks. Although exhausted from his prolonged trip to New Orleans and sleepy at this early morning hour, he was eager to see his wife and children. Surprised to see the gas lights burning brightly at this time of day, he smiled, assuming that Mary had waited up to welcome him home. As soon as the carriage rolled to a stop, he jumped to the ground and rushed inside without a word to his coachman.

His heart sank when he entered the front room. Huddled on the floor against the back wall of the empty room, Mary and the children shivered under a thick layer of blankets. "What's wrong?" he demanded.

"They took everything," she sobbed, clutching Katie closer to her. The commotion awoke the younger children, all of whom began to whimper.

"What? Who took everything? What's going on? What did they take?"

"Everything!" Her voice was a shrill wail. "Everything, all the furniture, all the fixtures, the livestock, your safe, even the bales of hay. Everything!"

"Who?" Shaking the sleepiness from his brain, he tried to understand what she was saying. He dashed into the adjoining rooms to discover that Mary's statement was accurate. Aside from the blankets that covered her and the children, each room was totally empty. Returning to where they were heaped together, "Who?" he repeated.

"Sheriff Wood," she sobbed. "He and a bunch of men showed up here four hours ago with some kind of paper attaching all our property."[161] She untangled

199

herself from the pile and stood to embrace her husband. "The way they pounded on the door, I thought the devil wanted in. Then they barged in and took everything. They loaded all our stuff in wagons and hauled it away," she said, collapsing in his arms. "I'm glad you're home. I'm so tired I'm sick."

"It'll be OK," he assured, squeezing her tightly. "Get yourself and the children dressed and we'll go to the hotel."

"But...." she weakly protested.

"No buts," he said. "Get the children ready, we can't stay here."

The coachman was nearly finished grooming the horse when Arnold dashed into the stable ordering him to re-harness the sleek mare. When the carriage returned to the front door, Mary and the children were waiting on the porch. The clock in the courthouse tower was striking five a.m. by the time the Arnold family arrived at the Hill House, just one square east of the town square[162]. After some trouble arousing the innkeeper, Rebecca Hill, known to one and all as "Aunt Beck," Phil managed to procure rooms for his family. "You get some sleep," he instructed his wife, "I'll go find out what the hell's going on."

"You might as well wait until the sun comes up," she advised. "There won't be anyone at the sheriff's office at this time of day, and anyway, we're going to need a lawyer."

Phil paused to consider that. "What kind of paper did the sheriff have when he barged in?"

"I don't know. It was the middle of the night and I was surprised and startled and scared." She started to cry again.

"Take it easy," he said, hugging her. "We'll get to the bottom of this. I guess that they must have had a court order. Did you read it?"

"No, I was too upset," she whimpered.

"Well, see to yourself and the children," he instructed. "I'll go wake up Will Wilson."

As he had arranged, his carriage was waiting in the stable, ready to travel. Climbing in beside the driver, he ordered "Will Wilson's house." After Arnold had purchased Wilson's home earlier in the year, Wilson had moved into another home on an adjoining property a little farther down Valley Creek. On the way, Arnold reflected on the fact that he and attorney Wilson had become friends was fortunate – he had a feeling he was, indeed, going to need a lawyer.

Bounding up the steps to the porch, Arnold pounded on the lawyer's front door. "Phil?" Wilson wondered as cordially as could be expected given the circumstances. "What the hell's going on?"

"That's just what I need you to find out," Arnold replied.

"Well, come on in," Wilson invited, motioning his visitor into the house. "Shall I make some coffee?"

"No, damnit! I need your help." Impatience laced his voice.

"I can see that you're upset," Wilson said, rubbing his eyes. "What's happened?"

"Sheriff Wood showed up at my house about midnight," Arnold began. "I was out of town. Mary said they barged right in waving some kind of paper at her and impounded everything we own. They loaded everything – everything – up and hauled it away." His words tumbled breathlessly from his mouth.

"Well," Wilson mused, "is your family all right?"

"Yes. Mary was pretty shaken up, but she and the children are at the hotel, asleep by now, I hope."

"Where?"

"The Hill House, but...."

"That's good." Wilson interrupted. "Why don't you go on back there and get some sleep yourself? It's Saturday, but I'll locate Sheriff Wood and find out what the story is."

"I'll go with you," Arnold sputtered.

"All right, if you insist," Wilson agreed. "It'll take me a while to get ready. Go on back to the Hill House and see to your family. I'll stop by there to get you on my way to the sheriff's office."

❧

Phil Arnold awoke with a start as someone was shaking his shoulder. As his eyes fell on the grandfather clock across the hall, he remembered sitting in the rocking chair just inside the door of the hotel to wait for the lawyer, but was surprised to see that the clock's hour hand pointed to two o'clock. The shadows told him that it was early afternoon. Shaking the cobwebs from his brain, he heard Will Wilson urging, "Wake up, Phil."

"What did you find out?" He stood and stretched.

"Well, it's interesting."

"Yeah?"

"Yeah. It seems as how somebody name of William Lent has filed a law suit on you all the way from San Francisco, California. Do you know him?"

"Yes, I know 'Simple Bill,'" Arnold said. "What's he suing me for?

Wilson allowed himself a slight smile. "$350,000, that's what for."

"Wow! That's a lot of money, but I meant...."

"I know what you meant," Wilson said, erasing his smile as he pulled a paper from an inside coat pocket. "He filed the suit against you, your wife, your cousin John Slack, Samuel Thomas, John Polk and J.H. Thomas."[163]

"Polk and Thomas? What the hell do they have to do with anything?" He was incredulous.

"I guess he thinks you might have valuables stashed away in their bank's vault, so he's just covering every possibility he can think of."

"Well, damn him!" Arnold exploded, "ain't dislodging my family in the middle of the night enough? He took my safe, too, you know?"

"Yes, I know. Not to worry, we'll get through this and get your stuff back."

"Anyway, why does he claim I owe him all that money?"

"Says here," Wilson read from the paper, "that 'Philip Arnold and John Slack confederated and conspired together with others for the purpose and with the intent of committing a fraud upon the plaintiff.'" Here he raised his eyes to Arnold's and informed, "That'd be Lent." Then he read on, "'And the public , and in furtherance of said fraudulent conspiracy procured from parties unknown to plaintiff a large quantity of precious and valuable stones of the value not exceeding $37,000, known as real diamonds, rubies and emeralds in the rough, and planted and scattered and caused to be planted and scattered in and upon certain lands in a certain district known as Colorado Territory to give said land the appearance and character of mineral lands in which said precious....'"[164]

"Enough!" Arnold shouted.

"There's several more pages here," Wilson informed, waving the papers in the air.

"I don't doubt that," Arnold almost smiled. "He didn't skimp on the words, did he?"

"Well, I read the thing through," Wilson said. "What it boils down to is he's claiming that you and Slack cheated him out of $350,000 by salting diamonds and other gems on some property in Colorado Territory and then committing fraud by getting him to invest in what you represented as a genuine diamond field."

"By hell," Arnold exploded, "I never sold one dollar's worth of property to Lent, nor have I ever had any contact with him, nor did he ever pay me one cent on any contract I ever had with him."[165]

"Take it easy," Wilson advised. "You'll have your day in court."

"I'll tell you one thing," Arnold raved on, oblivious to his attorney's comment. "Lent has been involved in numerous shady deals and has deceived many prospective buyers of mining stock in which he had an interest. He and his ring have floated on the people of this country and in Europe – most of them of the working class – $40,000,000 worth of mining stocks. If you take a look at those stocks, you'll find the name of William Lent on 'em as either President or Director."

Without pausing for breath, he went on, "If Mr. Lent makes it appear to a court that I have defrauded him out of one cent, I promise that I will give him every cent he has sued for, and no man under the sun can say that Philip Arnold ever violated a promise."[166] Out of steam, he collapsed into a chair.

"Take my advice and just forget about it for the next few days. Let me handle it."

Having had virtually no sleep in the prior 48 hours, Arnold took that advice to heart. He made his way upstairs and into bed where he slept until the bright Sunday morning sunshine woke him.

At dinner that evening, the Arnolds were amazed to find that the Hill House had a famous guest, none other than the "Boy General" from the Civil War, George Armstrong Custer. Dressed in an outlandish buckskin outfit with a red silk scarf wrapped around his neck, Custer held court from the head of the dinner table with his wife, Libby, sitting adoringly at his right side. "Mr. Arnold," he said, "we are honored to have a man of your notoriety among us."

"It is I who is honored, General." Even though Custer wore the insignia of a Lieutenant Colonel on his epaulets, everyone still addressed him by his wartime brevet rank. "Might I ask what you're doing here?"

Obviously pleased to have a fresh audience, Custer launched into a lecture with the confidence of one accustomed to the spotlight. "After the war, the army retained only a few of us select officers. I was assigned to the Seventh Cavalry," he began. "Then the powers that be in Washington City decided to break up the Seventh and station small contingents at various locations throughout the South. It was my fortune – or misfortune – to draw Elizabethtown. We've been in command here since September." Libby's face lit at his emphasis on the term "we," but her adoring smile faded just a bit as she was reminded of the duration of her stay.

"I see," Arnold said, "part of the occupation of the South. What are your duties here, may I ask?"

Custer laughed. "We're to suppress the local activities of the Ku Klux Klan and ride herd on the moonshiners."

"What? There's no Klan activity around here," Arnold opined.

"As astute an observation as ever I heard," Custer said, a condescending note in his voice. Glancing at his wife, he added, "That should give you some idea of how boring we find this country. At least it leaves one time to write, but I do long to get back on the plains and see some action once again."[167] Pausing for a bite of his roast beef, he changed course. "I understand that you own a good deal of property hereabouts, Mr. Arnold."

"Oh, I have a few holdings. Why do you ask?"

Glancing at "Aunt Beck" out of the corner of his eye, Custer said, "with all due respect to you, Mrs. Hill, Libby and I are looking for a house to rent where we'd have a little more room for our belongings and a modicum of privacy." Returning his attention to Arnold, he asked, "Would you happen to own such a property?"

"No. I'm sorry, but aside from my personal residence, all my holdings are farm lands and vacant city lots."

"I see," Custer intoned. "Since you mention your personal residence, and an elegant home it is, I might add, what is it that brings you to the house of 'Aunt Beck?'"

Arnold knew that his story was known to everyone in the county by now and every occupant of the Hill House was surely acquainted with each detail of his plight. Still, everyone at the table leaned forward in anticipation of getting the word "straight from the horse's mouth." "Oh, I've had a spot of legal difficulty," he announced, trying to sound casual.

"So I understand," Custer said. "But, come now, would you care to supply any of the juicy details?" He avoided eye contact by carefully spreading apple butter on a biscuit.

"Suffice it to say that a lawsuit has been filed against me," Arnold said evenly.

"Yes, yes, we know that much," Custer pressed on, his arrogance plainly displayed by the smug grin on his face. "I'm eager to learn the contents of your safe the sheriff has impounded, among other things."

"Autie," Libby Custer admonished her husband using the pet name he'd worn in his family since his childhood inability to manage 'Armstrong,' "perhaps…."

Her effort was too late. Rising to his feet, Arnold said, "The contents of my personal safe, sir, are none of your damned business. By the way, I might add that I, too, look forward to your return to the plains." With a curt nod to Mrs. Custer, he left the table. Retiring to his room, Arnold spent the rest of the day composing a "card" to the newspapers, recounting his side of the entire diamond story.[168]

The next day, the attorneys and Phil and Mary Arnold gathered in Sheriff W.D. Wood's office where some of Arnold's property had been taken for secure storage. The Louisville attorney representing Lent introduced himself to Arnold and Wilson. Smiling as he shook hands, he tried to show no personal animosity as he said, "I suppose it would be too much of a pun to say that this is in the sheriff's office for safe keeping," as he patted Arnold's iron safe. "I'm John M. Harlan, representing Mr. Lent."[169]

Wilson introduced himself and Arnold and Mary. "Well, W.D., are you ready to perform your duty?"

"I am," answered the sheriff. "Mr. Arnold, would you be so kind as to open this safe?"

Having already discussed his rights and responsibilities with his lawyer, Arnold made no protest as he spun the numbered dial. He twisted the handle, and as the heavy door swung open with a rusty squeak, he stepped aside. "There you go."

Harlan and Wilson made a visible effort to restrain themselves from crowding around as Wood withdrew a sheaf of papers from the safe. Shuffling through the documents, he announced, "These are bonds from McCracken County, Kentucky, dated March 1, 1869. They bear seven percent interest semi-annually and mature in twenty years. The total worth would be, uh," Wood paused, calculating in his head, "$45,500."

"I paid $34,125 for those," Mary informed.

Inspecting another paper from the safe, Sheriff Wood said, "This is a Bank of California draft signed by Thomas Brown and dated October 15, 1872. The value is," he paused while he scanned the note, "uh, $197,183.10. It's payable to P. Arnold."

In the ensuing stunned silence, the sheriff extracted more documents. Shuffling through, he announced, "These are several notes for $1,000, $200, $4,000 and $200, that totals up to $5,400." Turning them over, he said, "each one is endorsed, 'I sign the within note to Mary E. Arnold,' and signed 'P. Arnold.'"

"My husband loaned those gentlemen my money and took their notes for it. That's why he assigned them to me," Mary said. "It was my money."

"Why did he transact business in such a round-a-bout method?" Harlan inquired in typical accusatory attorney fashion.

With a glance at her attorney, Mary answered, "I do not know." Saying nothing, Phil stared out the window, ignoring the inquiring looks from Harlan and the Sheriff.

Wood returned to the safe. "Here's $260.50 in bills and silver," he said.

"Forty dollars of that belongs to my mother," Mary insisted.

"Gold coins amounting to $335," Wood said, jingling the coins in his hand as he deposited them on his desk.

"This is all entirely my money," Mary insisted. In response to the attorney's questioning looks, she fished a slip of paper out of her purse. "This is legal, ain't it?"

Wilson took the paper from her. "What is it?" Harlan asked.

"Well, the spelling and grammar leave a little to be desired, but it appears to be an agreement signed by Philip and Mary Arnold way back in '68. He agrees to give her all the money he can spare," Wilson said, turning the paper over to inspect the back.

"That proves this is all mine, don't it?" she pleaded.

The attorneys stared at each other, neither knowing what to say. "Here's some jewelry," Sheriff Wood said, breaking the silence. "Necklaces, rings, a jeweled cross, ear rings and a gold watch and chain." He added these items to the pile on his desk.

"Most of that stuff belongs to my daughter, Katie," Mary said.

"It would be difficult to establish a value for those," Wilson opined.

"We're here only to inventory the contents," Wood reminded. He checked the slip on which he'd been recording the values. "The total of the notes, bonds and cash is $248,678.60," he said. "We'll list the other items under 'Value Unknown.'"[170]

Outside the office, Arnold turned to his wife. "Mary, you go on back to the Hill House. I want to confer with Will. I'll be back there in a little while."

"They're makin' out that I stole the money that bought my home and all my property," Arnold said to his lawyer as Mary walked away.

"Well, that's exactly what the lawsuit alleges," Wilson reminded. "The claim that the diamond property was 'salted' amounts to fraud."

"I'd agree with that," Arnold declared, "but if any salting was done, it was after I left there."

"You'll have your day in court. You just go home and lay low. I'll start getting our ducks in a row."

"Speaking of that," Arnold pleaded, "can't you get 'em to release my furniture so I can at least go home?"

"That's my number one priority."

As Arnold started to walk away, several men led by banker John Polk approached. "How are you doin', Phil," Polk asked.

"I've had better days," Arnold replied, shaking hands. "What are you boys up to?"

"Well," Polk said, "we actually came down here just to tell you that the whole community is behind you. If these damned California sharps think they can come in here and intimidate us, they'd better go back to the Golden State and think some more. If there's anything you need, you just let us know. We assure you that any and all resources in this town are at your disposal."

⁊

"How the hell did you find me here?" Bill Lent demanded.

"I assure you, sir, that there is little that happens in Louisville that the *Courier-Journal* doesn't know about," the reporter said, suppressing a slight smile. "Especially the comings and goings of important personages such as yourself."

"But to track a man down in his hotel room…." Lent sputtered.

This time the reporter made no effort to hide his smile. "You have the good taste to choose to stop at the Galt House. While it is certainly the most elegant hotel in town, it also happens to be the one where our renowned editor, Mister Henry Watterson, spends his leisure in the Gentlemen's Club downstairs. You may rely upon the fact that nothing happens within these confines that escapes 'Marse Henry's notice."

"Well," Lent spat impatiently, "what is it that you want?"

"We'd love to publish your side of this diamond hoax story," the man said, expectantly poising a pencil above his pad. "You know, give the public your view of this lawsuit you've got up against Philip Arnold and John Slack."

"Get out," Lent roared. "I'll tell you nothing. Get out of my sight before I call hotel security." He bounded across the room and flung the door open. "Get out! I'll tell my story in court."

"But sir, Mr. Watterson…."

Grabbing the reporter by the front of his shirt, Lent physically threw him out of the room. "Damn Watterson! Damn you! Damn Kentucky!" he shouted at the figure rapidly retreating down the hallway.

Slamming the door, Lent took a deep breath and crossed over to the desk. Pulling writing materials from the drawer, he began making a list of topics he wanted to discuss with his attorney, John Harlan, who was due in about an hour. He had listed only the top two items when he was interrupted by a rap on the door. "If it's that damned reporter…." he mumbled to himself. When he opened the door, he was surprised to see an impeccably dressed Asbury Harpending standing in the hall leaning on a silver-headed cane. "Is there anybody who doesn't know I'm here?" Lent wondered.

"Oh, I have friends," Harpending said with a smile. Accepting Lent's motion to enter, he stepped into the room. When the door closed, he added, "I am a native Kentuckian, you know?"

Lent waved his visitor to a chair. "I don't care if you're a native of Mars. So what's on your mind, Asbury?"

"I do have more than a passing interest in your pending law suit, you know. I'm here to give you whatever advice and help I can."

"That's what I hired Harlan for," Lent said, sitting.

"Have you seen this?" Harpending asked, sliding a newspaper across the table.

Lent picked it up and read: "I see by the papers that Arnold and Slack are to be prosecuted and eminent counsel has been employed. I have employed counsel myself – a good Henry rifle – and I am likely to open my case any day on California Street. There are several scalps I would like to string on a pole – I don't include Janin, your expert. His is of no consequence; send him to China where he will find his equals in the expert business.

"As you are all going into the newspapers, I'll take a fling at it myself some of these days. I'm going to the fields on my own hook in the spring with fifty men and will hold my hand against all the experts you can send along. If I catch any of your kid glove gentry about there, I'll blow the stuffing out of 'em."[171]

"That's some mighty big talk Arnold's spewing out there," Lent said with a sigh. "I reckon my attorney can deal with him." He pushed the newspaper back across the table.

"Mr. Harlan is a fine lawyer," Harpending opined, "but I fear that, as he lives in an ivory tower, there's a few practical matters that he might not understand."

"I've been assured that he knows the law forwards and backwards."

"Oh, I'm sure he does," Harpending said with a dismissive wave of his hand. "I'm talking about the difficulty of serving the papers on Arnold, for instance."

"What's any difficulty about that? Everybody knows exactly where he's at."

"Yes, but that's a different issue. He's a big hero around here – the local boy who went off and out-smarted us California sharps. You can bet your last share of diamond mine stock that the community of Elizabethtown will rally 'round him." Harpending laughed at his small joke.

Lent saw no humor in the remark. "Even these damned Kentuckians have to obey the law don't they?"

"Well, yes. The letter of the law anyway. But they don't have to be in any hurry and they don't have to go out of their way to obey."

"What are you saying?"

"I'm merely suggesting that some difficulty may be had in bringing Arnold 'to law' as they say in these parts. I suggest you attempt to come to some out-of-court agreement with Arnold. In the unlikely event you ever do get him to court, you'll never get a judgment against him, and if you do, you'll never collect."

"Why," Lent sputtered, "you know as well as I do that he's guilty of salting that so-called mine and defrauding the whole bunch us. As guilty as sin!" He slammed his fist on the table.

"Yes, I know that. But, Bill, knowing it and proving it are two different things. Proving it in a Kentucky court is still yet another matter. He maintains that he does not owe me or you or anybody else anything, and, if he sticks to his guns, you'll never get a cent out of him by legal proceedings no matter what the proof."[172]

"Well, you know, don't you, that a California Grand Jury indicted Arnold?"

"No!" Harpending exclaimed. "I didn't know that and I'm surprised. What charge did they indict him under?"

Lent finally found something to smile about. "Nobody knows. A San Francisco lawyer stepped up to represent Arnold and Slack and even he couldn't get 'em to reveal the indictment."[173]

"I don't guess it matters much anyway," Harpending observed. "They'll never get him extradited; you can take my word for that. I'm telling you, Bill, this business is like a hog wallow; the more you stir it, the worse it's gonna stink. My advice is to settle with him, if possible, cut your losses, go home and avoid further embarrassment."

❧

Although Philip Arnold felt his wife's exasperation, he really didn't know what he could do to alleviate the situation. "Phil, you've got to get us out of here," she pleaded. "That Custer woman is driving me crazy. She complains constantly about everything – except her perfect husband, of course – and nothing ever suits her. She even dislikes sweet old 'Aunt Beck.'"

"I know," he empathized. "She's a handful, that's for sure."

"Handful? She's high and mighty is what she is. You don't have to stay here all day and put up with her like I do. And Custer himself! After he gets done with what little business he has for the day, he gives us a break while he goes to his room and writes, but when he gets bored with that, he comes to the parlor and plays the organ, for goodness sakes! His playing is simply awful but he thinks it sounds good, and that he's doing us a favor by providing some entertainment.[174] We have got to get out of here."

"Well, I'll go see Will right now. Maybe he's made some progress on getting our property released."

"I'd give anything to get out furniture back and get out of here," she pleaded.

A little ole $350,000 would do it, Phil thought, but decided to say nothing. Instead, he simply walked out the door happy to be away from Mary's complaints. He realized that she was bearing up pretty well in the situation, but he had his own troubles, too. While lawyer Wilson had advised that there was little chance of the Lent suit coming to trial anytime soon, still Arnold always had to be on the alert for process servers. Will Wilson was in his office, studying some papers. "Did you talk to the judge?" Arnold asked.

"I did," Wilson said, glancing up from his papers. "Judge Cofer says he'd love to release the attachment on your property and he will as soon as he can, but his hands are tied until the next session of circuit court."

"When's that gonna be? Mary is driving me crazy."

"I know, believe me, I know," Wilson said with a smile. "The feud between her and Libby Custer is the talk of the town." As his smile faded, he added, "The next court session starts a week from tomorrow, February 10."

"Is there nothing we can do until then?"

"Well, I reckon you could buy all new furniture, but then they'd probably attach that, too. Just tell your wife that I'm sure the Judge will release the attachment at least on your furniture next week. Then you'll can move back home."

☙

"Your Honor, will you hear my petition now?" Wilson addressed the judge, waving a legal document in his hand.

"Yes," Judge Cofer said. "Go ahead."

"Thank you, Your Honor. We feel that the attachment of my client's property now in force is grossly unfair. Mrs. Arnold maintains that the household fixtures – and even the land their home sits on, for that matter – is her property, bought with her own money, and is, therefore, not subject to any action filed against her husband. In view of these facts, we petition the court to dismiss the attachment."

Lent's lawyer, John Harlan, leapt to his feet. "Judge, I object! My client's suit names Mrs. Arnold as well as her husband as a defendant. Whose name the property is in is of no consequence...."

"He makes it sound as if Mary Arnold stole the money that bought her furniture," Wilson interjected. "If he thinks...."

"Settle down, both of you," Judge Cofer said soothingly. "We'll get this sorted out. It appears from the petition and affidavit that the plaintiff was, at and before the commencement of this action, has been ever since and is now a resident of the state of California, whereas the defendants, Philip Arnold, Mary Arnold, J.H. Thomas and John Polk were and are now residents of the Commonwealth of Kentucky. Are we all in agreement about that?"

"Your Honor?" Harlan said, not liking the direction the discussion was headed.

"Yes, sir?"

"That gives rise to my petition which may obviate the need for some of this discussion."

"Very well," the Judge said. "What's on your mind?"

"First of all, due to circumstances beyond our control, we ask that the defendant John Slack's name be removed from our suit."

With a dismissive shake of his head, the Judge said, "So ordered."

Harlan rose to his full height and moved a step farther from the judge's position. "My client has reasons to believe, and does believe that," he paused and took a deep breath before adding, "due to local prejudice and influence he will not be able to obtain justice in this court." Ignoring Judge Cofer's glare, he continued, "We therefore petition that this court take no further action and that this case be removed for trial into the United States Circuit for the Kentucky district."

Judge Cofer stared at Harlan for a long moment. "Very well," he said with a sigh, "I'll take the matter under advisement." Consulting his calendar, he said, "all parties are to be back in this court on February 22, 1873. I will give you my decision at that time."

When the parties returned on the appointed date, Judge Cofer addressed the attorneys and defendants. "I have carefully studied the law which applies here," he began. "An act of Congress passed in 1867 is clear on the point. When any party to a case requests that it be removed to federal court, the state court is directed to grant that request and to proceed no further with the case. Now, Mr. and Mrs. Arnold, for me to release your property, as I am inclined to do, would amount to 'further action.' Therefore, I cannot dismiss the attachment and I declare this case closed in this court."[175]

Chapter Twenty

Even though the likelihood of his legal difficulties reaching resolution anytime soon seemed remote, Philip Arnold had decided that spending an afternoon preparing their home for occupancy would be good for his family's morale. Mary had taken to the idea immediately and prepared a picnic lunch. As soon as they arrived, the children ran into the back yard whooping like wild Indians. Mary dove right into scrubbing the floors while Philip cleared cobwebs from the ceiling corners.

After several hours' work, Mary took a break. Gazing out the front window of their home, she observed that the greening grass and the balmy breeze were chasing the last traces of winter from the yard. The redbuds and daffodils were in full bloom and the fragrance of the flowering crabapple tree down by the creek wafted through the open window. She inhaled a deep draft of the warm air and reluctantly turned to resume her housework.

Just as she turned from the window, a movement near the far corner of the yard caught her eye. Moving back to the open window, she put her hands on the sill and cautiously peered out in the direction from which she'd seen the movement. Scanning the landscape and seeing nothing, she concluded that Phil's constant warnings about being on the lookout for strangers were beginning to cause her to imagine things. Still, something had caught her attention. Watching intently, her heart skipped a beat when she saw a man dart from behind one tree to another halfway between the creek and the house.

"Phil!" she screamed.

"What is it?" Phil replied from his study at the rear of the house.

"There's somebody out there," she shouted. "Come and look."

"In our yard?" he asked, moving into the front room.

"Yes," she whispered. "Look toward the bridge."

"I don't see nothin'," he remarked, leaning out the window.

"I saw him, over there by the milk cellar," she insisted. "He was behind a tree."

"OK, be still," Phil said, kneeling by the window. "We'll just watch quietly for a minute."

She moved beside him, kneeling on the floor. In a moment, she squealed, "There he is," pointing out the opening.

"I see him," Phil whispered. "Go get my rifle, make sure it's loaded and have it ready by the front door. Then get the children inside."

"Don't go out there."

"Do as I say," he ordered. As soon as she disappeared into the next room, Phil walked to the front door. When he heard Mary coming back into the room, he opened the door and stepped onto the porch, leaving the door open. Keeping a close eye on where he'd last seen the man, he walked slowly across the yard, staying near the porch. Suddenly, a man stepped into plain view. In a glance, Arnold took in his rough, seedy appearance and concluded he was probably a hobo just off the nearby Louisville and Nashville Railroad tracks.

"What is it you want here?" Arnold demanded.

"Nothin'. Only just lookin' around. Say, who owns this nice place?" The stranger's manner was agreeable as he glanced around the yard.

"I do," Arnold replied, somewhat less apprehensive and appreciative of the compliment. He waited for the intruder to speak again.

"Wish 'twas mine," the tramp said, looking around approvingly. "A feller could live here right comfortable, I allow. Say, stranger, what might your name be?"

Arnold retreated a step closer to the porch as the man neared him. "Arnold," he said trying to remain calm.

"What? You wouldn't be that Philip Arnold everybody's talkin' about, would you?"

Arnold moved quickly onto the porch. If his name was familiar to the man, he was no hobo just passing through. "That's me. What's it to you?"

Reaching inside his shabby coat, the man withdrew a folded sheet of paper and handed it to Arnold. Instinctively, Arnold accepted the paper. "I have a writ from the Circuit Court of Hardin County to serve on you. It's in the great diamond case of Lent vs. Arnold and Slack."

Recovering, Arnold flung the paper to the floor boards and reached through the open door for his rife. By the time he fumbled for it, turned and brought the weapon to his shoulder, the man, now obviously a detective, sworn and hired as a process server, was already fading into the shadows across Valley Creek.[176]

❧

"What the hell's goin' on, Will," Arnold demanded of his lawyer, having beat a hot trail to the attorney's office as quickly as possible after assuring his wife that everything was OK.

"Evidently Mr. Lent and his attorneys aren't keeping their employees current on the status of things," Wilson said with a slight smile. "The writ they served on you is more than a month old and is as worthless as last year's crow's nest. Judge Cofer has referred the case, as requested, to federal court, so the county court has no standing."

"Yes, I know. I thought the Judge was on our side."

"He is," Wilson assured, "but the law was clear; he had no choice."

"So now we start all over again in federal court in Louisville?" Arnold sank into his chair with a long sigh. "I'll never get my property back."

"Don't despair. Well, starting over is one option," Wilson said.

"Yeah?" Arnold perked up a bit. "What's another?"

The lawyer leaned back in his chair. "I have a sneaking suspicion that Mr. Lent just might be willin' to settle if we made him a good enough offer."

"What makes you think that?"

"I've been in touch with some folks I know out in San Francisco," Wilson advised. "They tell me that the prevailing sentiment among the diamond investors out there is to just forget this whole affair and avoid as much further embarrassment as possible. I happen to know that more than one of those California investors has counseled Lent to settle it out of court and cut his losses."

Arnold sat back to consider that idea. At length he said, "Well, I'm pretty damn tired of this business. I've had this lawsuit hanging over my head for more than three months now. My wife is on my case about living in the hotel – not that I blame her, the Custers are insufferable – and the children are very uncomfortable."

"As I said, there might be an easy way out." Wilson leaned toward his client and placed his elbows on the desk. "All I have to do is get in touch with Lent's attorney."

"What kind of offer are we talkin' about? How much do you think he'd take?"

The lawyer again leaned back in his chair. "Well, if the suit went all the way to a court and he won the judgment, you'd be ordered to pay him the $350,000." He paused to stroke his chin while thinking. "How would you feel about offering a third of that?"

Arnold flinched. "That's about $117,000. A hell of a lot of money."

"Yes, it is," Wilson agreed. "But, you can afford it, and it's certainly better than the $350,000 you might have to pay."

"Well," Arnold began with a deep sigh, "if he'd accept that amount, would it make the whole stinkin' business go away?"

"Yes, it would. Would you like me to contact Mr. Harlan?"

"Damn it, Will," Arnold exploded, "I don't owe him nothin'."

"Take it easy, Phil, we're only just talkin'." Seeing Arnold make an effort to calm himself, the attorney used his most soothing voice to ask, "How much would you say your peace of mind is worth?"

Arnold considered that comment. "I don't know how you put a price tag on that. Well, let's find out if old 'Simple Bill' is willin' to settle."

Before Wilson could say anything, his clerk knocked on the office door. "A gentleman to see you," he announced.

"Tell him to wait; I'm with a client," Wilson said.

"I told him that. He says Mr. Arnold will be interested in what he has to say as well."

With an intrigued glance at Arnold, Wilson said, "All right, show him in."

Arnold was shocked to see Asbury Harpending walk into the room. As usual, Harpending was impeccably dressed, his navy blue suit and vest spotless and his necktie perfect. "Hello, Phil," he addressed Arnold pleasantly. "Mr. Wilson, I presume?" He extended his hand to the attorney.

Wilson stood to shake hands. "You have the advantage of me, sir."

"I'm sorry," Arnold sputtered. "Will, this is an old friend, Asbury Harpending." Wilson and Arnold exchanged perplexed glances.

"Have a chair, Mr. Harpending," Wilson said, gesturing as he returned to his seat. "What can I do for you?"

Harpending took the chair next to Arnold across the desk from Wilson and squirmed a bit making himself comfortable. "I'm here on behalf of Mr. William Lent," he began. Arnold and Wilson both leaned toward him expectantly. "For your benefit, Mr. Wilson, suffice it to say that Mr. Lent, Mr. Arnold and I, along with several other gentlemen, have been, uh, shall we say 'associated' in many adventures over the last twenty years or so."

"I see," Wilson said, trying not to let his impatience show.

"Well, to come right to the point," Harpending paused to glance at Arnold then Wilson, "I think Mr. Lent could be influenced to settle the legal action against Mr. Arnold and Mr. Slack and the rest of the defendants in consideration of a certain sum of cash."

Arnold and Wilson both suppressed their amazement that this should drop out of the clear blue at the very time they were discussing such a proposition. "I would think such an offer would have come through Mr. Lent's attorney," Wilson said.

"What figure did you have in mind?" Arnold interjected.

"Please understand that I have no legal standing in the matter," Harpending said with a smile. "I'm simply trying to help out a couple of old friends. On that basis, I thought that if I acted as an intermediary, we might put an end to the discomfort being endured by everybody involved." He paused a beat before adding, "Mr. Lent is willing to terminate his legal action in consideration of $150,000."

After a long moment, Wilson broke the silence. "Phil?"

Arnold turned toward Harpending with a deep sigh. "Asbury, I do appreciate your efforts here. Are you sure Lent will accept that amount?"

"Yes. Let me assure you that it took some fancy talking, but he's willing to forget it and go home if you'll pay him $150,000."

"We will insist that my client be granted immunity from any further litigation," Wilson said.

"That's agreeable," Harpending answered, directing a benign smile at Arnold.

Arnold looked to his lawyer, who avoided his eyes by turning his head toward the window. "All right, Asbury," Arnold said, extending his hand. "Even though I don't owe him a damned cent, I'll do it."[177]

છ૭

On March 24, 1873, John M. Harlan, representing William Lent, and William Wilson, representing Philip and Mary Arnold, met in a private room in Louisville. On behalf of the Arnolds, Wilson turned $150,000 in cash over to Harlan. Each party agreed to pay their own legal fees. Lent also agreed to pursue no further action against Philip or Mary Arnold or John Slack, and the court ordered Sheriff W.D. Wood to return the Arnold's property, which had been attached the previous December. [178]

Evidently determined to have the last word, Philip Arnold, declaring himself to be the injured party, published a card in the newspaper:

"To the editor of the news:

"In your last issue there appeared an editorial article in relation to the settlement of the case of Wm. M. Lent against me lately pending in the United States Circuit Court at Louisville, which is incorrect in some of the statements. The settlement was made between me and John B. Slack on the one side and Wm. M. Lent, W.C. Ralston, Geo. S. Dodge, A. Harpending and George D. Roberts on the other side. The settlement was a complete wipe out of everything between us, as duplicate agreements now in the possession of the parties will show, and I paid to the attorney of Wm. Lent, through my attorney, the sum of ($150,000) one hundred and fifty thousand dollars (and not fifty thousand as you stated) upon the considerations named in the agreement. I did not owe the above named gentlemen one cent, but I paid the money to purchase my peace and to get loose from this most powerful and world-renowned ring, and besides, I could not afford to lose the time I would have necessarily have had to lose in attending to the suit for four times the money I paid."[179]

Chapter Twenty-One

Friday, August 14, 1874
Elizabethtown, Kentucky

Mary Arnold was most certainly not a happy woman as she accompanied her husband to the Louisville and Nashville Railroad depot near their home. "Why are you going to Louisville?" she asked, a tear in her voice. The carriage rolled along in silence for several long moments before he spoke.

"Just some business I need to take care of," Philip said emotionlessly. He avoided her eyes by staring straight ahead into the back of the coachman.

"I wish you'd stay home," she pleaded. She wondered just what kind of business needed attending to over a weekend, but decided not to ask. Getting no response to her plea, she continued, "Ever since that man showed up in our yard, the children and I have been scared out of our minds."

"I know," he said as they rolled to a stop at the train platform. "But you know that's all over. As part of the settlement, they agreed to pursue no further legal action, so there's nothing to worry about. Nobody can touch us now."

"Still, I see no reason for you to go, not today anyway," she said as the coachman helped her down to the floor boards.

"It'll only be a day or two," Philip said peering anxiously down the track. He was eager for the train to appear and end this discussion. He paced to the far end of the platform.

"Philip," she pleaded, trailing him down the platform. Before she could continue, a whistle sounded just around the bend, announcing the train's arrival. She said something, but her voice was drowned out by the hiss of steam and the screech of brakes as the locomotive ground to a halt.

"I'll be home Monday or Tuesday at the latest," he shouted as he grabbed his valise from the carriage and hurriedly ascended the single step into the passenger car.

"All aboard!" the conductor yelled, waving a flag to the engineer. With a clanging of the bell, the wheels began to slowly turn, moving the train north along the track toward the Falls City.

The short trip took only about an hour, so evening shadows were just beginning to creep between the buildings as the train moved into downtown Louisville. Philip Arnold smiled as he stepped down onto the platform. He liked Elizabethtown and was happy to live there and be a part of the community, but sometimes a man just needs to get away. Elizabethtown was a nice little town, but, as Custer liked to point out, it did not offer much in the way of entertainment. After all, was a little recreation in the big city too much for a man of his experiences, tastes and resources to ask?

"Rufer's Hotel," he instructed the cab driver. Visions of cabarets and good times danced in his head as the taxi rolled through the streets of the big city.

❧

A loud pounding at the hotel room door startled Philip Arnold awake. Shaking the alcohol-induced cobwebs from his brain, he slowly sat up and gradually became aware of his surroundings. The hammering at his door became more insistent. A gruff voice commanded, "Open up!"

Almost unaware of his movements, Arnold got out of bed, crossed the room and unbolted the door. Before he could touch the door knob, the door flew open and a large man dressed in a seedy brown suit quickly stepped into the room. "Philip Arnold?" he demanded.

"Yeah," Arnold responded, his head reeling. "What is it you want?"

The man spun the confused Arnold around and slapped steel handcuffs on his wrists. "I'm City Detective Gallagher," he announced, rotating his prisoner again to face him. "I have been ordered to arrest you subject to a warrant issued by the Governor. Get your pants on; you're goin' to jail."

Arnold slept most of the morning away in the Jefferson County jail. By the time his Elizabethtown friend and attorney, Will Wilson, arrived, he had recovered most of his faculties. "What the hell's goin' on, Will?"

"The governor of Kentucky issued a warrant for your arrest based on a request from Governor Newton Booth of California," he said, consulting a paper in his hand.

"What!" Arnold screamed. "The bastards have violated the agreement. They can't do this!" he raved, waving his arms wildly. "They agreed to no further litigation! I paid $150,000 to ensure this would not happen! They can't do this to me!"

"Calm down," Wilson advised. "This is something different." He crossed the cell to sit on the cot and motioned his client to join him. As Arnold sat, Wilson studied the writ in his hand. "Seems as how a man by the name of George Hudson, a San Francisco attorney, arrived here last Wednesday and contacted Louisville attorneys Dupuy and Middleton," he said. "Middleton and Hudson took the California warrant to the capitol in Frankfort to get Governor Leslie to issue an extradition order. The governor was out of town, but Lieutenant Governor Carlisle honored the request and issued the warrant for your arrest. You were unlucky enough that the *Courier-Journal* announced your arrival at Rufer's Hotel just at the same time Middleton got back to town. He promptly went to the police station to get the city detective to execute the warrant."

"Damn it, Will, they can't do this!"

"I told you, this is not the Lent business. This doesn't involve Lent, or Roberts or Ralston or Harpending. It's an entirely different matter."

"Well then, what the hell is it about?"

"Seems as how somebody named L.L. Treadwell has filed a suit against you, charging you with obtaining money from him under false pretenses and claiming you owe him $75,000. Do you know this Treadwell?"

"I know of him," Arnold said with a sigh. "He's another one of the California investors who thinks he's smarter than everybody else. What I don't know is how the hell he figures I owe him any money. I never had any sort of business transaction with him, not at any time."

"All right," Wilson said calmly. "I had a chance to study the California law. It stipulates that obtaining money under false pretenses is a misdemeanor punishable by one year's imprisonment and a fine of up to $1,000, but no action will be taken if the money is refunded. I don't guess you want to pay Treadwell $75,000, do you?"

"I told you!" Arnold shouted, leaping to his feet. "I never had any transaction of any kind with the man. Damn him, he's simply trying to blackmail me."[180]

"Well," Wilson said with a deep sigh, "that's not all."

"What!" Arnold exploded. "What else can go wrong?"

"There's another California warrant." He shuffled the papers in his hand. "This one, handled by the same local lawyers, is on behalf of a John T. Pantlind who is...."

"Pantlind!" Arnold screamed. "What the hell's going on here, Will? Is this 'everybody get a piece of Philip Arnold week'?"

Ignoring his client's outburst, Wilson went on, "Pantlind is the administrator of A.C. Hepner's will. Did you know this Hepner?"

"Yeah," Arnold said, thinking. "Jim Cooper and I had some dealings with him on some mining properties in New Mexico four or five years ago. I sure as hell don't owe him any money though."

"He, or rather Pantlind on his behalf, claims you and Cooper signed a bond on November 8, 1870, agreeing to pay him, or his heirs or assigns, $4,100 within six months. As you never did, he wants the $4,100 plus six percent interest."

"Well ain't that just peachy?" Arnold asked rhetorically, sitting on the cot. "Cooper and I did take an option on some mines from Hepner and Pantlind. We did so with the understanding that we had a right of purchase should the properties prove valuable, otherwise, as proved to be the case, the bonds were null and void and to be returned without purchase. Not only did we give the bonds back, they were so destitute that we gave them some meal and flour and bacon, and I personally loaned Pantlind $100. Hell of a way to reward my generosity!"[181] After a thoughtful pause, he added, "Why the hell ain't he goin' after Cooper too?'

In answer, Wilson merely shook his head. "Well, you know, Phil, that in the eyes of some, your settlement with Lent was an admission of guilt." As Arnold started to protest, Wilson stopped him with an upraised palm. "I know, but I'm just saying that anybody who sees it that way might just be trying to jump on the band wagon and see if they can squeeze some money out of you too."

"It ain't gonna work!" Arnold shouted. "I don't owe anybody anything and I will not pay one cent to anybody." Calming a bit, he asked, "Can you get me out of here Will?"

"Not right away," Wilson answered. "Give me a day or two to file some papers with the court."

On August 22, Philip Arnold appeared, with counsel William Wilson, before Judge W.L. Jackson in the United States courthouse in Louisville. Wilson argued that the charges against his client were simply misdemeanors and, hence, would not fall within the Governor's purview. Therefore, Wilson submitted, Arnold's detention was illegal. Representing the State of California, Louisville attorney J.R. Dupuy, maintained that every action had been performed according to the law and hence the warrant was in order. After careful consideration, Judge Jackson decided that the warrants were indeed valid and ordered that Arnold be detained in the Jefferson County jail until he could be handed over to the custody of the San Francisco attorney George Hudson, who was, at the time, out of town to be transported to California for trial.[182]

❧

A disappointed and disgusted Philip Arnold languished in jail for the next two weeks waiting for the California agent Hudson to return. He used the time to make a few plans of his own. Finally, on September 5, his attorney Will Wilson arrived and handed him the morning's *Courier-Journal*. "There's a column there you'll find interesting," Wilson commented, handing him the paper.

The column began by saying that the paper had received a letter from "a gentleman in San Francisco." It says here, Arnold read on, that I am "'really arrested upon a criminal indictment relating to operations in the diamond chimera, and the action of L.L. Treadwell's attorney in these premises is entirely deceptive.'"

"Yeah, I read it," Wilson said. "You got any idea who this 'gentleman' might be?"

"Could be Harpending, but I wouldn't think he'd squeal like this," Arnold said. "Could be Ralston, but more likely Roberts or Dodge."

"How 'bout Lent?" Wilson asked.

"Nah. After the agreement he signed, he knows we'd come after him."

"Exactly what I was thinking of doing," Wilson advised.

"It says that Treadwell 'fully realizes that there are several wealthy and influential residents of this city, leading citizens in the fullest sense of the term, who will make considerable sacrifice rather than Arnold should appear and tell all he knows.'"

"That would be Harpending, Ralston and Lent?" Wilson inquired.

"I suppose so," Arnold agreed. "This goes on to say that 'Treadwell hopes to affect a compromise on this account. He has studiously endeavored to suppress statements of the case here.' Damn, this is interesting. Later on here, it says, 'Now we believe that Arnold will not be returned here. We think that Treadwell is really seeking a compromise, and cares nothing at all about an expose of one of the greatest swindles of the last decade.'"

"Like I said before," Wilson said, "he's simply trying to squeeze some money out of you. I wonder if the 'gentleman' knows what he's talking about."

"It would seem that he does," Arnold commented. Then, sitting up with a start, "Will, did you see this?"

"What?"

Looking down the newspaper page, he said, "Here's a card from Treadwell. 'In the account of the arrest of Philip Arnold at Louisville on the 15th inst., published in your issue of the following day, I find in your statement of the cause of such arrest that you have erroneously connected my name with the diamond swindle and stated that I had been defrauded by the said Arnold of a considerable sum of money in that notorious undertaking, whereas I never had any connection, in any manner whatsoever, with the diamond company, never invested one dollar in it nor lost any money by it.'"[183]

"Well then," Wilson observed, "either Treadwell or the 'gentleman' is a liar."

"Or both," Arnold said. "Damn it, Will, when are you gonna get me out of here?"

"The wheels of justice grind slowly, Phil. I'm workin' on it."

"I know you are," Arnold acknowledged with a sigh, "but I'm suffocatin' in here. Besides, if they ever get me to California, my goose will be cooked good and proper."

"Don't let that worry you any," Wilson assured. "I promise you that you will not go to California."

"I will unless you can get the judge to turn me loose." His voice was laced with worry.

Wilson moved closer to his client so he could speak softly. "You have friends, Phil," he whispered. "There are plans in place made by well-drilled, determined and true men. They assure me that come what may, you will not be transported beyond the Mississippi River. There's a densely wooded spot in Indiana where you'll exchange your seat in the car as a prisoner for one in the coach as a hero." Wilson moved to the bars to look up and down the corridor, ensuring that no one was within earshot. Coming back to Arnold, he continued in a soft voice, "Should you be placed on a train, they have plans to take it over and affect your escape. In case there should be any objection to the program, 'persuaders' will be on hand to secure a compromise.[184] Just sit back and relax; it'll be OK."

Two days later Phil was relaxing on his cot when the jailer approached. "A lady to see you," he announced, unlocking the cell.

Arnold leapt to his feet in anticipation. To his utter surprise, Mrs. E.H. Bonner, a lady he and Mary had known in New Mexico and California, swept into the cell in a swirl of burgundy-colored satin and French perfume. A few wisps of her strawberry blond hair escaping the band of her wide-brimmed hat tumbled over her forehead, adding a touch of mystery to her green eyes. "I know you're a world traveler," he said, shaking her hand, "but what in heaven's name are you doing here?"

"Oh, I'm just on an eastern tour," she began. "I missed the train for Lexington yesterday and so was forced to remain here overnight. When I learned this morning that you were lodged in jail here, I just thought I'd stop in and pay my respects to an old friend in trouble. This is ridiculous!"

"I'm glad I'm not the only one who thinks so," he enthused. "Please sit," he invited, motioning to the cot. I wish I could offer finer accommodations. Do you know anything about this mess I'm in?"

She took the end of the cot farthest from where Arnold sat. "Well, I know that you, as well as my husband, had an interest in the Pyramid Mountain Silver Company."

"That's right," Arnold interrupted, "we were all together in New Mexico. I sold my interest to George Roberts."

"Yes, I know," she said. "What you don't know is that Roberts turned around and sold it to Treadwell. You will also be interested to learn that Treadwell filed a similar charge against Roberts. He wanted $50,000 from Roberts."

"That is interesting," Arnold said. "Has anything happened?"

"The case was heard and dismissed in San Francisco last week," she informed. "Anybody knows that we sell a mine for what we have in sight and the purchaser takes his chances. The miner sells for all he can get from the speculator, and it's a legitimate transaction. Buyer beware."

"Of course," Arnold agreed. "Everybody who's ever been involved in any such dealings knows the rules, although it seems Mr. Treadwell somehow managed to remain ignorant."

"Well, I know you to be an honest and energetic miner, prospector and adventurer," she said with a smile. "I think you're the victim of a swindle and an outrage and I'm going to write a card to the newspaper to make my opinions and knowledge public before I leave here. I don't know if it'll do any good, but I'm going to do it."[185] She rose to leave.

Arnold banged his tin cup on the bars to summon the jailer before turning to shake her hand. "I appreciate beyond words such an endorsement from such an intelligent and refined lady as yourself. I don't know if it'll do any good either, but it certainly cannot hurt anything, and I do not have words to express my appreciation."

She stepped through the door as the jailer held it open. "Please say hello to Mary for me. I wish you the best of luck."

The next day, Arnold and Wilson appeared before Judge Stites. "I see that you charge that committing Mr. Arnold to the custody of Mr. Hudson rather than the jailer was an illegal action," the judge began.

"Yes, Your Honor," Wilson said. "My brief also contends that the indictment was defective, that the affidavit did not sustain it, the warrant did not indicate that the proper papers had been presented to the governor, and that the papers were not made out in accordance with the Fugitive Justice Act of 1793."

"So, I see," Judge Stites commented, stroking his goatee. After studying the papers, he considered for a long moment before speaking. "I conclude that as the warrant failed to show with any degree of certainty that Mr. Arnold was actually charged with having committed any crime in California, said warrant is fatally defective. That being the case, all charges against Mr. Arnold are hereby dismissed."[186]

❧

"It looks fine to me, Phil," Wilson said leaning back in his office chair, "but I'll be damned if I can see what you think you're going to accomplish." He handed the sheets of paper back to Arnold.

Chapter Twenty-One

"A man is entitled to have his say, ain't he?"

"He certainly is. But are you sure you want to make all these sordid details public?"

"I'm damned tired of having my name drug through the mud and they don't hesitate to do that in public. I'm gonna set the record straight."

"Well, all right. I suggest you take your statement to the County Clerk and have it certified before you send it to the paper."

To the editor of the Courier-Journal
Elizabethtown, KY., Sept. 14, 1874.

I hope you will permit me, through the columns of your widely circulated paper, to state a few facts in reference to my late arrest and imprisonment, that those who desire to know the truth may judge as to whether I was really a fugitive from justice and whether the proposed extradition was in good faith intended to vindicate the laws and maintain the dignity of the great State of California or to gratify the mercenary ends of certain individuals who, under the pretense of justice, desired to make merchandise of a citizen of Kentucky under color of law.

In the years 1870 and 1871 I had certain transactions with one Harpending and Roberts in reference to supposed diamond discoveries, and they were the only persons with whom I ever had any dealings in reference to said discoveries. It appears that on the 30th of December, 1872, an indictment was obtained against a person of my name, in which it was charged that said person had obtained money under false pretense on the 17th of August, 1872, in the County and City of San Francisco, from the said Harpending and Roberts and one Ralston, they being the only complainants in said indictment. Early in April 1872, about eight months before said indictment was found, I left the City of San Francisco with my family, and returned to my home in Kentucky. But before my departure from the city and county of San Francisco my property was advertised for sale in the city, and was sold publicly, and the fact of my intended departure was notorious for weeks before, and I left the city in open daytime, in the presence of thousands, and without the slightest fear or apprehension on my part that I would be, or that I had been, accused of any public offense against the laws of California.

I reached my home with my family in the latter part of April, 1872. On the 17ᵗʰ of August 1872, the date of the alleged offense, I was in Laramie, in Wyoming Territory, about fourteen hundred miles distant from the City of San Francisco, and I state most positively that I was not in said city at any time during the month of August, 1872 or in the State of California, on account of any mining discoveries, or upon any representations in reference to any diamond discoveries. The truth is that the only money I ever received in reference to these matters was in the State of New York, and not in California.

*I had no knowledge that any such indictment had been obtained until in the year 1873, when a civil suit was instituted against me in Kentucky by one Lent who sued in his own interest and as the representative of the complainants in said indictment, to wit: the said Harpending, Roberts and Ralston. From the time I left California in April 1872, I was not in the State again until October, 1872, and during all this time it was well known by said parties and others in California that I was living with my family, at my home in Elizabethtown, Kentucky. Lent came in person in 1873, and instituted the civil proceedings in Hardin County. This civil suit was based on the business transactions which I had with two of the complainants in said indictment, to wit: Harpending and Roberts, and on the 25ᵗʰ day of March, 1873, this civil suit was compromised with said parties, and I was released and fully discharged from all responsibility or supposed liability, directly or indirectly, growing out of said suit or said mining discoveries, and I have the receipts and acquittances from **all** the complaining parties and from all with whom I had any dealings in reference to said mining interests.*

Now, in view of these facts, and knowing that the offense charged in said indictment was only a misdemeanor under the laws of California (the punishment whereof is a fine not exceeding $1,000 or imprisonment not exceeding one year in the county jail, [)] and knowing that the same statute provided that where the matters complained of were compromised by the parties in interest, the court having jurisdiction of the offense, in its discretion, might dismiss the prosecution on account of such compromise, I was satisfied that this was an end to the matter – and it was an end of the case so far as the parties in interest were concerned. Now, if I had really fled

228

from California to avoid justice, is it or not remarkable that the matter was permitted to slumber until August, 1874, and most especially when all the parties complaining knew of my place of residence, and when some of them actually came to Kentucky and instituted suit against me in my own county, in 1873.

What consideration or motive has prompted an outsider, one L.L. Treadwell, a man with whom I never had any business transaction, to volunteer and make his affidavit before Governor Booth which led to my arrest and imprisonment?

Did this man Treadwell make his affidavit in good faith before the Governor of California to vindicate the laws of that State; and did the man George Hudson, who came as an accredited agent of a great State, leave the golden shores and cross the plains to bring a fugitive to justice, or was the whole proceeding a deep-laid plan to rob and blackmail a citizen of Kentucky under color of law? Was it that Treadwell might extort money from your correspondent upon the supposition that, rather than be dragged from his family and friends and transported to another State three thousand miles from his home, he might again be induced to buy his peace? Let us look into this matter, that a candid and impartial world, and especially that the good people of California and Kentucky, may know the truth and judge accordingly.

On the 6th of August, 1874, his Excellency, the Governor of Kentucky, issued his warrant for the arrest of your correspondent, and on the 22nd of the same month Judge Jackson, of Louisville, ordered that the body of your correspondent to be placed in the custody of said George Hudson, to be conveyed by him to the State of California. But instead of proceeding at once on the long journey, the agent readily consented to delay the matter ten days, during which time I caused my friends and counsel to apply to the Governor and see whether or not, upon a rehearing of the case, he might be induced to recall his warrant, but not being prepared then to present all the facts, and especially the blackmailing business hereafter explained, the application proved unavailing. I then, with the advice of my friends and counsel, determined to sue out a new writ of habeas corpus, but before doing this I determined in my own mind to sound the man Hudson to the bottom and see what sum it would require to purchase my liberty. It is proper for me to state that even before I was committed to jail Hudson hinted that the matter might be compromised for twenty-five thousand dollars, and that he did not desire to take me to California.

While the case was pending before the Governor, I made an arrangement with Hudson for him to select an escort to go with me to California at my expense. I was to pay Hudson $100 to pay his expenses, and $471 for the expenses, etc., of the escort which he agreed to select. I paid this sum over to him, and was induced to believe that he really intended to furnish the escort, but he finally told me, after he got this money, that he had no intention of taking me to California: that he wanted the $25,000, and that if he started with me he would take me to Philadelphia and keep me in jail until I paid it.

As stated before, I determined to develop this robbery and blackmailing business, in the hope that it might in some way result in my liberation. Hudson insisted on a compromise, and I finally notified my lawyers that I had abandoned the idea of taking out another writ, and at this they were greatly surprised and disappointed, and insisted that I should sue out the writ. But I told them that they would please call on me no more; that I had no further need for them; that I was making my arrangements to start to California. I then notified Hudson that I was ready to see and negotiate with him. He promptly obeyed, and was soon in the jail, but we had great difficulty in agreeing on a plan. The difficulty was to agree on a man to hold the money until I was liberated and who should accompany me to the place where I was to be turned loose. Hudson very readily agreed to give up to me his power of attorney, the paper which showed him to be the Agent of California under the hand and seal of Governor Booth. He also proposed to give up to me Judge Jackson's order, which was his only authority to convey me to California, and agreed to write on the back of the order the following release, to wit:

"For value received I hereby release the within named Philip Arnold, and this I do as agent of L.L. Treadwell, and also as agent of California."

All these papers were be to delivered up to me before I left the jail. He also said that Treadwell also had a suit pending against Roberts and proposed to transfer to me the benefit of this suit, and he also said he had a warrant for Harpending and proposed to give me the benefit of this, and read to me his *power of attorney and his warrant for Harpending. But the trouble was to find a man to hold the $25,000. I proposed several reliable men in the city, but Hudson would agree on no one except John W. Beckly, who is a near relative of Treadwell, and who had returned from California about two months ago, as he said himself. I finally agreed to see Beckly, and talk the matter over with him, and, accordingly, Beckly was soon in the jail and the whole plan revealed fully to him, to which he readily consented. I and Hudson were to go to Cincinnati, by way of the Ohio and Mississippi railroad, and put up at the Gibson House, while Beckly was to go to Cincinnati by way of the Short line, and also put up at the Gibson House; and there the money or certificates of deposit were to be paid over to Hudson by Beckly, and I was to be dismissed, and to go hence without day [delay.]*

Now I had no intention of carrying out this arrangement – none whatever; but my object was, if possible, to develop and bring to light this blackmailing business, under the belief that, if this fact was made clear, the Governor would not let me go into the custody of this man Hudson; and when the mercenary purposes came to light, they might result in some way in my liberation. After the plan of escape was agreed on, Hudson was extremely anxious to start, and I put him off by telling him that I must have a few days to raise the money. After these negotiations with Hudson, I called for my attorneys again and notified them of what Hudson had proposed to do in the way of selling out, and also notified them to proceed at once and take out the writ of habeas corpus.

I will now mention a few circumstances which will clearly show that Hudson was a blackmailer, and even should Beckly deny the agency which I have mentioned; but I am assured that if he was called on oath he would come out like a man.

I had a subpena [sic] issued for Beckly, and I had it served on him the day I was brought out before Judge Stites, and he obeyed the summons. I also had some of the police subpenaed [sic.] Hudson also appeared the first day I was brought out, but during the argument of counsel it was hinted that before the trial was over the fact would be made clear that Hudson had offered to sell out for $25,000. A short time after this hint, Hudson disappeared and was seen no more on that day, and when I was brought out the next day Hudson failed to put in his appearance. It was matter of inquiry *as to what had become of the man. Some thought perhaps he had gone to Frankfort for a new warrant, but the most rational supposition was that when he heard the hint about the $25,000, which had been thrown out by counsel, and when he saw that Beckly had been subpenaed [sic], and that Beckly was in attendance, and that Beckly knew all the facts with reference to the blackmailing, Mr. Hudson promptly paid his bill and left for his California home.*

In conclusion, I only wish to say that I am a citizen of Kentucky. I was born and reared in this proud old Commonwealth and claim that protection which is due to a peaceable and law-abiding citizen. I have been guilty of no crime, and while I recognize the fact that those who are charged with a felony, or some other crime should be extradited, I do not recognize the right of citizens of other States to arrest and imprison a citizen of Kentucky for mercenary purposes as this was clearly the purpose of my late arrest as no impartial mind can deny.

PHILIP ARNOLD

Philip Arnold says the statements made in the foregoing letter are true.

PHILIP ARNOLD

Subscribed and sworn to before me by Philip Arnold this
September 14, 1874.

C.M. FRAZIE
Clerk Hardin Circuit Court[187]

Chapter Twenty-Two

Monday, June 17, 1878
Elizabethtown, Kentucky

Following the Treadwell affair, the Arnolds enjoyed a time of happiness, peace and profit. Mary was happily engaged with the rapidly maturing children – Tom and Dick were teenagers, and Katie was now married to David May, Mary's brother's son[188] – and the womens' society around town while Philip immersed himself in agricultural and business affairs. His biggest business deal concerned the local banking firm of Polk and Thomas. Although the transaction was kept secret at the time, during the Great Depression[189], when lack of funds had forced the bank to suspend business, Arnold had supplied the money to keep the bank afloat. He remained involved behind the scenes until April 1877, when the arrangement became totally above board as Phil was named the senior partner in the banking firm of Arnold and Polk. By 1878, the firm had become popular and highly respected locally.

Back in 1873, Custer's wish to return to the plains came true when he was ordered to the Dakota Territory to become engaged in the "Indian Wars." Three years later, the news of his demise at the Little Big Horn was described as a "bloody massacre" in all the papers. In Elizabethtown, however, "General" Custer's inglorious end met with mixed reactions among the Kentuckians with whom he had been so snobbish. Otherwise, American's centennial year passed in Elizabethtown, much the same as everywhere else in the United States, amid patriotic parades and band concerts.

In the fall of 1877, Arnold had accomplished his dream of constructing a building on the previously purchased lot on the northwest corner of the public square. Much to the mutual satisfaction of the parties involved, The Gilded Age building, a handsome two-story brick structure, was leased to and occupied by the prosperous dry goods business of Berry and Hargan.[190]

Additionally, Phil had greatly expanded his farming interest, molding his holdings into "the best improved farm in Hardin County."[191] At various times, he stocked the farm with thoroughbred horses, sheep and swine, buying and selling as the notion struck his fancy. Money was apparently no object; his main concern was that he not be required to personally perform any of the necessary labor. Out of respect for Arnold's standing, the diamond business was never mentioned except in a light-hearted way, such as the newspaper posting about a huge hog Arnold owned. The article declared that the "one thousand pound hog is a cross of the Berkshire and Poland China, just as his thousand dollar mine was a cross between salt and fiction."[192]

On this sunny June morning, however, Philip Arnold was a troubled man. Back in April 1876, when the local banking house of L.M. Longshaw was encountering credit difficulties, Polk and Thomas, with Arnold's blessing, had graciously loaned their competitors $8,000 in Louisville City Hall bonds. The loan was due on January 15, 1877; on that date Longshaw was to repay the principal along with six percent interest.[193] When the due date arrived, rather than repay what was due, Longshaw began a shell game of changing his collateral for the note. Arnold soon tired of that tactic and filed a law suit for the $360 interest he claimed due plus another $300 for his trouble.

Then on May 3, 1878, after Arnold was officially part of the bank, Harry Holdsworth, a clerk in the banking house of L.M. Longshaw wrote a confidential letter to his former employer, a credit agency in Cincinnati. Initially, he defamed the firm of Arnold and Polk: "Messers Arnold and Polk, bankers at this place went to protest in New York for $150 last week, for lack of funds, this we think very strange and coupled with this, they have not discounted any paper for the last sixty days, but are rediscounting their paper in Louisville, and to a customer of ours (who is one of the best men in the Co.) who applied for a loan at their bank for $50 today; they said they could not discount for the next month or two."

Holdsworth then insulted Philip Arnold personally: "Arnold is the wealthy man of the concern, but I think he will not last long. Polk has not one dollar in the world and is actually nothing more than Arnold's clerk. Arnold made what money he has by salting mines in Arizona with diamonds and selling them at great profit. For this little speculation, he was arrested and laid in jail for some time, but was released on some small technicality and has since been enjoying his ill-gotten gains."[194]

This letter was somehow leaked and published for the world to see in the *Courier-Journal*. When Holdsworth's letter came to Arnold's attention, he was livid. Polk and Arnold promptly filed suit against Holdsworth, who brazenly admitted authorship of the letter, and Longshaw. Claiming that the letter "reflects on the credit and standing of [our] bank and also upon the present standing and character of [myself,] " and that the comments were "false, malicious and defamatory,"[195] Arnold asked for $25,000 damages.

On this Monday morning, Philip was walking to work along the public square, twirling, as was his custom, a silver-headed cane. As he neared his office in the bank, he saw Holdsworth approaching. Stiffening, he brought the cane to his side and slowed his pace. Both men stopped leaving a space of about three feet between them. "I understand, sir, that you claim responsibility for the letter," Arnold spat, his anger rapidly approaching the boiling point.

"I do," Holdsworth replied, his brazenness slipping a couple of notches now that he was face-to-face with the much larger man.

"Then you are nothing more than a common scoundrel and an ordinary liar," Arnold shouted. Before Holdsworth could reply, Arnold's anger spewed forth and he struck his advisory with his heavy walking stick. As Holdsworth recoiled from the blow, Arnold struck again and again, raising welts on Holdsworth's skin and bloodying his head.

Henry Kennedy, standing nearby, rushed to Arnold's side and gripped his arm. "Enough, Phil! You'll kill him."

"No better than the blackguard deserves," an infuriated Arnold screamed. Jerking his arm away from Kennedy, he shouted, "Get away from me or I'll kill you, too!"

Another bystander, Henry Kurtz, said to Kennedy, "Look out Henry, he's got a pistol."

Kennedy let go of Arnold, who stood trembling in rage as Holdsworth, bloody and bowed, limped away as quickly as his condition allowed.[196]

"Take it easy, Phil," Kennedy advised.

Making a concerted effort to calm himself, Arnold slowly turned to face Kennedy. "The next time I see him," he said evenly, "I'm gonna kill that little son of a bitch."

Chapter Twenty-Three

Glad that the long day was at last finished, Philip Arnold heaved a deep sigh as he walked out the front door of Arnold and Polk's bank. Fumbling in his pocket, he found the key and turned to lock the door. From behind him, a voice asked, "Hey Phil, how ya doin'?"

He turned expectantly to see his friend, J. Berry Taylor approaching. "Why hello, Cap," Arnold greeted, using Taylor's military rank as a mark of respect. Taylor shook hands waiting for an answer to his greeting.

"Well, to tell you the truth, I've had better days," Arnold admitted.

"Yeah? What's goin' on?

"I guess you know the trial in my suit against Holdsworth and Longshaw was scheduled to begin yesterday," Arnold said, pocketing the key.

"Was scheduled?" Taylor was puzzled. "I suppose that means it did not begin as planned?"

"You suppose correctly," Arnold said, turning to face Taylor. "The judge continued it 'til February. That does aggravate the hell out of me. Not only does Longshaw owe me money, it's high time Holdsworth was brought to the trough to answer for the insults he's heaped on me."

Taylor could see the rage rising within his banker friend. "Come on over to Lott's. I'll buy you a beer," he offered. As the two men started for the saloon across the square, Taylor asked, "Why was the case continued?"

"Just some more of Longshaw's stalling tactics," Arnold spat as they walked into the dank interior of Lott's saloon. Bellying up to the bar, they ordered beer.

"Well, forget about it for a while," Taylor advised. "Here's to ya," he said, hoisting his mug. Both men drank deeply and sat the mugs on the bar. "How's things out on the farm?"

Relaxing a bit, Arnold was about to answer when he saw Harry Holdsworth, in the company of Henry Kennedy, push through the swinging doors. The slight relief Arnold had just experienced vanished as the new arrivals eyed Arnold and Taylor as they moved into the room. Sensing trouble, Kennedy hailed the men at the bar. "Why, hello, boys," he said jovially, "how 'bout I buy you both a beer?"

Taylor opened his mouth to answer, but said nothing as he observed the hard-set of Arnold's face. The four men stood in silence for a moment before Arnold addressed Holdsworth, his voice a harsh rasp. "You have done me a mortal injury, and now you are following me up!" Before Holdsworth could protest, Arnold pounced on him and threw the smaller man to the floor. Sitting astride the prostrate Holdsworth, Arnold rained blows on his adversary's head and shoulders with his fists.

Charles Lott ran from behind the bar. "Here now, that's enough of that," he shouted. As Arnold drew back for the next blow, Lott seized his arm in mid-swing.

Arnold turned on Lott with the rage of a wounded tiger. "If you touch me, I'll kill you," he snarled.

As Lott made another move as if to intervene, Taylor stopped him. "It's their fight, let 'em alone."

Hearing the ruckus, City Marshall Warren, who happened to be in the Bryan, Warren and Company store next door, dashed into Lott's. He found Arnold still beating on Holdsworth while the latter cried, begging Arnold to stop. Elbowing his way through the crowd, the marshall pulled Arnold to his feet and roughly shoved him across the room. "Enough!" As C.W. Wintersmith, another bystander, moved to Holdsworth's assistance, Arnold evaded Warren enough to get in a kick at the still prone Holdsworth. As Arnold's foot lashed out, a look of utter contempt covered his face.

Wintersmith helped the bruised and bleeding Holdsworth to his feet. "I can't see!" Holdsworth cried as blood gushed over his forehead and eyes.

"Come on," Wintersmith said, "I'll take you to the bank and get you cleaned up."

Wintersmith's arm supported Holdsworth as the two men left Lott's heading for Longshaw's bank. In the washroom, after Holdsworth wiped the blood from his face and staunched the bleeding, he turned to Wintersmith. "Get me that shotgun from behind the door," he demanded.

"Now, Harrry, you'd better let well enough alone. You know Arnold is crazy."

"I'll be damned if I let him get away with this," he shouted. "If you don't want to help, just get out of my way." Holdsworth drew a double-barreled shotgun from its station behind the door to the office, checked the charge and started for the front door.[197] Rather than trail along, Wintersmith decided to just go home.

With fire in his eyes and a deliberate step, Holdsworth snuggled the shotgun in the crook of his left arm and started back down the street toward Lott's Saloon. Arnold was standing on the board sidwewalk out front, conversing with Berry Taylor, his face at a right angle to Holdsworth's line of approach. At someone's shout, "Here he comes!" Arnold turned to observe his adversary purposely striding toward him. Seeing the shotgun in his arms, Arnold instantly took in Holdsworth's intention and reached inside his vest to withdraw a revolver. Perhaps surprised that Holdsworth had nerve enough to return to the fray, his arm quivered a bit as he fired twice at the man some thirty feet distant. Although usually a better shot, in this case, both bullets missed Holdsworth, who quickly ducked behind a tree. Whatever the reason for Arnold's poor marksmanship, one of his shots shattered the front window of B. Kauffman and Company's store across the street.

Peeking around the tree, Holdsworth fired the first barrel of his weapon. The shot missed Arnold, but did strike two bystanders. Enraged even further by this turn of events, Arnold advanced toward Holdsworth's refuge, firing as he moved. Of the three shots he fired, one lodged in the tree, one missed completely and the other wounded local farmer James Anderson. By this time, Arnold was within a few feet of the shotgun's muzzle. Holdsworth discharged his remaining barrel at close range. The buckshot ripped into Arnold's right shoulder, tearing out a fist-sized hunk of flesh. As Holdsworth discarded his empty weapon and ran, Arnold, despite his serious wound, managed to fire his remaining shot. Its only effect was to hasten Holdsworth's retreat toward Longshaw's home.[198]

Berry Taylor helped Arnold onto his horse. The two men rode side by side to Arnold's home on the edge of town. When Mary, who had heard the gunshots, saw the horses approaching, she dashed onto the porch. Seeing her husband's blood soaked shirt, she screamed, "Captain Taylor, what's happened?"

"The situation with Harry Holdsworth boiled over," Berry said, helping Arnold off his horse. They had a first class shootout right on the public square." Mary and Taylor helped Phil onto the porch. "Make him as comfortable as you can," Taylor advised. "I'll go for the doctor."

By the time Doctor Pusey arrived, Mary had gotten her husband to bed and stopped the bleeding as best she could with a compress. The doctor shooed her from the room so he could examine and dress the wound.

"How bad is it, doctor?" she asked when he emerged from the bedroom.

"Well, it's serious, but not life threatening," Pusey advised, wiping his hands. "He's lost a lot of blood, so he'll be weak for a while." His voice trailed off.

Sensing that he was withholding something she pleaded, "Yes? Please go on."

"Well," the medical man said with a sigh, "it's possible that he may lose his arm." The doctor paused, waiting for her reaction. As she said nothing, he added, "Keep him quiet; I'll check back in the morning."

☙

Although the doctor had pronounced Philip Arnold's wound not serious, it was very painful and bothersome and gave him no amount of trouble over the next six months. On August 28, 1878, when Harry Holdsworth was tried in county court for the shooting, Arnold was too weak to attend. In Arnold's absence, his partner John Polk testified that "Arnold is at home sick and not in a condition to attend the trial in this case at the present term, having been severely wounded by the defendant Holdsworth within the last thirteen days past, and Arnold is now and has been, since said wounding, under medical treatment."[199] All the eye witnesses gave their testimony, and when Holdsworth's attorney, Turner Wilson, attempted to introduce evidence pertaining to the cane-whipping, Arnold's lawyer, Will Wilson, objected. Judge Lancaster upheld the objection, deciding that "it was not competent evidence." At the end of a long hot day, Holdsworth was put under a $400 peace bond and the case was held over to the October term. [200]

On October 22, Philip Arnold was indicted for "unlawfully shoot[ing] at H.N. Holdsworth with a pistol loaded with powder and leaden ball, with intent to kill said Holdsworth." The witnesses, once again, told their stories, and at the end of the day, Philip Arnold was placed under a $500 peace bond and trail was set for the April term.[201]

The next day, although the attorneys were ready, the trial of Holdsworth for shooting Arnold was postponed until the April term.

Three days later, October 26, Philip Arnold was indicted for "carrying a concealed deadly weapon, other than an ordinary pocket knife." Again, with Arnold not present, the judge merely tacked an additional $100 onto Arnold's bond.[202]

❧

The Arnolds ushered in the new year, 1879, with little celebration as the various legal troubles loomed, and Philip was slow in recovering from his wound. Early in February, with him quite ill in addition to his undiminishing pain, Mary summoned the doctor.

Doctor Pusey entered the front room and greeted Mary agreeably. Ignoring his pleasantries, "Phil is very sick," she informed.

"Well, I'd best have a look," the doctor said, heading for the bedroom where Phil had lain since the shooting.

At length, he finished his examination and emerged back into the parlor. "Well?" Mary asked expectantly.

"It's pneumonia," he announced. "He's in no condition to deal with it, so we'll have to keep a close eye on him."

Mary, in company with the older children, spent a long Thursday night keeping watch over her restless husband. When the doctor arrived on Friday morning, February 8, he immediately ordered the family from the room. After a seemingly endless time, Doctor Pusey emerged, his face graven. Although the words were unnecessary, he whispered to Mary, "He's gone."

When the services were held the following Monday, many residents proclaimed it the largest funeral Elizabethtown had ever seen. Many local businesses closed and the circuit court and county convention were adjourned out of respect for Philip Arnold's memory.[203] Following the graveside service, the Arnold children escorted their mother to her home. Katie May helped her mother to a rocker in the front room, while Tom poked up the fire and Dick

241

carried in more wood. "Is there anything else I can do?" Katie asked, kneeling by the chair. The boys and Nora gathered near, each placing a hand on their mother's shoulder.

"No," Mary answered, "I'm okay."

"Mother," Tom said, "we'll take care of everything – anything – you just tell us what you need."

With a push from her foot, Mary rocked back in her chair and closed her eyes. In a soft voice, she said, "I'll be just fine."

Katie May studied Mary's face as she rocked contently. Was it simply her imagination, or did she detect just the slightest hint of a smug grin at the corners of her mother's mouth?

Epilogue

Thursday, August 15, 2012
Bardstown, Kentucky

So, there we go, that's the story of Philip Arnold and the great diamond hoax. Yes, I know you have questions, but before we get to those, there a few loose ends to tie up. The law suit of Arnold and Polk v. Longshaw and Holdsworth over the $8,000 loan that started all the trouble was finally called to be heard on February 17, 1879. As Philip Arnold was nine days dead at that point, the case was promptly dismissed, each party to pay their own court costs and attorney fees.[204]

Two months later, April 25, 1879, the indictment against Holdsworth for shooting and wounding Arnold was called in Hardin Circuit Court. The jury, amazingly, found Holdsworth not guilty, and that was the end of that.[205]

Later in the year, August 22, Mary Arnold, as Philip's widow, attempted to reinstate the suit against Longshaw and Holdsworth. At the hearing, Longshaw insisted that he had not agreed to pay any interest. In Philip's absence and there being no written agreement, nothing came of this action, either.

That brings us to James Anderson, the bystander wounded when a bullet fired by Arnold passed through his stomach. His wound was initially thought to be fatal, but by February 1880, he had recovered enough to file an action against Arnold, seeking $25,000 damages. Only, now, his case was against Mary. The county court dismissed the case with Mary agreeing to pay all costs.[206] Anderson was dissatisfied with that verdict, so appealed. On April 12, 1881, when the Kentucky Court of Appeals upheld the lower court's decision, Anderson ran out of options.

Finally, on April 24, 1882, the case of Commonwealth of Kentucky v. Philip Arnold for shooting, with intent to kill, at Harry Holdsworth was heard in Hardin County Court. Noting that "the statue in reguard to the verification of claims against deceased persons does not apply to the Commonwealth," the court ordered Mary Arnold to pay thirty percent of the $500 bond ($150) plus thirty percent of the $50 damages claimed ($15, probably for the broken glass) to Commonwealth's attorney, Joe Haycraft.[207] When she turned over the $165 three days later, the Philip Arnold story finally ended.

Now, the questions. The first question, which lurks in one's mind for most of the book, is how in the world could he pull this off? Many things have changed since 1872, but one which has not is human nature. Then, as now, everybody wants to get in early on the next big thing. Then it was diamond mines, now it's some internet project or an ultra 3D television device, but greed remains the prime motivator.

Another factor contributing to Arnold's success is what I called "El Dorado fever," the infectious malady that struck everybody who went to Arnold's diamond field. Even the King expedition's leader, who went there already knowing it was a swindle, said "that night we were full believers in the veracity of Janin's report and dreamed of the untold wealth that might be gathered."[208]

That highlights the next factor, ignorance. When Charles Lewis Tiffany, who later admitted that he knew nothing about uncut diamonds, valued the sample at $150,000, Arnold surely had to hide his astonished grin from the investors. Likewise, the investors and even the geologists (including Henry Janin) knew little about diamonds in the raw. Even the government men, Clarence King and Sam Emmons, were singularly unknowledgeable in this area. Emmons admitted as much, noting, "the origin and manner of formation of diamonds is one of the yet unsolved problems of geology."[209]

The final piece of this puzzle is Arnold's skill and intelligence. Beyond doubt, he was a silver-tongued con man worthy of Bernie Madoff's admiration. He was also smart enough to educate himself with sufficient geological data to locate a spot where diamonds might actually occur. And, he ensured that that site was so remote that no one would accidentally stumble upon it. Then he played his cards perfectly at every step, beginning with refusing to even show George Roberts what was in the package he desired to deposit in the safe on that foggy evening in 1870. Arnold agreed to the investors' demands when necessary, acceded to their requests when proper and made his own demands when the timing was right. But even with that, you have to figure that the diamond hoax succeeded far beyond Philip Arnold's wildest dreams. In his report to the stockholders of the San Francisco and New York Mining and Commercial Company, Clarence King expressed his appreciation: "This is the work of no common swindler, but of one who has known enough to select a spot where detection must be slow, and where every geological parallelism added a fresh probability of honesty. The selection of geological locality is so astonishingly considered, the salting itself so cunning and artful, the choice of all conditions so fatally well made that I can feel no surprise that even so trustworthy an engineer as Mr. Janin should have brought home the belief he did, since as his report states, he was not allowed to prospect exhaustively." [210]

Asbury Harpending published his book in 1913, primarily to demonstrate that, contrary to common opinion, he was one of the dupes rather than a perpetrator. That goal colored many of his statements and observations, but he did express, albeit grudging, admiration of Arnold's cleverness: Speaking of the brazenness of scattering not only diamonds but rubies, emeralds and sapphires all at the same site, Harpending wondered, "Why a few pearls weren't thrown in for good luck, I have never been able to tell. Probably it was an oversight." [211] In its day, the diamond mine "find" consumed gallons of printers' ink, spurred the formation of many speculation companies and sent hordes of prospectors to Arizona and New Mexico in search of the rumored American El Dorado. Harpending pointed out, quite properly, I think, that a public offering of stock would easily have garnered many millions of dollars in subscriptions. Asbury offers the fact that they did not do so as proof that he and the others were on the up and up.

Next, a question for everybody (and that includes me) is where did Arnold's money go? The first place to seek an answer, Philip Arnold's will, provides no clue. "For the natural love and affection which I have for my beloved wife, Mary E. Arnold, I give and devise to her absolutely and in fee the whole of my property both real, personal and mixed...." [212] So, whatever money he had passed to her without accounting. Her will uses exactly the same wording to pass her property along to her daughter, Nora. Again there is no accounting, although Mary did note that she had already given Katie, Richard and

Thomas $10,000 each. [213] It seems reasonable to assume that the property left to Nora was worth approximately the same as what was given to the other children, so she must have been worth at least $40,000, a far cry from the original $500,000.

Before his untimely demise, Philip Arnold bought a large amount of Hardin County real estate (see Appendix A.) From the time of his death until her own death in 1904, Mary also engaged in several transactions. While there are quite a few dealings and the deed books do not give all the details, it would appear that nothing large enough to make much of a dent in the hoax money occurred in land speculation. Worth a note in passing is the fact that many of those land deals involved law suits, both personal and involving Arnold and Polk's bank. There's another interesting book in those deed records.

The newspapers make several references to Arnold's farm enterprises. Not only did he buy lots of properties, but evidently spared no expense in outfitting his farms with barns, fencing and other improvements. Additionally, he dabbled in thoroughbred horses (at which, as any knowledgeable person will readily verify, one can lose a fortune very quickly,) swine, sheep and any other variety of livestock which struck his fancy.

Finally, and perhaps the most likely use of the money, is Arnold's lifestyle from 1872 until his death. There are no details, but the newspapers offer several tantalizing hints as to his activities. For example, he wrote to the *Courier-Journal* on December 14, 1872, "On my return from New Orleans last night...." Why has he in New Orleans? How long had he been there? He was arrested in Louisville on August 15, 1874, leaving us no clue as to why he was there. Was dashing off to the bright lights something he did on a regular basis? Again, it seems reasonable to assume that he spent plenty of money living high and wide.

For a fact, the basement and yard of Arnold's home across Valley Creek on Poplar Avenue (which is now the Lincoln Trail Battered Spouse Refuge) have been dug up and thoroughly explored, even to the extent of dynamiting the old well from which the Arnolds' obtained their water, all without result. By now, despite the persistent rumors, the folks around Elizabethtown are pretty sure he didn't bury any of his loot to be found by future generations.

What became of John Slack? That question has bugged a lot of people, including Asbury Harpending. As late as 1913, when Harpending published his side of the story, he said, "I have always considered that a deep mystery hung over his fate. It seems not unlikely that he died somewhere in the western country, probably among strangers and never participated in the profits of the diamond fraud at all."[214] We still know little of Slack's monetary take from the hoax, but Bruce Woodard, who spent eight years researching this story in the 1960's, traced Slack from the diamond fields to St. Louis. There he found work making wooden coffins, eventually becoming president of the company. This would lead one to speculate that he may have invested some money to gain that position. However that may be, his company suffered greatly in the Great Depression of 1873, so Slack moved on to a gold mining camp near White Oaks, New Mexico. The fact that White Oaks was a rip-roaring boom town evidently convinced Slack that is was a lucrative venue for a coffin maker. At any rate, he apparently made out all right until White Oaks' mining petered out. In 1887, he applied to the government for, and received, a Mexican War Veteran's pension. Slack evidently kept his mouth shut concerning the diamond hoax; upon his death on July 26, 1896, the local papers reported that, "Mr. Slack was one of the oldest and most universally respected residents of White Oaks.... He was always honest and just in his intercourse and dealings with his fellow men and generous to those who gained his ready sympathy and confidence." The evaluation of his estate showed he was worth $1,611.14 at his death.[215]

Mary Arnold died on August 8, 1904. The local paper reported her passing, noting that she (like Slack) was "one of [Elizabethtown's] oldest and most respected residents." Mary also, "experienced the vicissitudes of both poverty and wealth, but always remained true to her friends. She was a woman of many noble traits of character, charitable in all things, straightforward in all business transactions, an excellent neighbor, an indulgent mother and a faithful Christian...."[216]

Speaking of the Arnold family, I mentioned the Arnold children several times in the text, but gave little information on them as they played no significant role in the story. Here's what I know from the census and the gravestones. The oldest daughter, Elizabeth, was born in Hardin County on March 5, 1857 and died there on September 6, 1863. Tom was born in 1862, followed by Richard in 1865. At the time of their mother's death, they were both living in Louisville. Katie (born May 8, 1859) married, as noted, her cousin Dave May, while Nora (born in 1870) married Jere O'Meara. The O'Mearas apparently lived in Oklahoma for a time while Katie lived out her life in Elizabethtown. Both the girls are buried there in the family plot. Ben Arnold, born July 7, 1874 died in Elizabethtown July 20, 1892, just after his eighteenth birthday.

Why did Ralston and Harpending and Dodge and Roberts and the rest of the San Francisco investors not come after Arnold and Slack? One conjecture is as good as another, but perhaps in the spirit of "all's fair in love and war and mining speculation" all of them, except Lent, decided to simply accept their losses and move on.

Finally, who benefitted and who suffered from the great diamond hoax? Beyond question, Philip Arnold gained greatly. John Slack probably got some of the money, how much is not known. According to Henry Janin, Harpending bought back Janin's stock for the exact same $10,000 he paid, so he made no money other than his "experting" fee. Harpending reports that "the losses … fell on the shoulders of the original dupes, W.C. Ralston, William M. Lent, General Dodge and myself. My impression is that the money obtained by Lent from Arnold, very nearly, if not quite, balanced his account. Perhaps he may have given a portion of this to General Dodge, his business associate. Mr. Ralston promptly repaid the 25 stockholders, who subscribed $2,000,000 for a half interest in the company, dollar for dollar. Not a man of them lost a cent."[217] So, Philip Arnold was the big winner, if he considered that the money was worth the trouble and pain it caused him, while Ralston, Harpending and Roberts sustained the loss.

Asbury Harpending returned to Kentucky late in 1872 and built a $65,000, twenty room frame house near Princeton. "Each sleeping room is equipped with a lavatory and running water. The bathroom tub is of copper and is said to have been the first bathtub installed in this section of Western Kentucky." The newspaper reports that, "in 1877, five years after completion of his mansion, Harpending suddenly disappeared."[218] As an explanation, Harpending himself said that after all the excitement he'd seen, he found the pace of a country gentleman a little slow. Evidently, he went back to California as in his foreword to the 1958 reprint of Harpending's book, Glen Dawson records, "Harpending spent more of his life in California than the last chapter of his book would indicate. Finally in 1918 he moved to New York…."[219] There, he dabbled in Wall Street, having never lost his appetite for speculation in financial matters, and made and lost another couple of fortunes before he died in New York City, January 26, 1923.

William Ralston was another victim of the Great Depression of 1873. In the aftermath of the Panic, the depositors made a run on the Bank of California, which resulted in one day withdrawals of $1,400,000. As a result, on August 26, 1875, Ralston's financial empire evaporated. The next day, while swimming in the Bay, as was his daily custom, he was observed to be in distress. A boat quickly arrived, but by the time they got him ashore, he was dead. "There was talk of suicide but the coroner's inquest, on which depended life insurance for Mrs. Ralston and four children, delved into the testimony, found that doctors observed evidence of an apoplectic stroke, none of drowning. This was borne out by the autopsy."[220]

The story of Philip Arnold and John Slack and the great diamond hoax has been told many times, including an episode of a western television show. In the show, which first aired on February 23, 1968, hosted by Robert Taylor, *Death Valley Days* presented "*The Great Diamond Mines*," starring Gavin MacLeod (of *The Love Boat* fame) as Philip Arnold and John Fiedler (who appeared on many, many TV shows, most notably as one of *Bob Newhart's* patients) as John Slack. The episode also featured Tod Andrews as William Ralston, Alex Leors as Henry Janin, Allen Wood as Clarence King and George Neise as Asbury Harpending. While presenting a reasonable version of the facts, reducing the story to a thirty minute format drained most of the zest from the diamond hoax tale. An interesting note in passing, the creative genius behind the series *Death Valley Days* was none other than the famous singing movie cowboy, Gene Autry.

The same tale has, of course, eventuated many, many times in human history, perhaps usually on a smaller scale. President Truman liked to say that "the only thing new in the world is history you don't know." This is so, Harry said, because "human nature never changes." All these years later, as we think of the saga of Philip Arnold and the great diamond hoax, we see the wisdom of Truman's observation.

Endnotes

1. Louisville *Courier-Journal*, December 16, 1872. In relating his side of the story, Philip Arnold gave the date only as "November 1870."

2. Wilson, Robert, *The Explorer King*, Scribner, New York, 2006. 236.

3. Ibid., 237. Although accounts vary, Roberts seems to have been the first person Arnold and Slack approached.

4. Hardin County, KY, marriage book C, page 78, certificate 774. Philip Arnold and Mary May were married January 30, 1855.

5. *Courier-Journal*, December 16, 1872.

6. Harpending, Asbury, *The Great Diamond Hoax*, University of Oklahoma Press, Norman, 1958. Originally published in 1913, in this book, Mr. Harpending journaled his very eventful life.

7. *Courier-Journal*, December 16, 1872.

8. Kentucky State Archives, Hardin Circuit Court Records in the case of Lent v. Arnold, 1872. The other witness, G.R. May, was Mary Arnold's brother.

9. The power of attorney is recorded in Hardin County Deed Book 6, page 245.

10. Woodard, *Diamonds in the Salt*, Pruett Press, Bolder, CO, 1967. 12. The date is approximate, given as "in the fall" (1870).

11. *Courier-Journal*, December 16, 1872.

12. DeFord, Miriam, *They Were San Franciscans*, Caxton Printers, 1941. 156.

13. www.shakespeareghosttown.com/history. That prediction proved accurate. Buoyed by the mines, Grant was renamed Ralston, in the banker's honor, in December 1870. In the next few years, the town had more

than 3,000 residents, mostly prospectors who discovered that Ralston and Harpending already owned all the valuable property. By 1875, Ralston was a ghost town. In 1879, brothers William and John Boyle breathed new life into the town by reopening the abandoned claims. Renamed Shakespeare by the Englishmen, some prosperity existed until the Panic of 1893 made it a ghost town once again. It remains so, a tourist attraction, today.

14 There's some confusion about were Harpending came from. In his book, he simply says "the western part of the state." Some references put his birth place at Henderson, but there is documentation that his father lived at Princeton and he did "return" there after this adventure.

15 Harpending, *Hoax*. 5.

16 Ibid., 10-15.

17 Ibid., 22-24.

18 Ibid., 32-60. The full title of Harpending's book is *The Great Diamond Hoax and Other Stirring Incidents in the Life of Asbury Harpending*. If half of the tales he relates are true, the man certainly led an eventful life.

19 Woodard, *Diamonds*. 17.

20 *Courier-Journal*, September 7, 1874.

21 Harpending, *Hoax*. 130. The Pyramid Company did fail, partly due to Harpending's troubles in Europe, partly due to Indian trouble, but mostly due to the fact that there was not much silver there. Harpending details his entire adventure in England in a couple of chapters.

22 Woodard, *Diamonds*. 15.

23 Harpending, *Hoax*. 176-177. Harpending says that with revenge as a motive, Cooper later confessed that he was the original author of the entire scheme.

24 Alter, Cecil, *James Bridger, A Historical Narrative*, originally published 1925, reprinted Long's College Book Company, Columbus, OH, 1951. 356.

25 Ibid., 357. Like many of Bridger's tales, this one is based in a fact. He was describing Yellowstone's Firehole River.

26 Ibid., 386.

27 Woodard, *Diamonds*. 21.

28 Harpending, *Hoax*. 145.

[29] Richerson, Margaret Settle and Jones, Mary Josephine, *Diamonds, Rubies and Sand*, Hardin County Historical Society, 1999. 1.

[30] Louisville *Courier-Journal*, December 16, 1872.

[31] Harpending, *Hoax*. 140-141. While not pertinent to this story, Harpending's troubles with the British press, Editor Samson and Baron Grant are interesting and detailed on pages 124 through 141 of his book.

[32] DeFord, *San Franciscans*. 161.

[33] Harpending, *Hoax*. 142.

[34] Ibid., 143.

[35] Ibid., 144.

[36] Harpending, *Hoax*. 147.

[37] *Courier-Journal*, December 16, 1872. In *Hoax*, (page 144) Harpending himself gives the time of his return as "May 1872." As that does not jive with the rest of the dates, apparently the date is either a typographical error or, as Harpending's account was written 40 years after the fact, his memory was faulty.

[38] Woodard, *Diamonds*. 23.

[39] Harpending, *Hoax*. 147.

[40] Woodard, *Diamonds*. 24.

[41] Ibid., 24.

[42] Wilson, *The Explorer King*. 242.

[43] Harpending, *Hoax*. 148.

[44] Woodard, *Diamonds*. 23.

[45] Harpending, *Hoax*. 148.

[46] Ibid.

[47] Ibid.

[48] Ibid., 150.

[49] Richerson and Jones, *Diamonds, Rubies and Sand*. 3.

[50] Woodard, *Diamonds*. 26.

[51] Harpending, *Hoax*. 150.

[52] De Ford, *San Franciscans*. 162.

[53] Woodard, *Diamonds*. 45.

[54] Ibid., 29.

[55] Ibid., 28.

[56] Richerson and Jones, *Diamonds, Rubies and Sand*. 3.

[57] Wilson, *The Explorer King*. 243.

[58] Foote, Shelby, *The Civil War, Fort Sumter to Perryville*, Vintage Books, New York, 1986. 534.

[59] Harpending, *Hoax*. 153.

[60] Woodard, *Diamonds*. 28.

[61] Harpending, *Hoax*. 152.

[62] Woodard, *Diamonds*. 30.

[63] Ibid., 152

[64] Hardin County Court records, Case of Arnold and Polk v. Longshaw and Holdsworth. Deposition of Samuel L.M., Barlow filed January 9, 1879.

[65] Harpending, *Hoax*. 154.

[66] Woodard, *Diamonds*. 31.

[67] Ibid.

[68] Richerson and Jones, *Diamonds, Rubies and Sand*. 4.

[69] Raymond, Rossiter, *Biographical Notices: Henry Janin*, cited by Woodard, *Diamonds*. 36.

[70] Report of the Commissioner of the General Land Office, cited by Woodard, *Diamonds*. 37.

[71] Harpending, *Hoax*. 153. In his report to the *Courier-Journal* (December 16, 1872), Arnold said Janin was paid $3,000, but as Harpending was the man who paid the fee, I'll take his word.

[72] Harpending, *Hoax*. 155.

[73] Ibid.

[74] *Courier-Journal*, December 16, 1872.

[75] Harpending, *Hoax*. 156.

[76] Ibid.

[77] Ibid.

[78] Ibid.

[79] Ibid., 157.

[80] Woodard, *Diamonds*. 39.

[81] *Courier-Journal*, December 16, 1872.

[82] Ibid.

[83] Woodard, *Diamonds*. 40.

[84] Ibid., 42.

[85] Harpending, *Hoax*. 162.

[86] Janin, Henry, *Engineering and Mining Journal*, September 3, 1872. The complete text of Janin's report.

[87] Ibid.

[88] Ibid.

[89] Kentucky State Archives. Receipt in the papers of Lent v. Arnold, Hardin County.

[90] Woodard, *Diamonds*. 169

[91] Harpending, *Hoax*. 161.

[92] Ibid., 160.

[93] Woodard, *Diamonds*. 58.

[94] Harpending, *Hoax*. 164.

[95] Woodard, *Diamonds*. 45.

[96] Ibid., 45.

[97] Harpending, *Hoax*, 172.

[98] Hardin County Deed Book 13. 340.

[99] *Courier-Journal*, December 10, 1939. MacIntyre's account, given to the Courier some 66 years after the fact, is fraught with errors. Whether due to faulty memory or perhaps MacIntyre's embellishment to enjoy his moment in the sun, his account has little value aside from the comedic.

[100] Ibid.

[101] Denver *Tribune*, August 7, 1872.

[102] Woodard, *Diamonds*. 63.

[103] *Courier-Journal*, December 10, 1938.

[104] Laramie *Daily Sentinel*, August 19, 1872.

[105] Harpending, *Hoax*. 168.

[106] Ibid., 169.

[107] Ibid., Other accounts put the number of men in the party variously from 10 to 30. As Harpending's 15 is a reasonable average, I'll go with his number.

[108] Woodard, *Diamonds*. 74-75.

[109] Ibid., 75.

[110] London *Times*, December 21, 1874.

[111] Laramie *Daily Independent*, October 14, 1872.

[112] *Courier-Journal*, December 16, 1872.

[113] Ibid.

[114] Laramie *Daily Independent*, October 14, 1874.

[115] *Courier-Journal*, December 16, 1872.

[116] Laramie *Daily Independent*, October 14, 1874.

[117] Wilson, *The Explorer King*. 239.

[118] *Courier-Journal*, December 16, 1872.

[119] Woodard, *Diamonds*. 81.

[120] Hardin County Deed Books. 1872.

[121] Richerson and Jones, *Diamonds, Rubies and Sand*. 11.

[122] Kentucky State Archives. Papers in the case of Lent v. Arnold.

[123] *Courier-Journal*, December 16, 1872.

[124] Richerson and Jones. *Diamonds, Rubies and Sand*. 11.

[125] Hardin County Historical Society, *Elizabethtown and Hardin County in September 1900*, Elizabethtown, KY, 1999. 15.

[126] Foote, Shelby, *The Civil War, Fredricksburg to Meridian*, Vintage Books, New York, 1986. 84.

[127] Wilson, *The Explorer King*. 246.

[128] Emmons, Samuel, field notes. Bancroft Library, University of California, Berkeley.

[129] Ibid.

[130] Wilson, *The Explorer King*. 247.

[131] Ibid.

[132] Emmons' field notes. Bancroft Library, University of California, Berkeley.

[133] Ibid.

[134] Ibid.

[135] Wilson, *The Explorer King*. 248.

[136] Emmons' field notes. Bancroft Library, University of California, Berkeley.

[137] Woodard, *Diamonds*. 109.

[138] Emmons' field notes. Bancroft Library, University of California, Berkeley.

[139] Ibid.

[140] Ibid.

[141] Ibid.

[142] Ibid.

[143] Woodard, *Diamonds*. 111.

[144] Wilson, *The Explorer King*. 249.

[145] *Courier-Journal*, December 16, 1872.

[146] Emmons' field notes. Bancroft Library, University of California, Berkeley.

[147] Ibid.

[148] Harpending, *Hoax.* 173.

[149] Woodard, *Diamonds.* 112.

[150] Harpending, *Hoax.* 173.

[151] Janin, Henry. *A Brief Statement of My Part In the Unfortunate Diamond Affair,* Bancroft Library, University of California, Berkeley.

[152] Woodard, *Diamonds.* 117.

[153] Ibid.

[154] Ibid.

[155] Statement of Edward M. Fry and John W. Bost, November 25, 1872.

[156] Janin, Henry, Report to stockholders, *Engineering and Scientific Journal,* December 10, 1872.

[157] Woodard, *Diamonds.* 118.

[158] Harpending, *Hoax.* 176-177.

[159] Ibid.

[160] Ibid., 177-178

[161] *Courier-Journal,* December 16, 1872.

[162] The house still stands. Today, it's the Brown-Pusey House and is open to the public.

[163] Kentucky State Archives. Original papers in the case of Lent v. Arnold, et al.

[164] Ibid.

[165] *Courier-Journal,* December 16, 1872.

[166] Ibid.

[167] Settles, Mary Jo, *Custer in Elizabethtown,* 1998. While in Kentucky, Custer wrote a series of articles originally published in *Galaxy Magazine* that resulted in the book, *My Life on the Plains.* He also did some recruiting. See appendix B.

[168] This resulted in the much referenced *Courier-Journal* article of December 16, 1872.

[169] John Marshall Harlan is the famous Kentucky lawyer and politician destined to become a United States Supreme Court justice.

[170] Kentucky State Archives. Lent v. Arnold papers. The Sheriff's list of the safe's contents is included.

171 *Courier-Journal*, December 19, 1872.

172 Harpending, *Hoax*. 185.

173 Woodard, *Diamonds*. 122.

174 Merington, Marguerite, *The Custer Story*, Devin-Adin Publishers, New York, 1950. 242.

175 Kentucky State Archives, Hardin County Circuit Court Order Book 12. 401 and 482. The order book laconically records, in every detail, what must have been an extremely heated session in the Hardin County Court.

176 *Courier-Journal*, March 5, 1873.

177 Harpending, *Hoax*. 186.

178 Kentucky State Archives. Original papers in the case of Lent vs Arnold.

179 *Courier-Journal*, April 4, 1873. Arnold was either confused or purposely lied as William Lent was the only plaintiff in this suit and the sole beneficiary of the settlement, as Arnold plainly knew.

180 *Courier-Journal*, August 16, 1874. The newspaper gives all the details of Arnold's arrest.

181 Elizabethtown *News*, August 20, 1874.

182 *Courier-Journal*, August 23, 1874.

183 *Courier-Journal*, September 5, 1874.

184 *Courier-Journal*, September 12, 1874

185 *Courier-Journal*, September 7, 1874.

186 *Courier-Journal*, September 9, 1874.

187 *Courier-Journal*, September 18, 1874. Although this "card" is a bit tedious, I agree that Philip Arnold should have his say, so this is it in its entirety, spelling, punctuation and grammar intact.

188 The 1880 census reported the Arnolds' ages: Mary 40, Katherine (May) 21, Tom 18, Richard 15, Nora 10 and Ben 7. The household also included four servants.

189 The disastrous economic event now referred to as The Panic of 1873 was called "The Great Depression" until the similar, but worse, conditions in the 1930's supplanted it.

190 Hardin County Historical Society, *Elizabethtown and Hardin County in September 1900*, Elizabethtown, KY, 1999.

191 *Courier-Journal*, December 24, 1873.

192 *Courier-Journal*, December 16, 1876.

[193] Kentucky State Archives. Original papers in the case of Arnold and Polk v. Longshaw and Holdsworth. The interest rate was to become a point of dispute – Arnold later claiming that it was 10 percent, while Longshaw contended no interest was due.

[194] Ibid. Although the handwriting is beautiful, the punctuation in this document leaves something to be desired. The testimony indicates that blotting out the signature was a common business practice.

[195] *Courier-Journal*, June 14, 1878.

[196] Kentucky State Archives, Arnold and Polk v. Longshaw and Holdsworth. There was considerable disagreement among the eyewitnesses as to whether Arnold was actually armed. In consideration of his rough and tumble mining experience and more recent legal woes, I would think he probably did carry a weapon as a matter of course.

[197] *Courier-Journal*, August 29, 1878. The article, detailing the trial testimony, describes the entire incident.

[198] Ibid.

[199] Kentucky State Archives. Original papers in the case of Polk and Arnold v. Longshaw and Holdsworth.

[200] *Courier-Journal*, August 29, 1978.

[201] Kentucky State Archives. Original papers in the case of H.N. Holdsworth v. Philip Arnold.

[202] Ibid.

[203] *Courier-Journal*, February 12, 1879.

[204] Kentucky State Archives. Original papers in the case of Polk and Arnold v. Longshaw and Holdsworth.

[205] Kentucky State Archives. Original papers in the case of Commonwealth v. H.N. Holdsworth.

[206] Elizabethtown *News*, February 27, 1880.

[207] Kentucky State Archives. Original papers in the case of Commonwealth v. Philip Arnold.

[208] King, Clarence. Report to stockholders, *Engineering and Mining Journal*. December 10, 1872.

[209] Emmons' field notes, Bancroft Library, University of California, Berkeley.

[210] King's report, *Engineering and Mining Journal*, December 10, 1872.

[211] Harpending, *Hoax*. 157.

212 Hardin County Will Book F. 233.

213 Hardin County Will Book G. 289.

214 Harpending, *Hoax*. 187.

215 Woodard, *Diamonds*. 169-172.

216 Elizabethtown *News*, August 13, 1904.

217 Harpending, *Hoax*. 188.

218 Princeton, KY *Leader*, December 29, 1977.

219 Harpending, *Hoax*. XII.

220 The Virtual Museum of the City of San Francisco, www.sfmuseum.net/hist10/wralston.htm.

Appendix A

Arnold Family Real Estate Transactions

While the number of the Arnolds' real estate transactions gleaned from Hardin County deed books is large, the relatively small amount of money involved provides little hint as to the disposition of the hoax money.

Book/page; Date; Acres; Price; Description; Deed Holder.

6/245; unknown; unknown; unknown; unknown; unknown.

6/257; 2/15/1864; 133; $1,629.25; old May place; Phil.

13/340; 7/23/1872; 34; $17,875.00; Arnold Home on Poplar Ave; Mary.

13/341; 7/23/1872; unknown; $5,000.00; this may be part of the above 34 acres; Mary.

13/270; 5/2/1872; 1,000; $1,000.00; bought from Mary's mother; Mary.

13/271; 5/1/1872; 133; $7,000.00; unknown; Mary.

13/352; 8/1/1872; 10.25; $200.00; unknown; Mary.

14/319; 4/29/1873; 47; $2,386.13; unknown; Both.

14/445; 6/14/1873; unknown; $90.00; unknown; Phil.

15/133; 12/6/1873; 262.5; $1,000.00; from Mary's Brother's estate; Mary.

15/145; 12/5/1873; 1050; $715.00; from Mary's Brother's estate; Phil.

16/288; 9/29/1874; 46.5; $200.00; from Mary's Brother's estate; Mary.

16/395; 11/24/1874; 59; $1,917.50; unknown; Mary.

17/23; 9/6/1875; 8; $320.36; unknown; Phil.

17/6; 3/22/1875; 55; $1,900.00; unknown; Phil.

17/53; 4/30/1875; 0.25; $30.00; half a town lot in the Haycraft addition; Phil.

17/56; 4/28/1875; 0.25; $90.00; the other half; Phil.

17/146; 8/12/1875; 0.5; $2,000.00; two town lots; Phil.

17/211; 8/12/1875; 0.5; $140.00; town lot; Phil.

17/253; 9/13/1875; 0.5; $125.00; town lot; Phil.

17/286; 9/18/1875; 0.5; $100.00; town lot; Phil.

17/401; 12/18/1875; 151; $751.20; unknown; Phil.

18/195; 5/17/1876; 215; $2,200.00; unknown; Phil.

18/236; 6/9/1876; 50; $350.00; unknown; Phil.

18/286; 7/27/1876; 120; $153.00; unknown; Phil.

20/82; 10/1/1877; unknown; unknown; unknown; unknown.

20/72; 10/1/1877; unknown; $8,000.00; site of Gilded Age Building on Town Square; Phil.

20/87; 10/8/1877; 1.5; $2,700.00; sold 3 town lots; Phil.

23/5; 8/20/1870; 22; $300.00; unknown; Mary.

21/427; 12/7/1878; 227; $1,120.00; unknown; Phil.

24/165; 11/20/1880; 7; $3,840.00; included a house; Mary.

23/444; 8/7/1880; 0.5; $100.00; town lot; Mary.

24/288; 2/19/1881; 0.5; $565.00; unknown; Mary.

23/174; 7/14/1877; 139; $973.00; sold, evidently date recorded incorrectly; Phil.

25/109; 10/7/1881; unknown; $1,150.00; sold a lot on Main Street; Mary.

25/110; 10/7/1881; unknown; $1,150.00; sold, Phil is dead by now; unknown.

26/332; 3/28/1881; 0.75; $9.38; lot; unknown.

22/117; 4/21/1879; 180; $320.00; buyer had already paid Phil all but $320; unknown.

26/601; 2/8/1883; 180; $317.01; buyer had already paid Phil all but $317.01; unknown.

28/172; 8/13/1883; 2; $27.75; unknown; unknown.

28/471; 4/4/1884; 7; $3,840.00; sold; unknown.

28/480; 1/21/1884; 3.75; $125.00; sold; unknown.

28/501; 8/1/1882; 0.5; $324.65; town lot; unknown.

29/441; 2/21/1885; unknown; $1; sold house and lot on Main Street to Mary's mother; unknown.

29/461; 2/28/1885; 77; $600.00; sold; unknown.

30/440; 12/11/1885; unknown; $2,000.00; sold part of town square to 2nd National Bank; unknown.

30/518; 1/16/1886; unknown; $500.00; sold Mother's house to brother; unknown.

30/521; 1/4/1886; 63; $2,000.00; sold to William Wilson; unknown.

31/632; 5/16/1887; 18; $51.00; part of a legal serttlement; unknown.

33/52; 6/12/1888; 77; $1,600.00;; unknown.

33/89; 8/31/1888; 0.5; $5,000.00; house and lot on Main Street; unknown.

33/549; 4/24/1889; unknown; $900.00; sold town lot; unknown.

35/141; 1/4/1889; 14.25; $71.20; sold; unknown.

36/2; 6/28/1890; unknown; $25.00; sold cemetery lot; unknown.

37/156; 9/21/1888; unknown; unknown; Mary and Will Wilson agree on property boundary; unknown.

37/207; 8/16/1892; unknown; $750.00; sold Main Street lot; unknown.

37/377; 10/4/1892; 151; $6,065.00; sold; unknown.

37/435; 9/30/1892; 1/2; $50.00; sold town lot; unknown.

40/581; 10/24/1896; 50.25; $400.00; sold; unknown.

42/287; 8/28/1897; 206; $4,647.25; sold; unknown.

43/425; 3/10/1903; 37; $6,000.00; sold; unknown.

Appendix B

Kentuckians in the Seventh Cavalry Regiment

Name (Company); Enlisted; Home; Service Termination.

Major Joseph C. Tilford (HQ); July 1, 1851; Boyle County; Detached Service.

First Lieutenant William Thomas Craycroft (B); June 15, 1869; Springfield; Detached Service.

Second Lieutenant John J. Crittenden (L); October 15, 1875; Frankfort; Killed June 25, 1876.

Private Harry Abbotts (E); October 18, 1875; Louisville; Detached Service – Hospital Duty.

Farrier Benjamin Brandon (F); November 1, 1875; Hopkinsville; Killed June 25, 1876.

Private Benjamin Brown (F); March 12, 1872; Taylor County; Killed June 25, 1876.

Private Thomas P. Downing (F); February 13, 1873; Lebanon; Killed June 25, 1876.

Private Samuel J. Foster (A); May 9, 1872; Clay County; Wounded June 25, 1876.

Private Harvey A. Fox (D); July 27, 1871; Mt. Vernon; Detached Service.

Private William George (H); May 1, 1875; Lexington; Wounded and Died July 3, 1876.

Private Curtis Hall (D); December 9, 1872; Louisville; Discharged December 9, 1877.

Private William M. Harris (D); August 25, 1871; Madison County; Discharged August 5, 1876.

Private James Hurd (D); August 30, 1871; Jessamine County; Discharged September 3, 1881.

Private Joseph Kneubuhler (HQ); March 14, 1872; Louisville; Detached Service.

Private Thomas Lawhorn (H); May 12, 1875; Caldwell County; Deserted February 7, 1877.

Private Frederick Lehman (I); October 17, 1871; Louisville; Killed June 25, 1876.

Private Hugh N. Moore (M); August 24, 1872; Louisville; Killed June 25, 1876.

Private Jacob Noshang (I); January 23, 1872; Louisville; Killed June 25, 1876.

Private William D. Nugent (A); August 5, 1872; Grayson County; Discharged August 5, 1877.

Private John S. Ragsdale (A); July 23, 1872; Hardin County; Detached Service.

Private Eldorado J. Robb (G); January 8, 1872; Warren County; Discharged January 8, 1877.

Private Benjamin F. Rogers (G); January 5, 1872; Madison County; Killed June 25, 1876.

Private Richard Rollins (A); November 26, 1872; Breckinridge County; Killed June 25, 1876.

Private George D. Scott (D); September 7, 1871; Garrard County; Discharged August 5, 1876.

Private Thomas W. Stivers (D); September 16, 1871; Madison County; Discharged August 5, 1876.

Private Elijah T. Strode (A); October 15, 1872; Monroe County; Wounded June 25, 1876.

Private Thomas B. Varner (M); August 24, 1875; Louisville; Wounded June 25, 1876.

Trumpeter Frederick Walsh (L); December 1, 1872; Louisville; Killed June 25, 1876.

Private William B. Whaley (I); September 24, 1873; Harrison County; Killed June 25, 1876.

Source: Arville L. Funk, "Kentuckians with Custer at the Little Bighorn," *The Filson Club History Quarterly*, Vol. 59, No. 4, October 1985.

About the Author

Ron Elliott, a native of Lincoln County, Kentucky, is a graduate of Stanford High School, Eastern Kentucky University and the University of Kentucky.

Ron's background includes working on the historic Apollo missions and a stint on Kentucky's Community College system facility. Having a relative involved in the assassination of Kentucky's would-be governor, William Goebel, piqued his interest in history and launched a writing career.

A much-in-demand member of the Kentucky Humanities Council Speakers Bureau, Ron is the author of several books, including *Inside the Beverly Hills Supper Club Fire, Through the Eyes of Lincoln and From Hilltop to Mountaintop*. His work is also featured in numerous magainze articles. He is the 2012 DAR Literary Award recipient.

Retired, Ron and his wife, Carol, currently live in Nelson County, Kentucky.

Index